CW01655956

Looking back at DELTICS

Strathwood

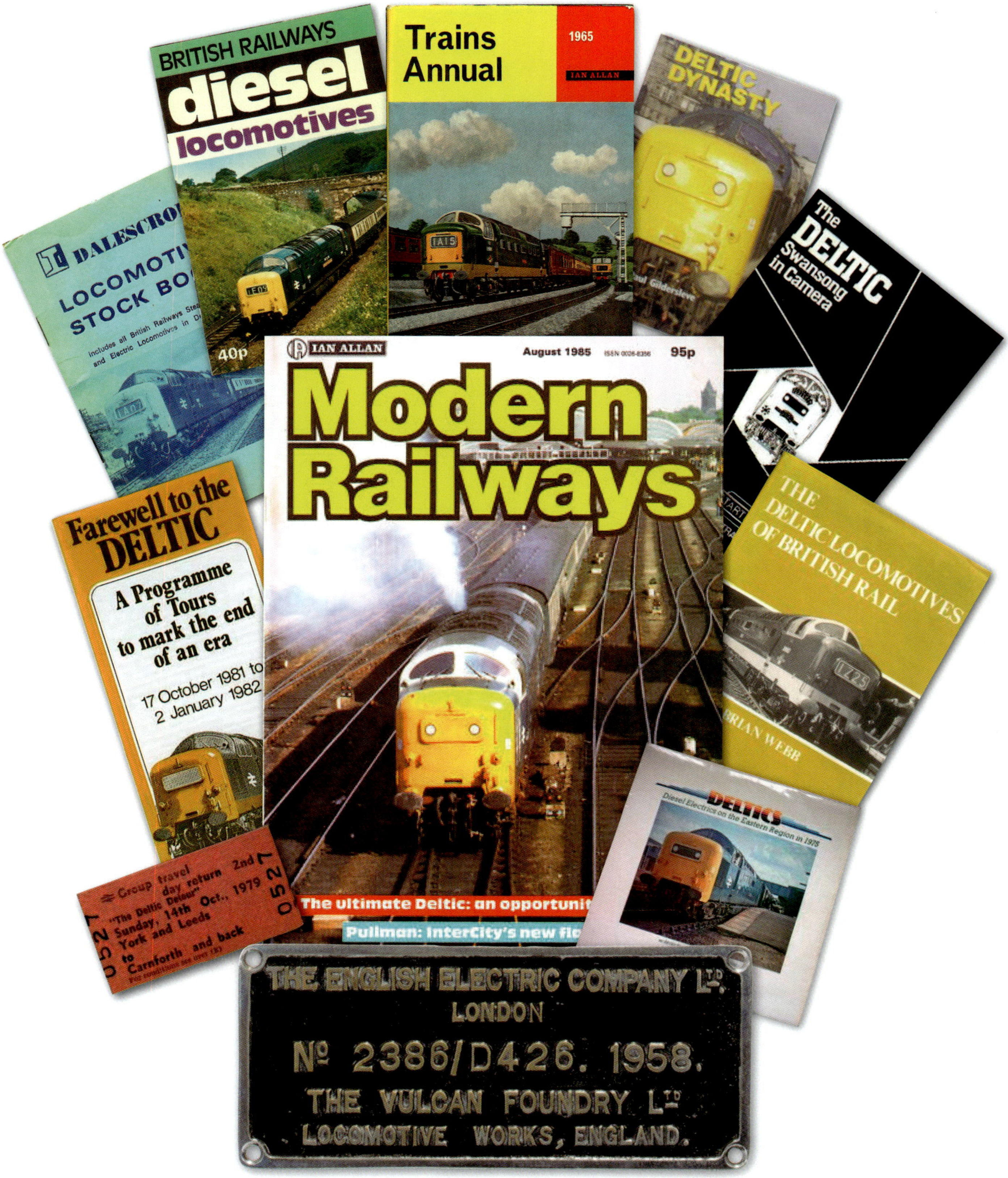
BRITISH RAILWAYS
diesel
locomotives
40p
Trains
Annual
1965
IAN ALLAN
DELTIC
DYNASTY
The
DELTIC
Swansong
in Camera
DALESCROFT
LOCOMOTIVE
STOCK BOOK
IAN ALLAN
August 1985
95p
Modern
Railways
The ultimate Deltic: an opportunit
Pullman: InterCity's new fle
Farewell to the
DELTIC
A Programme
of Tours
to mark the end
of an era
17 October 1981 to
2 January 1982
THE
DELTIC LOCOMOTIVES
OF BRITISH RAIL
BRIAN WEBB
DELTICS
Diesel Electrics on the Eastern Region in 1975
Group travel
day return
2nd
"The Deltic Detour"
Sunday, 14th Oct., 1979
York and Leeds
to
Carnforth and back
0527
THE ENGLISH ELECTRIC COMPANY LTD
LONDON
Nº 2386/D426. 1958.
THE VULCAN FOUNDRY LTD
LOCOMOTIVE WORKS, ENGLAND.

Looking back at DELTICS

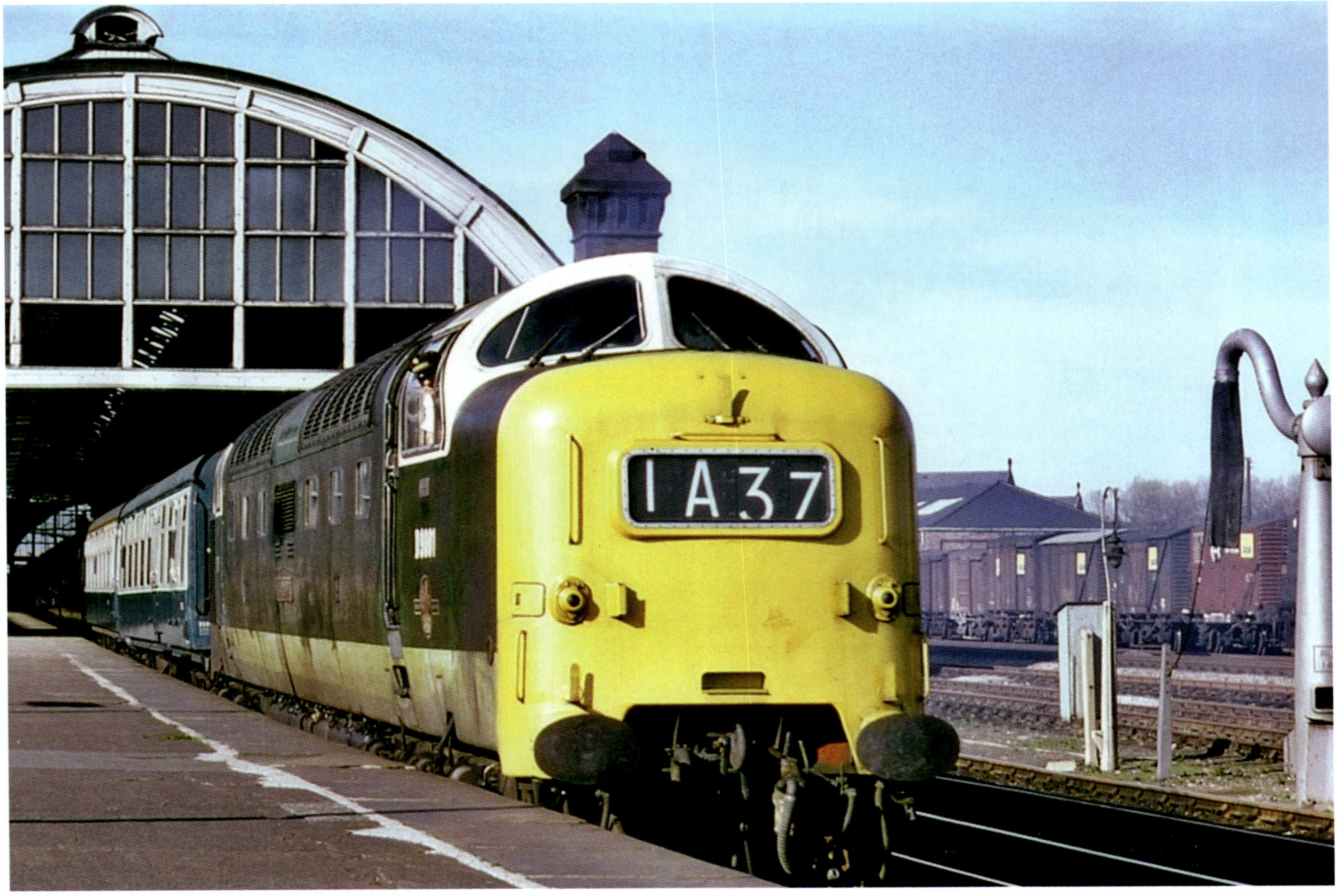

Cover: Recently adorned with full yellow nose ends D9001 St. Paddy has made the Darlington stop with the 14.00 Edinburgh to Kings Cross known as the up Heart of Midlothian on 17 April 1967. ***Bill Wright***

Kevin Derrick

Strathwood

Looking back at DELTICS

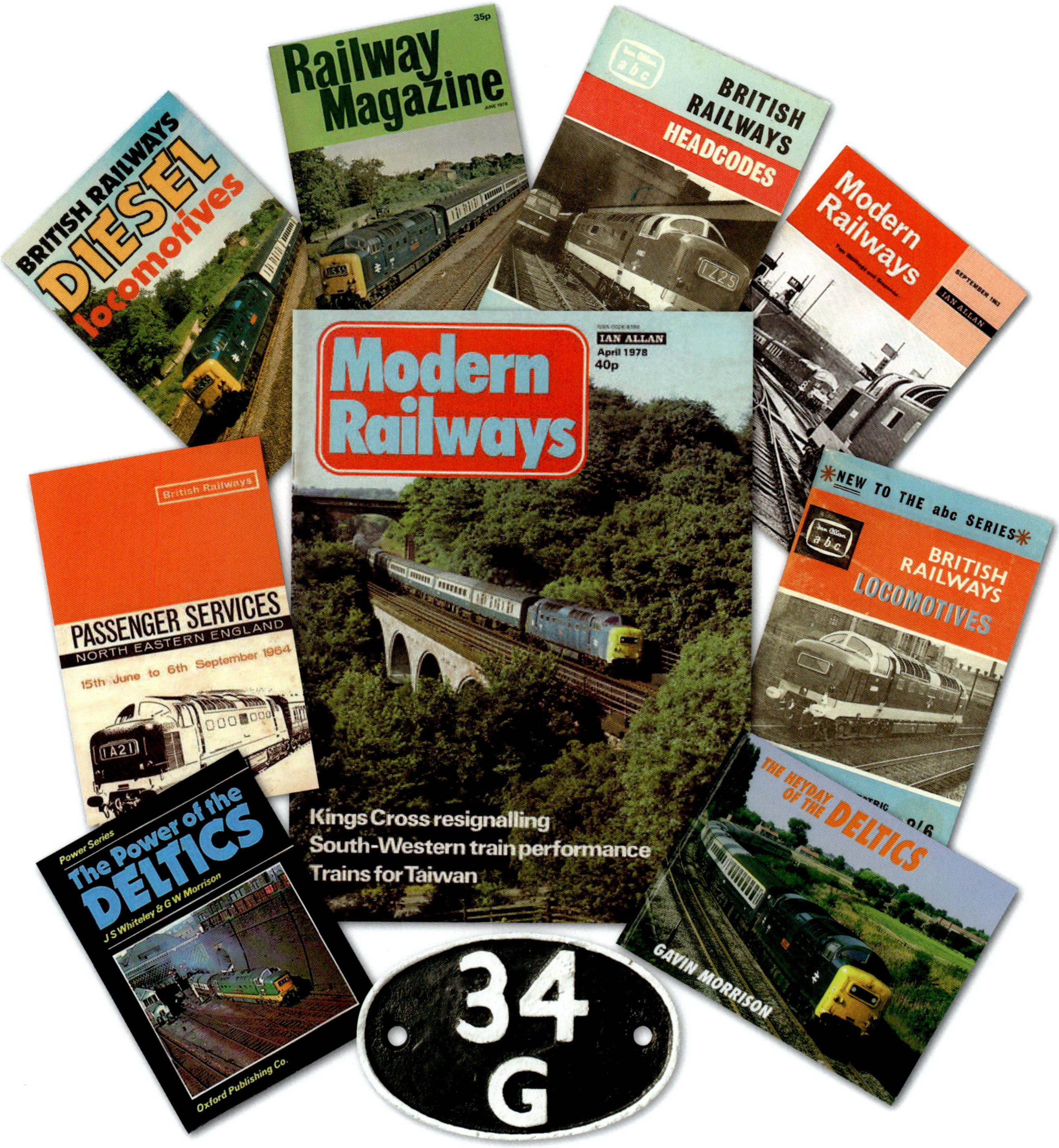

First published 2011

ISBN 1-905276-46-X
ISBN 978-1-905276-46-2

All rights reserved. No part of this book may be reproduced or transmitted in any form or by any means, electronic or mechanical, including photocopying, recording or by any information storage and retrieval system, without written permission from the Publisher in writing.

Copyright Strathwood Ltd 2011

Published by Strathwood Ltd, Glenavon House, Kinchurdy Road,
Boat of Garten, Inverness-shire, PH24 3BP. Tel 01479 831139

Proudly printed in the United Kingdom

Contents

Page

Introduction

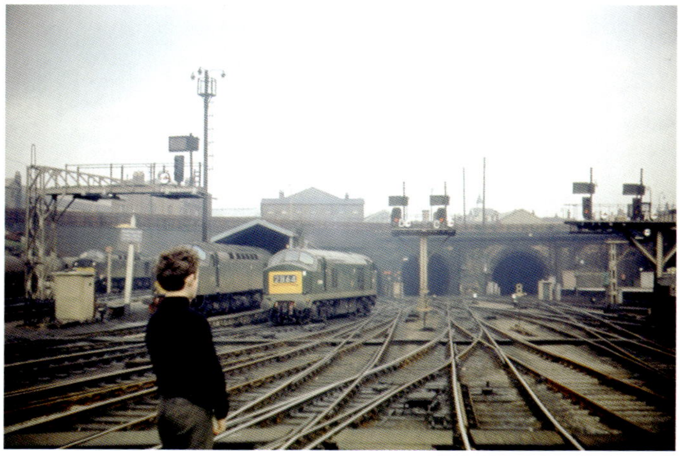

We have already taken a brief look at both versions of the production Deltics in the Type 5 and Type 2 power catagories and the prototype in the earlier release in this series Looking back at English Electric Locomotives. We can now take a chance to examine all thirty three locomotives a little closer during the late 1950s through to the early 1980s, when their mainline careers were to have offically ended. We have elected not to cover the intervening years of preservation which have now outlasted the production Deltics original twenty years of active service.

English Electric's brave venture to create the Deltic protoype at their Dick Kerr Works near Preston in 1955 must be regarded as a huge success. As whilst it never resulted in anymore than a direct order for just twenty two production Deltics. The prototype's notoriety as the most powerful diesel locomotive in the world, at the time brought the English Electric Company's sales team a real advantage and prestige in their attempts at gaining not only British Railway's orders but also overseas railways, particularly throughout the former Commonwealth countries railways systems. This was at a time when Great Britain desparately needed not only the work within the economy but also the valuable foreign exchange on those export orders.

It must also be regarded that Deltic's success certainly put paid to any attempts by North American producers being given the opportunity to tender for business within the country at the time. Ironically it would be the Baby Deltics as the least successful of the English Electric mainline designs that would be among the first to arrive on British Railways in 1959. One cannot but wonder had they arrived earlier with their inherent problems that the Eastern Region's order for twenty two of the Type 5 locomotives may have gone elsewhere, with double headed Brush Type 4s perhaps being the solution to increased loads and decreasing journey times on the Eastern Region before electrification.

Indeed the concept of the Class 50s and the London Midland Region's use of them doubleheading was born with the English Electric prototype DP2 utilising a spare Deltic body and bogies which gave birth to the next diesel type to be officially rated to 100mph in 1967.

Almost thirty years after the Deltics departed from everyday service and enthusiasts are still treated to the sound of those Napier Deltic engines under full power with mainline work on passenger and freight from time to time as well as on the nation's preserved railways, long may it continue.

Kevin Derrick
Boat of Garten 2011

Above: A young spotter looks out to the station throat and seems to disregard the movement of D5904 around the stabling point on 26 March 1965, surpising perhaps after the classes absence from the capital for a long period of rebuilding. ***Gilroy A Kerr***

Below: An impressive Deltic line up for the cameras at York on 5 November 1981 with 55015 Tulyar, 55022 Royal Scots Grey and 55009 Alycidon joining 55002 The King's Own Yorkshire Light Infantry in the early winter sunshine. ***Strathwood Library Collection***

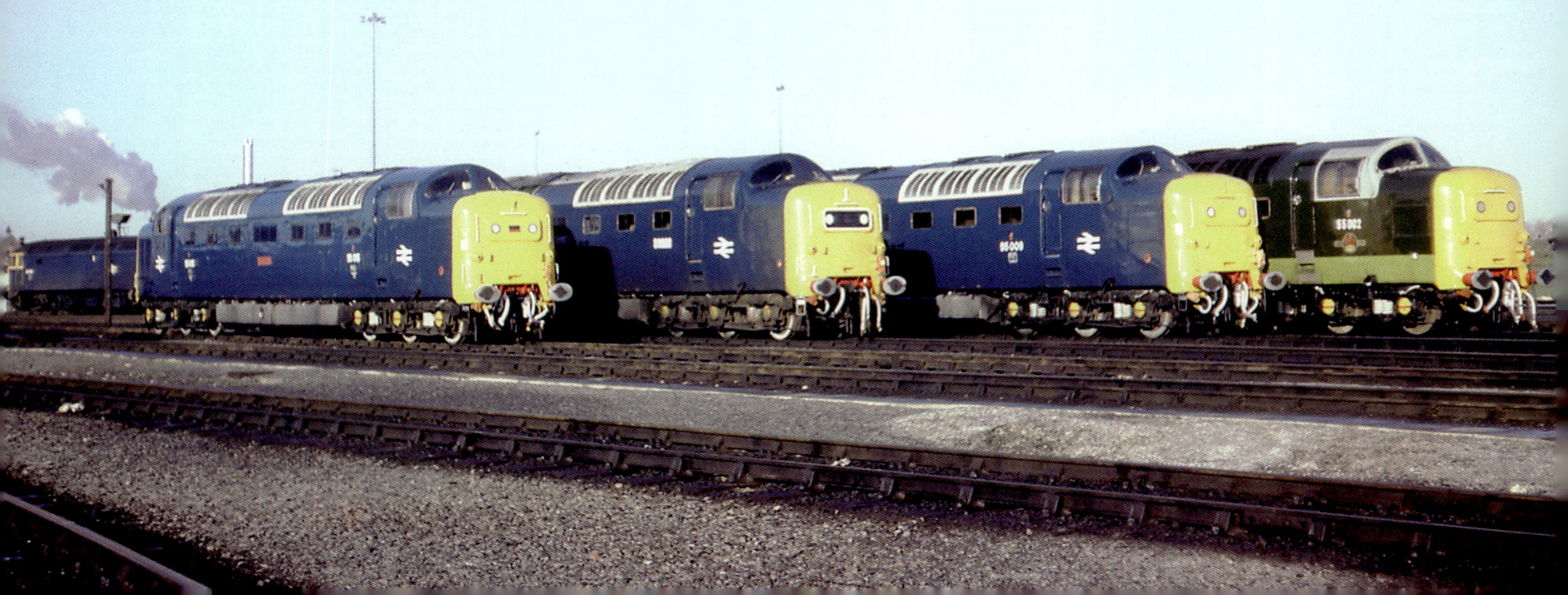

Enterprise

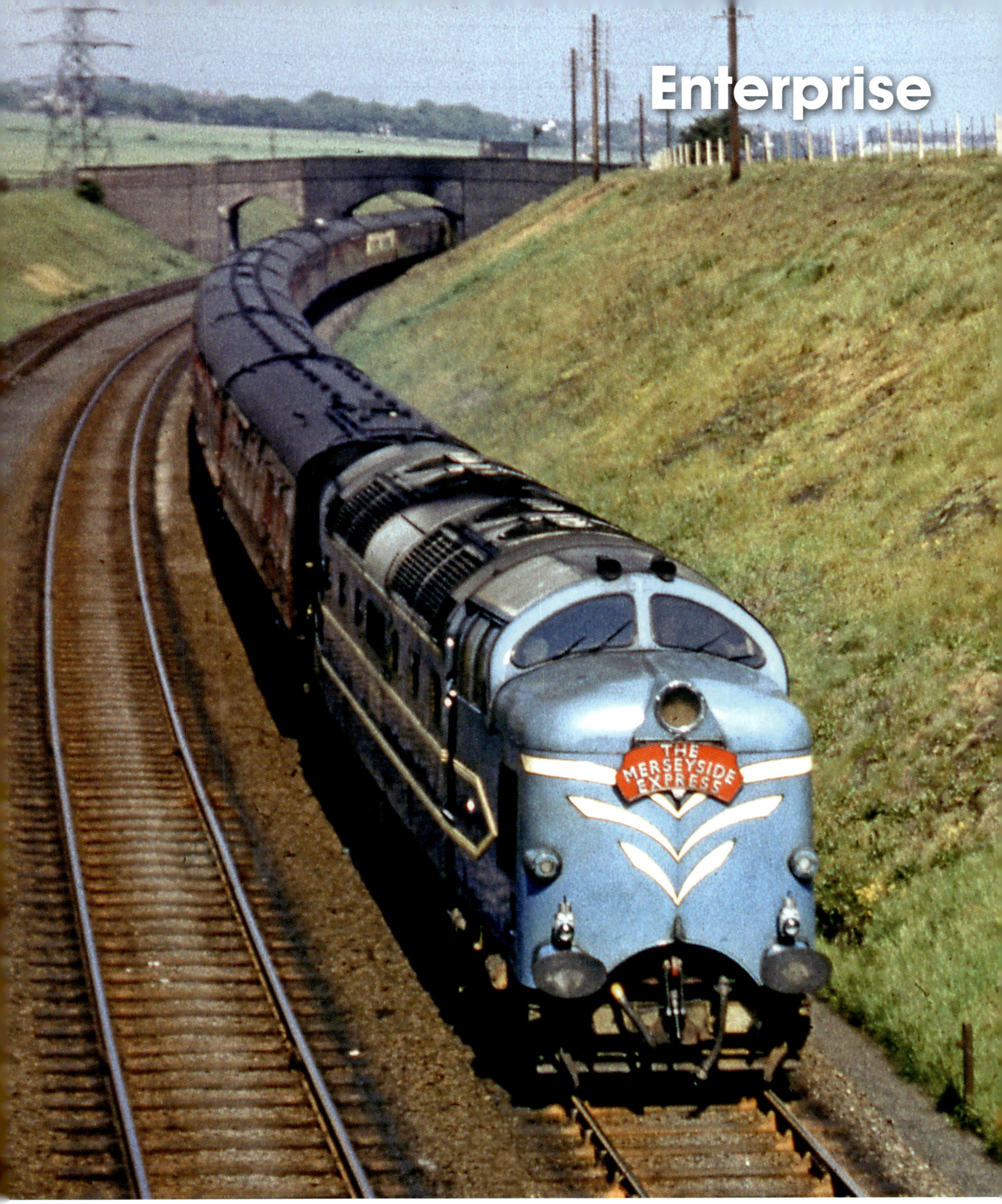

DELTIC was first sent into traffic on the West Coast Main Line in late October 1955 in the care of 8C Speke Junction which was convenient for fitters as required from English Electric's Vulcan Foundry at Newton-le-Willows and the Dick Kerr Works at Preston. When this view near Halton Junction was recorded in June 1957 the locomotive was rostered for the up Merseyside Express which was one of 1B Camden's turns. ***Rail Photoprints/The Late R A Whitfield***

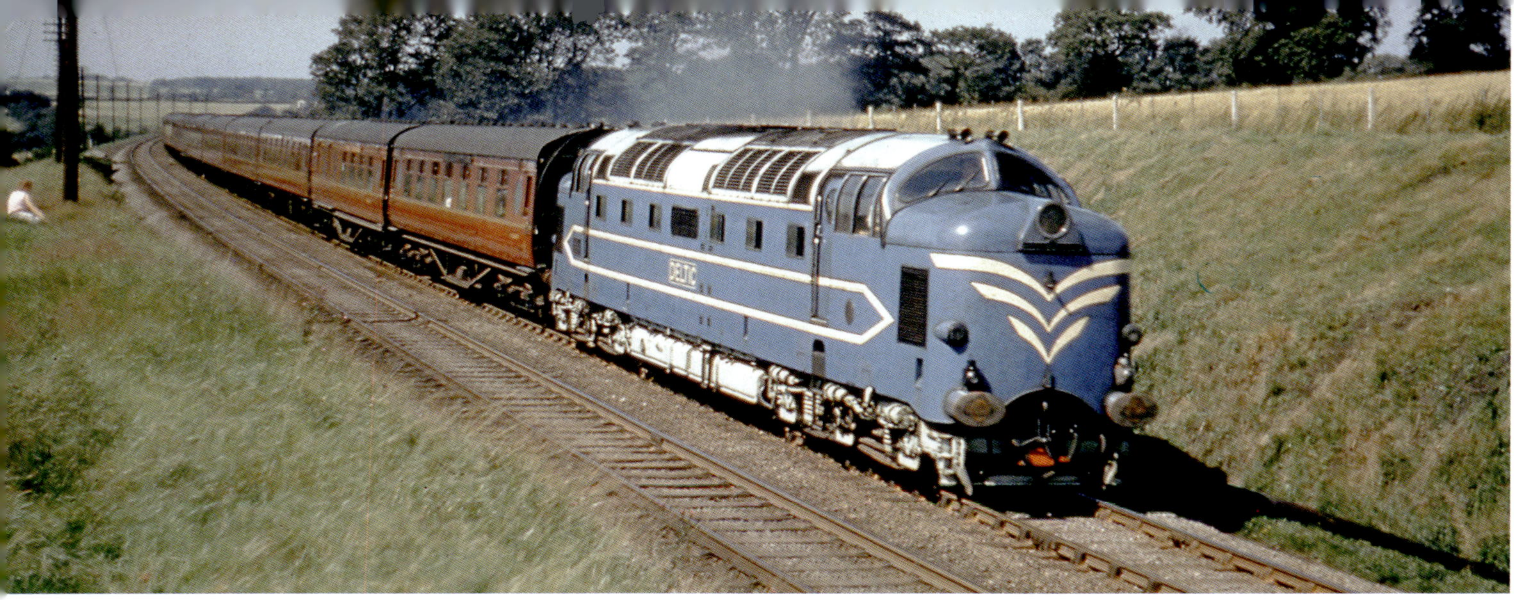

This view at Acton Bridge of DELTIC on an unknown up service most likely dates from the late summer of 1958, as by January of 1959 the locomotive had been moved to the Eastern Region and 34B Hornsey depot for its next series of trials. ***The Late Pat Whitehouse***

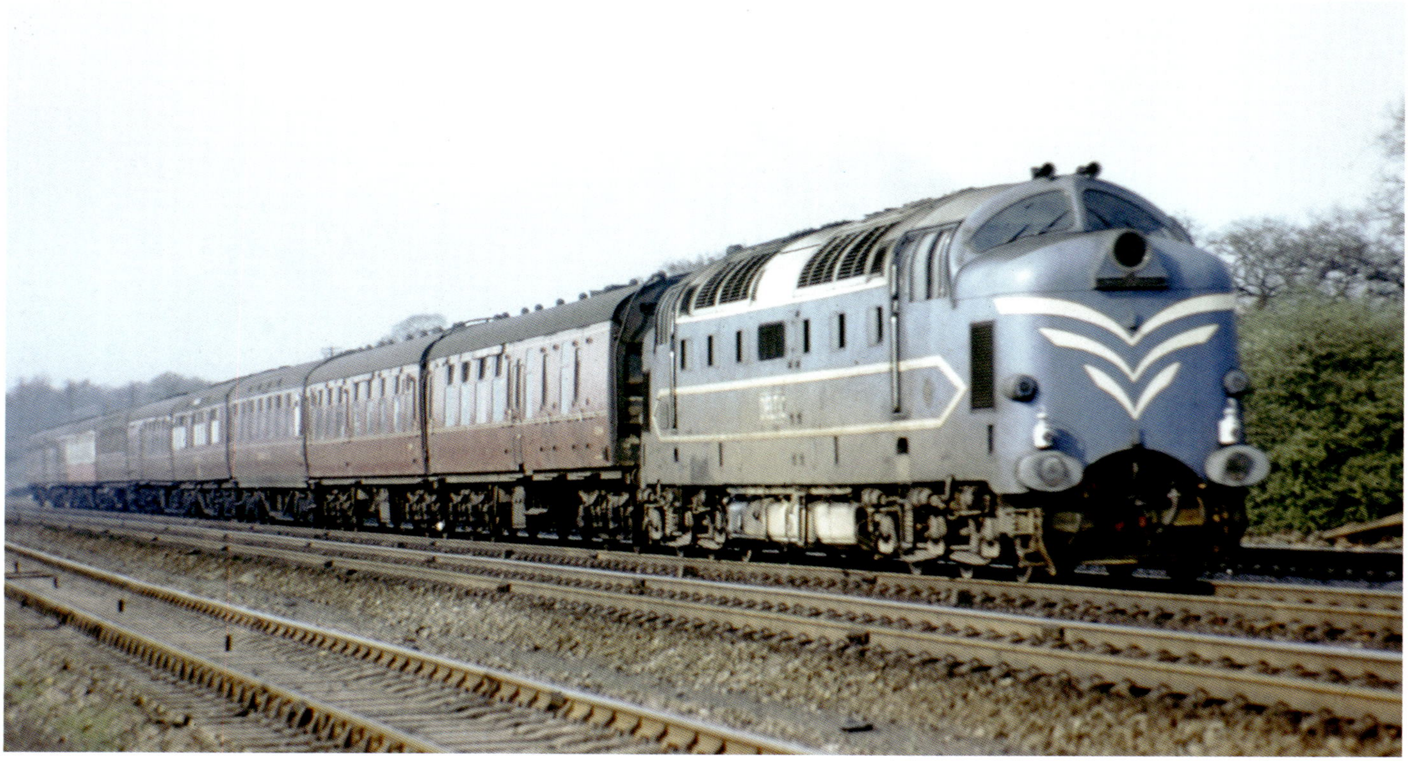

These two views from 1960 show the prototype engaged on express workings firstly near Brookmans Park and then near Retford. ***Both Strathwood Library Collection***

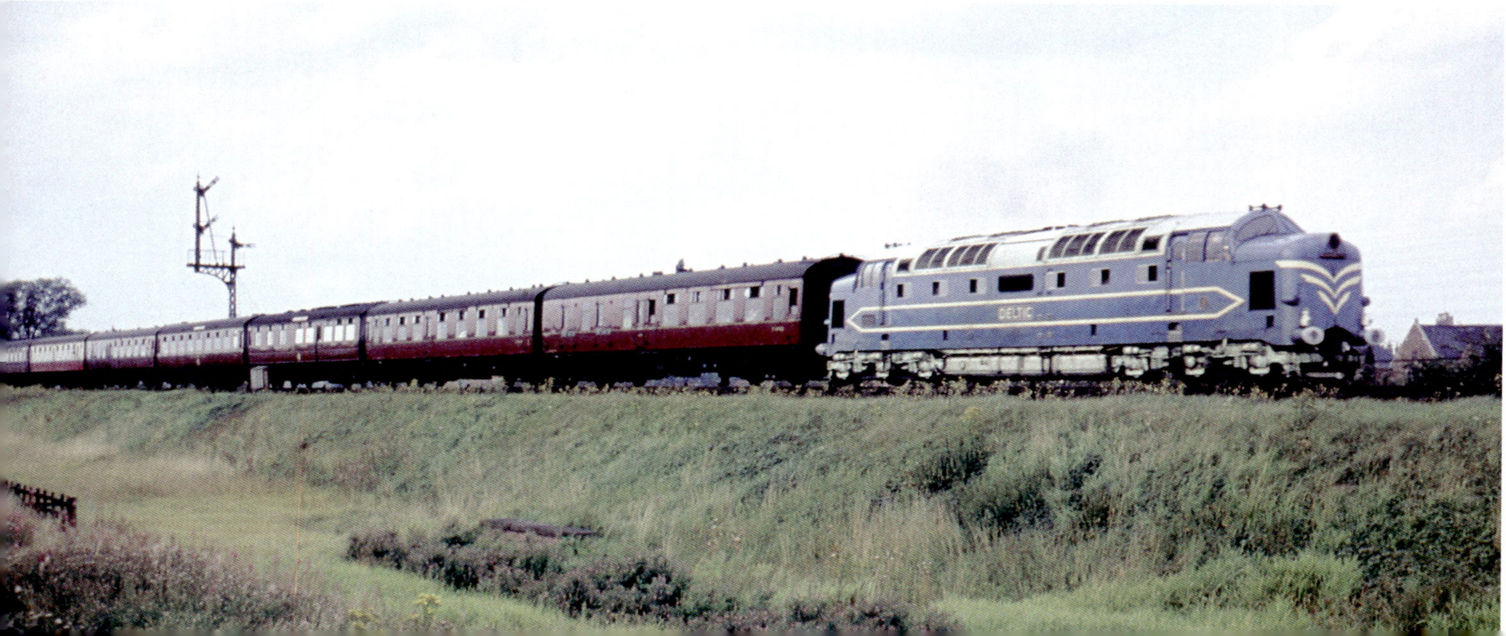

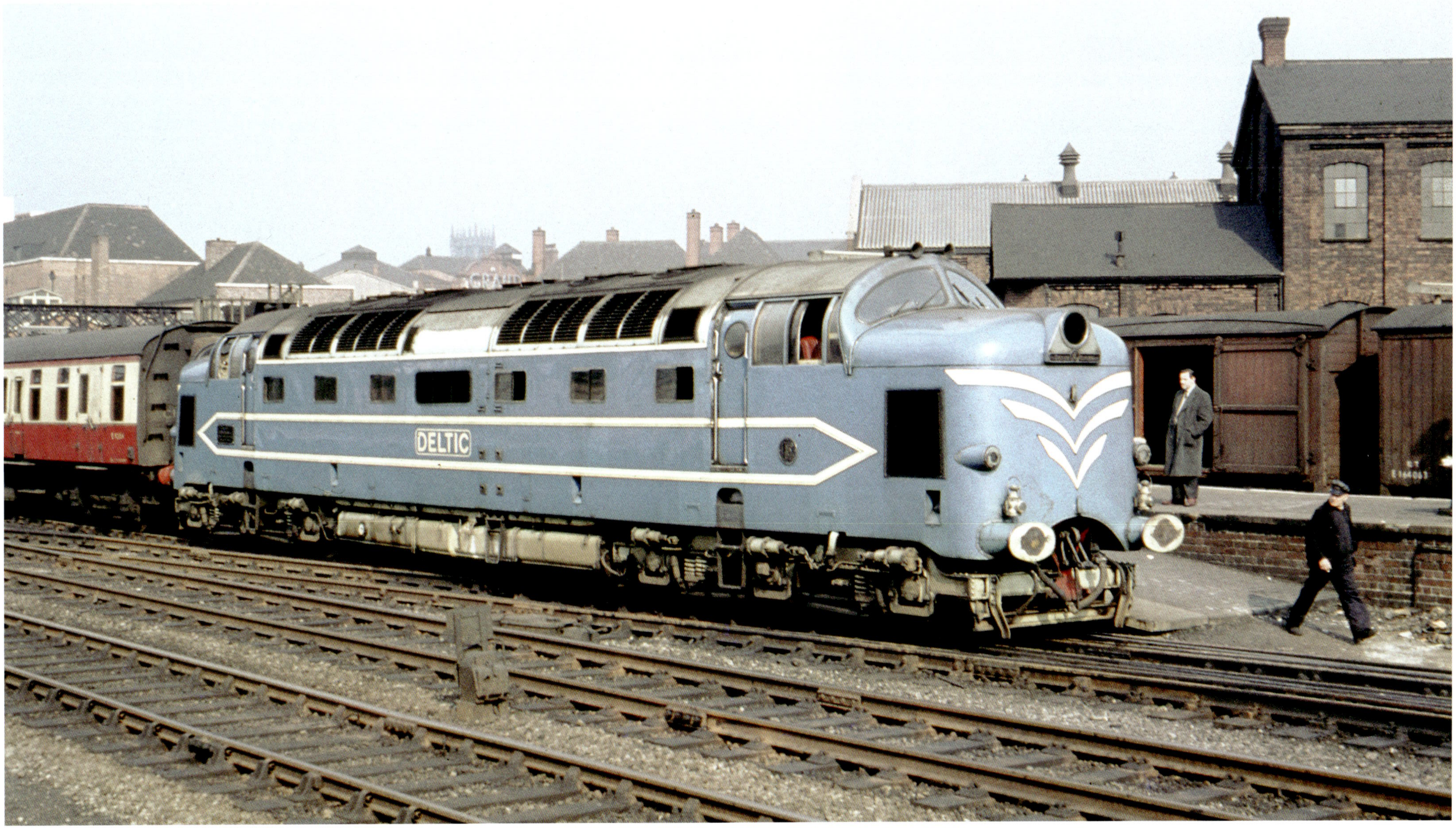

With what would soon become a familiar throb of Napier Deltic engines for many years at Doncaster this significant prototype stands with an up express in 1960. Although known as DELTIC this English Electric project was to have been allocated the number DP1 and the name ENTERPRISE. The locomotive suffered a major engine failure during March 1961 and was returned to English Electric having completed in excess of 450,000 miles of tesiting and everyday service. Attempts to consider a full repair and export to Canada as a sales drive for more orders came to nought. So the management at Engilsh Electric decided to restore the external appearance of the locomotive and donated it to the Science Museum in London where it would remain on public display for the next thirty years, until it joined the National Railway Museum's collection at York. ***Strathwood Library Collection***

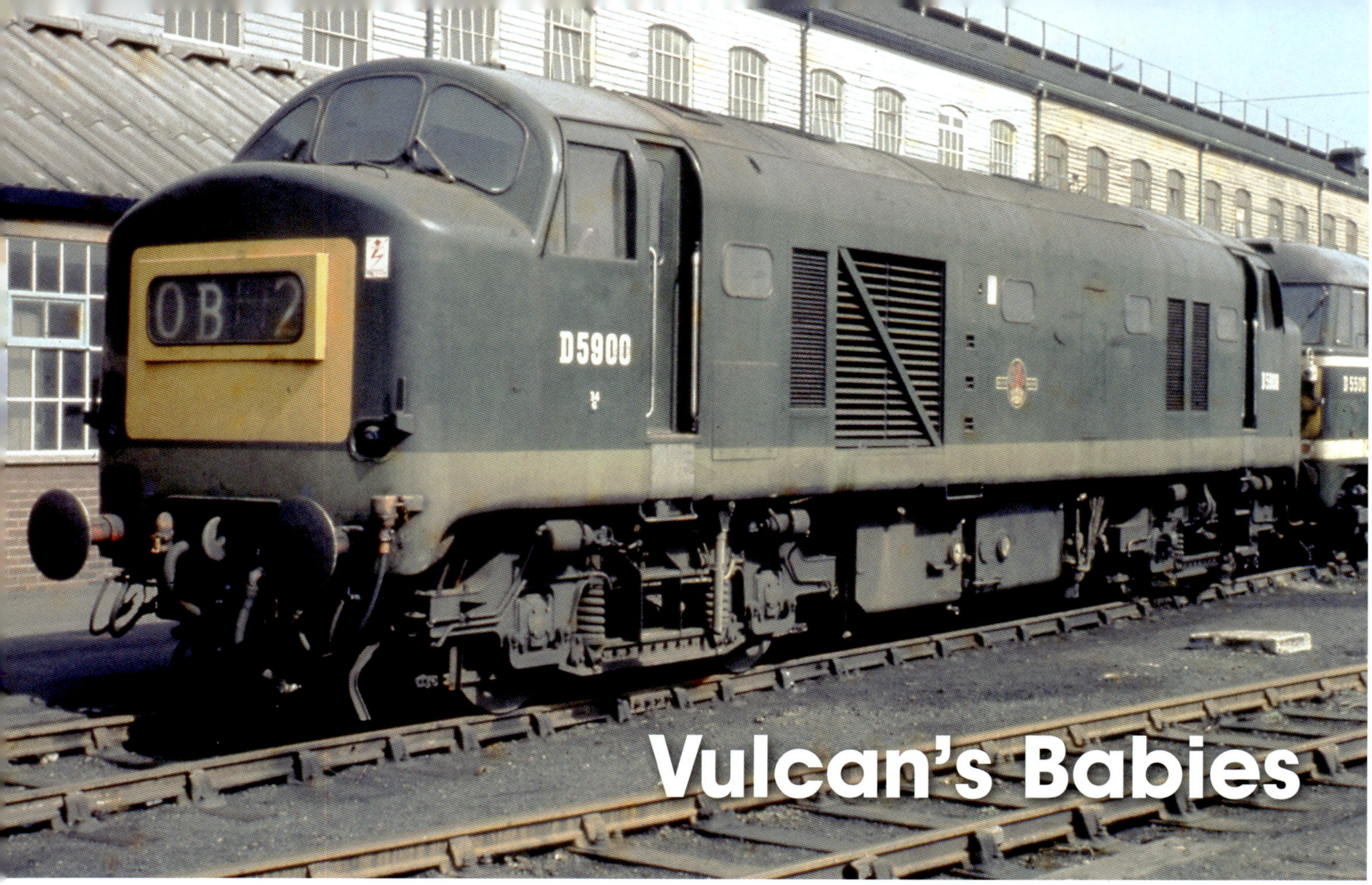

Vulcan's Babies

Seen awaiting repairs outside Doncaster Works on a visit in mid April 1968 was D5900, just how effective the works attention must have been we are not sure, as on 30 December the locomotive would become the second of the class to be withdrawn from service and remained stored at Hornsey until June the following year when it went to George Cohen's yard at Kettering for scrapping which took place during August 1969. ***Strathwood Library Collection***

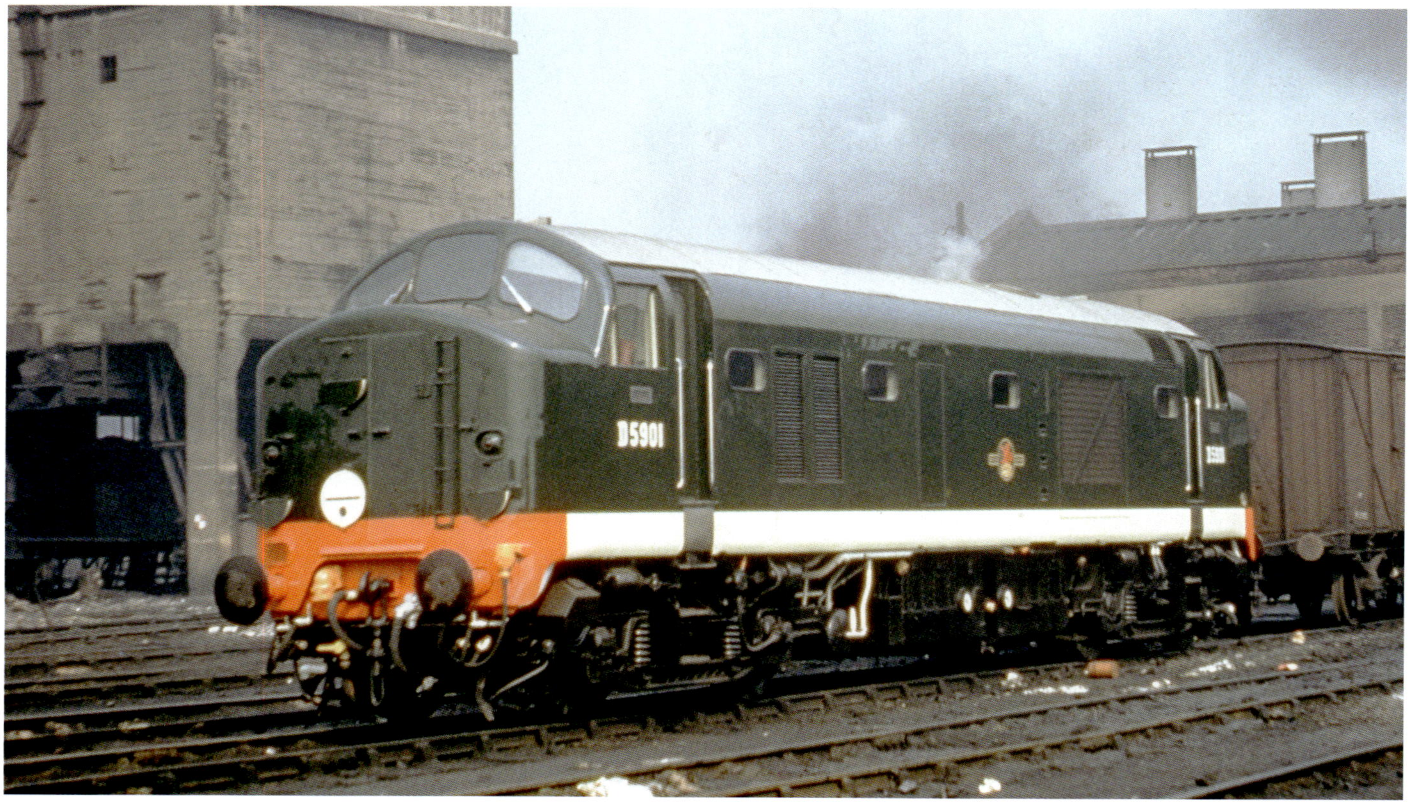

For two months from mid April 1959 the ten Baby Deltics could be seen arriving ex works from Vulcan Foundry to take up service firstly from here at 34B Hornsey joining their big brother the prototype DELTIC which was also based here from the start of 1959. In this original condition D5901 is seen awaiting acceptance on 22 May 1959. It has to be said a chance was missed when D5901 was cut up in early 1977 at Doncaster Works to save the last survivor of this troubled class which had found work with the Research Department at Derby since August 1969. ***Strathwood Library Collection***

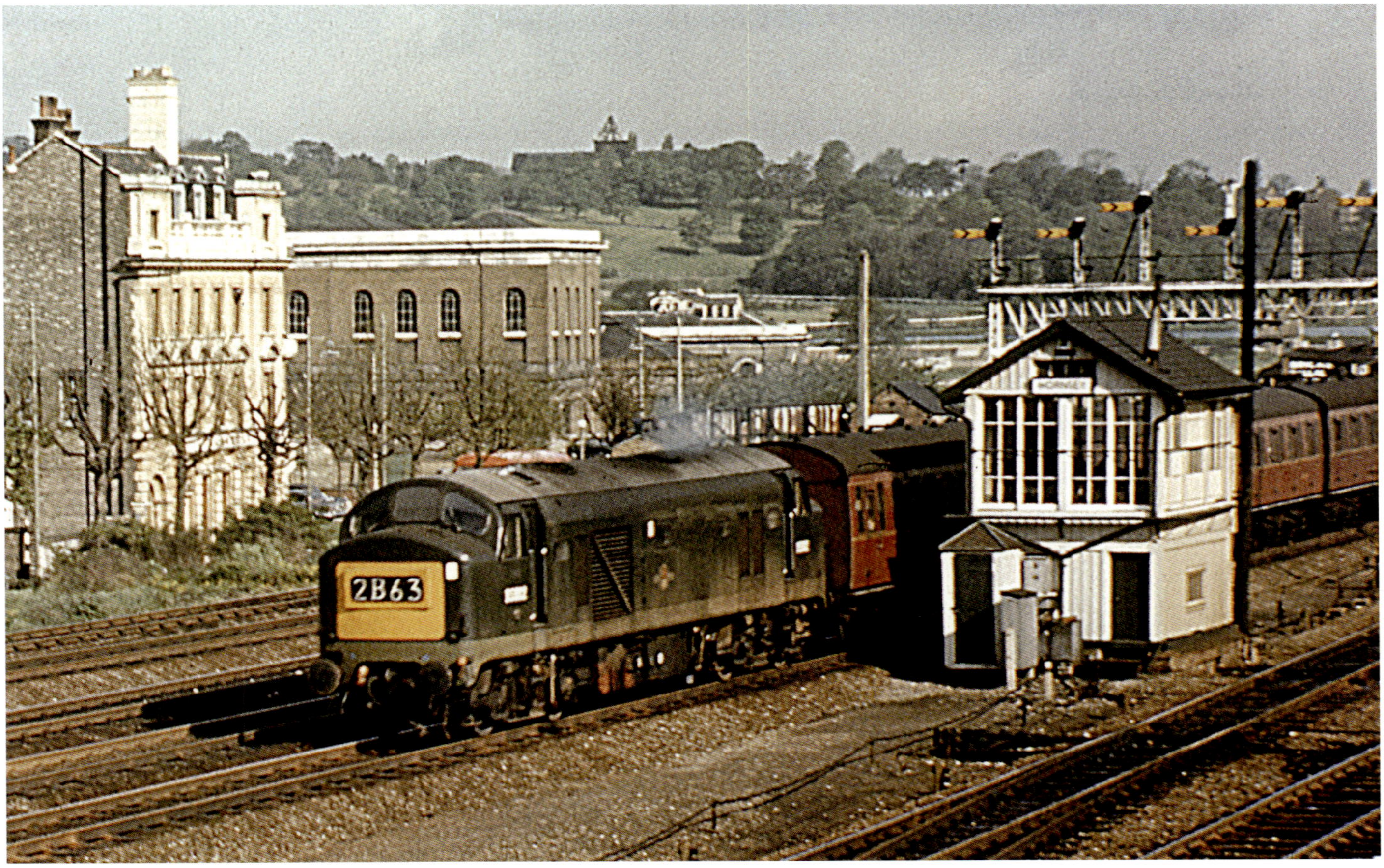

Right from the start the class were beset with problems with the deliveries of D5900-D5902 being delayed as they were too heavy for the specification agreed, making D5903 the first to enter service. Very soon many of the class were experiencing regular power unit problems and were unable to work their expected outer suburban diagrams with confidence from Kings Cross. As they started to be declared failures during 1963 they were stored at Stratford whilst arrangements were made with English Electric, who were keen to maintain good relations with British Railways for an agreed rebuild programme. In rebuilt condition D5902 passes Hornsey in April 1967 heading for Kings Cross with a commuter service. ***Rail Photoprints/Mike Jefferies***

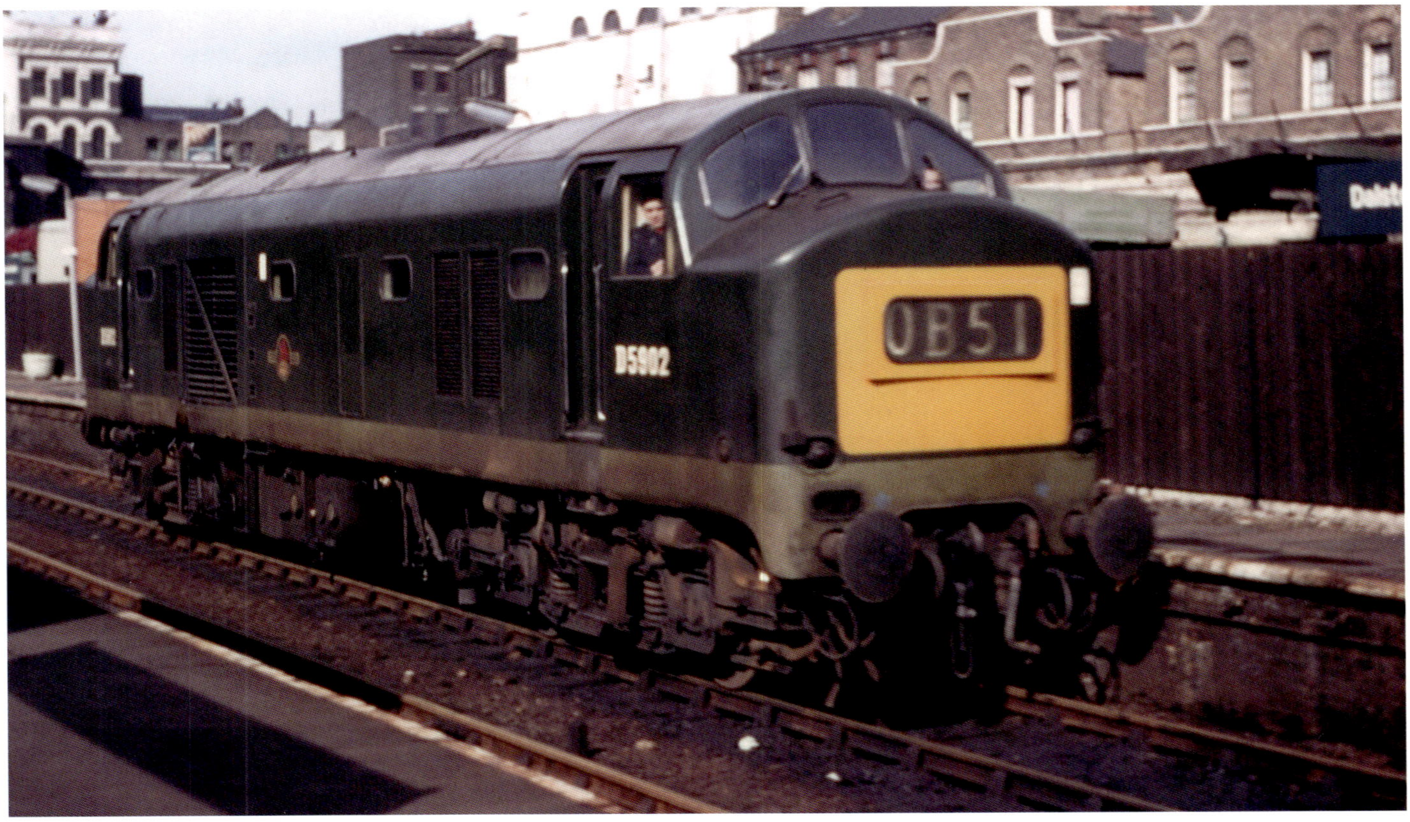

The same locomotive is seen running light engine through Dalston Junction in 1969, during November the same year it went into storage again at Stratford once withdrawn. Remaining here before being hauled to George Cohen's yard at Kettering in September 1970, where the cutters set to work having already disposed of D5907, D5900 and D5904 a few weeks beforehand. ***Grahame Wareham***

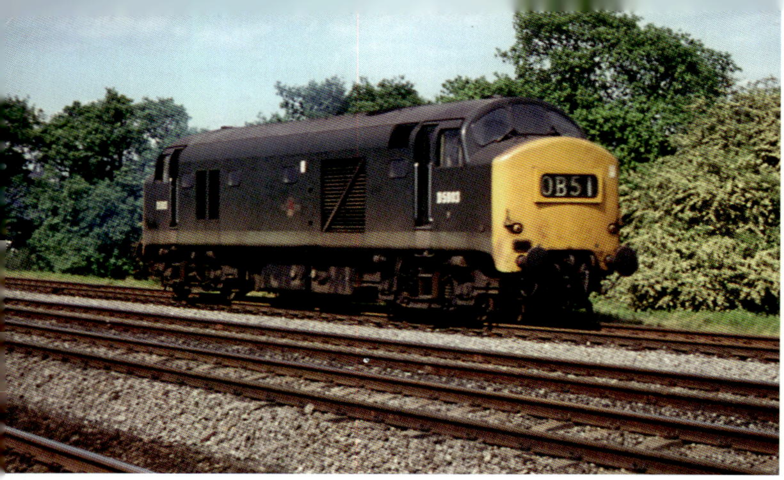

On 6 June 1968 D5903 now sporting full yellow ends was seen with another light engine movement on the up slow line at Brookmans Park. ***D Twibell/Transport Treasury***

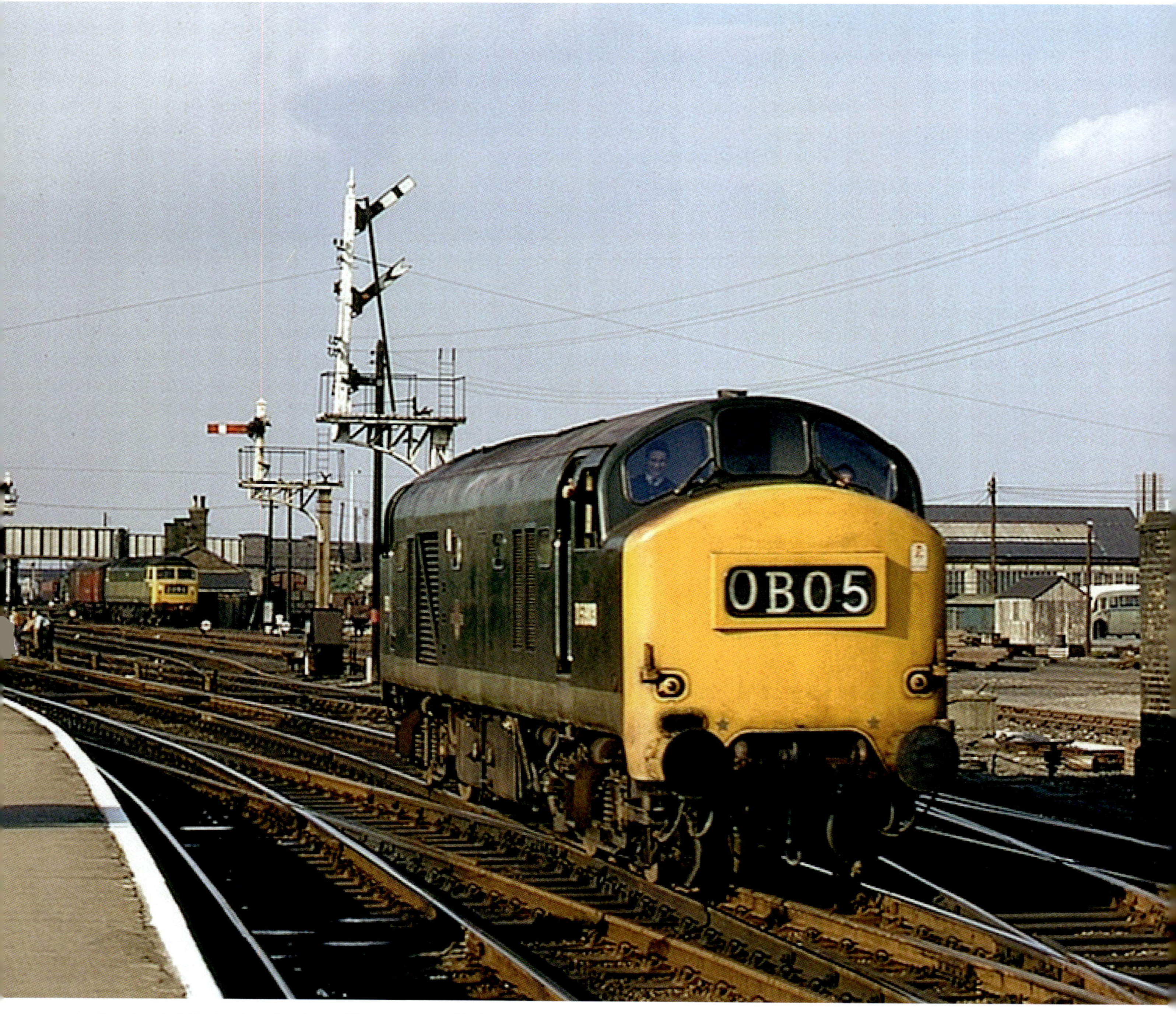

Just a shortwhile before being withdrawn on 30 December 1968 our cameraman witnessed yet another unproductive working for D5903 as its jolly crew brought it light through Peterborough on 7 October. By October the following year the locomotive would become the fifth of her type scrapped at Kettering. ***Bill Wright***

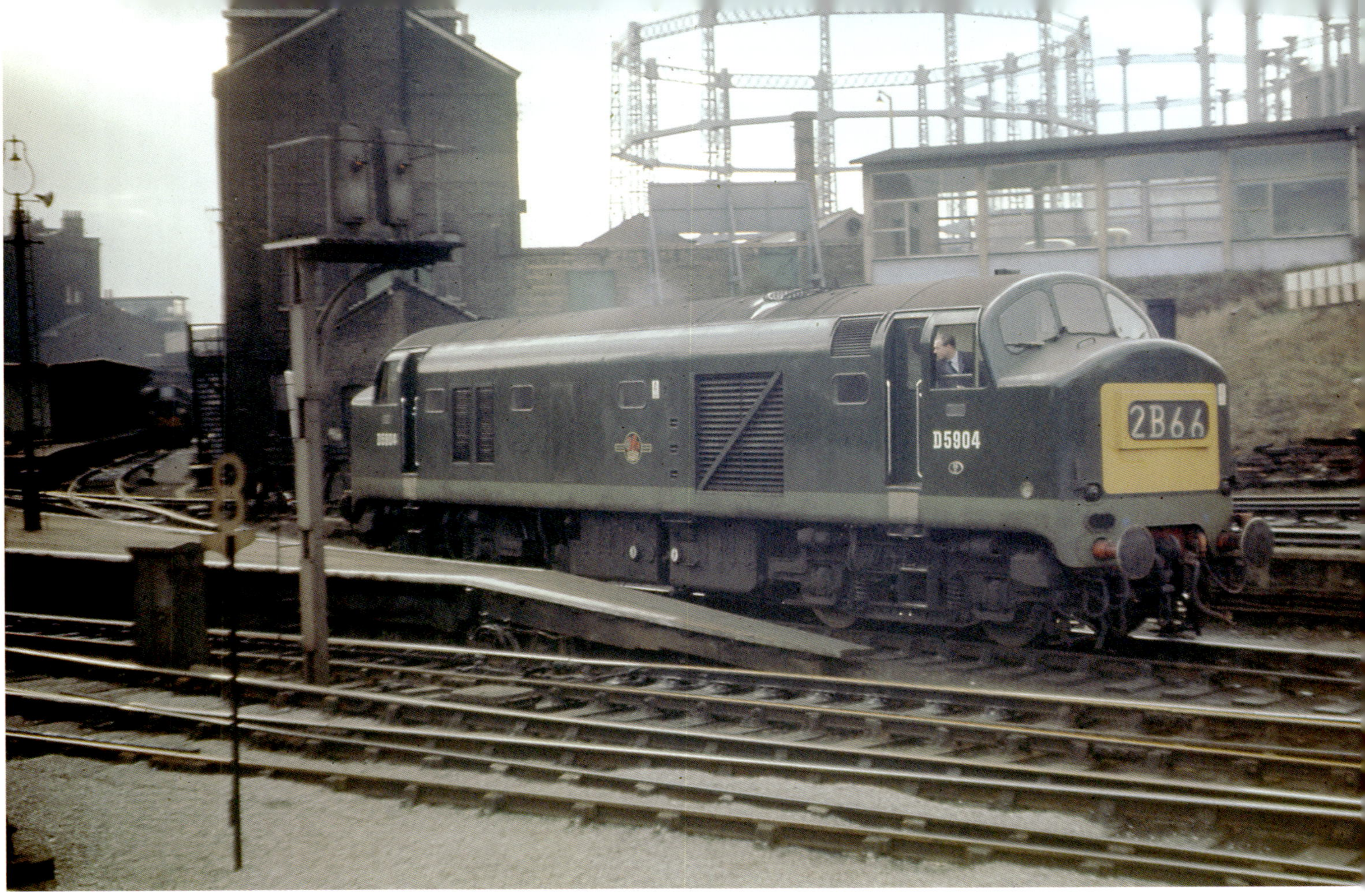

With D5904 trailing exhaust smoke across the suburban platforms at Kings Cross in 1965, it seems we are struggling to find Baby Deltics actually working trains attracting much attention of the photographers of the time. This example was another George Cohen victim in August 1969. ***Len Smith***

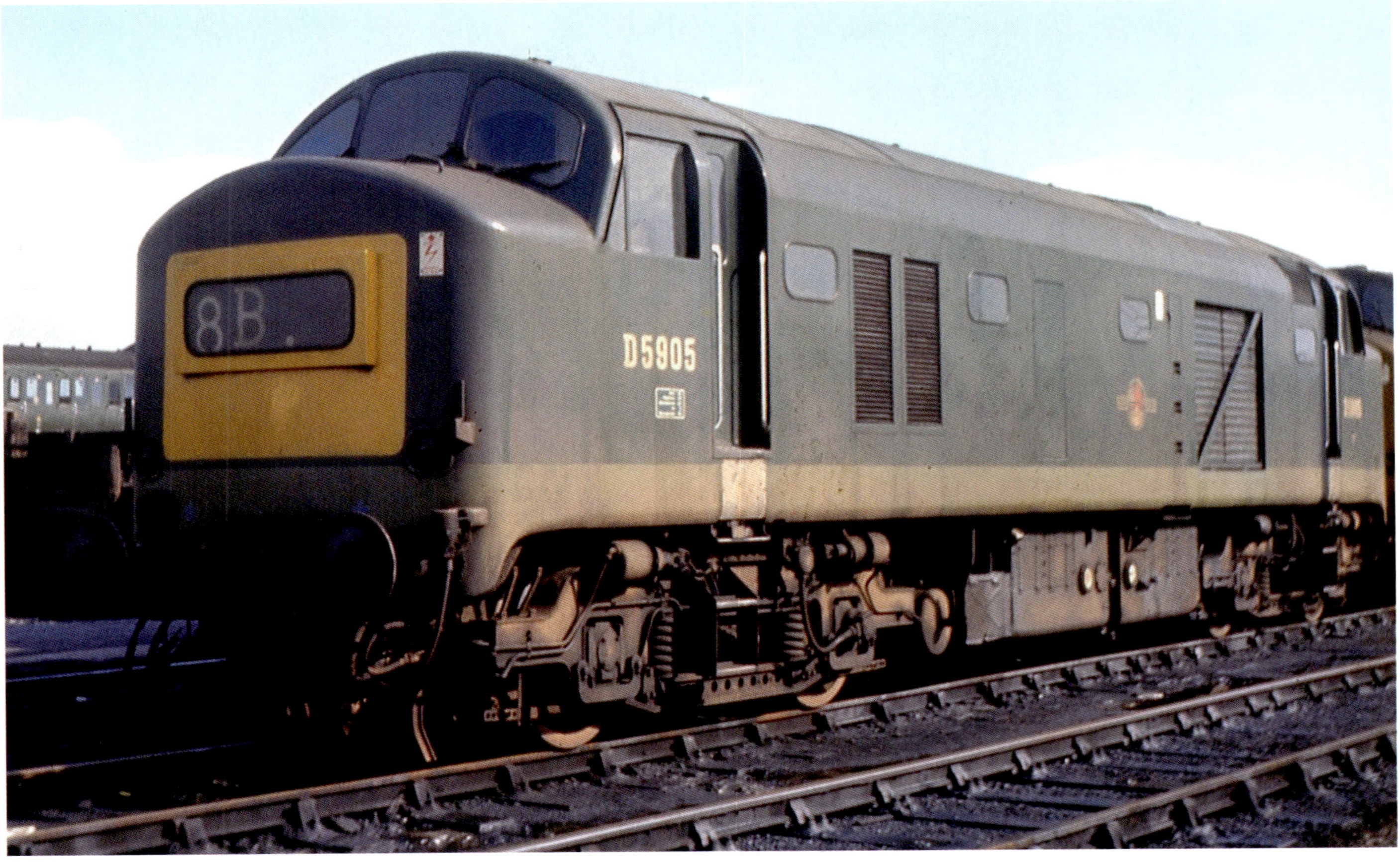

This time we visit Hitchin depot on a weekend in April 1970 to capture D5905 coupled ahead of classmate D5909 in the yard. Some work was found for the class at weekends on permenant way workings but for a short while this pairing of D5905 and D5909 could often be seen on trains of North London's waste to and from Ashburnham Grove. ***Grahame Wareham***

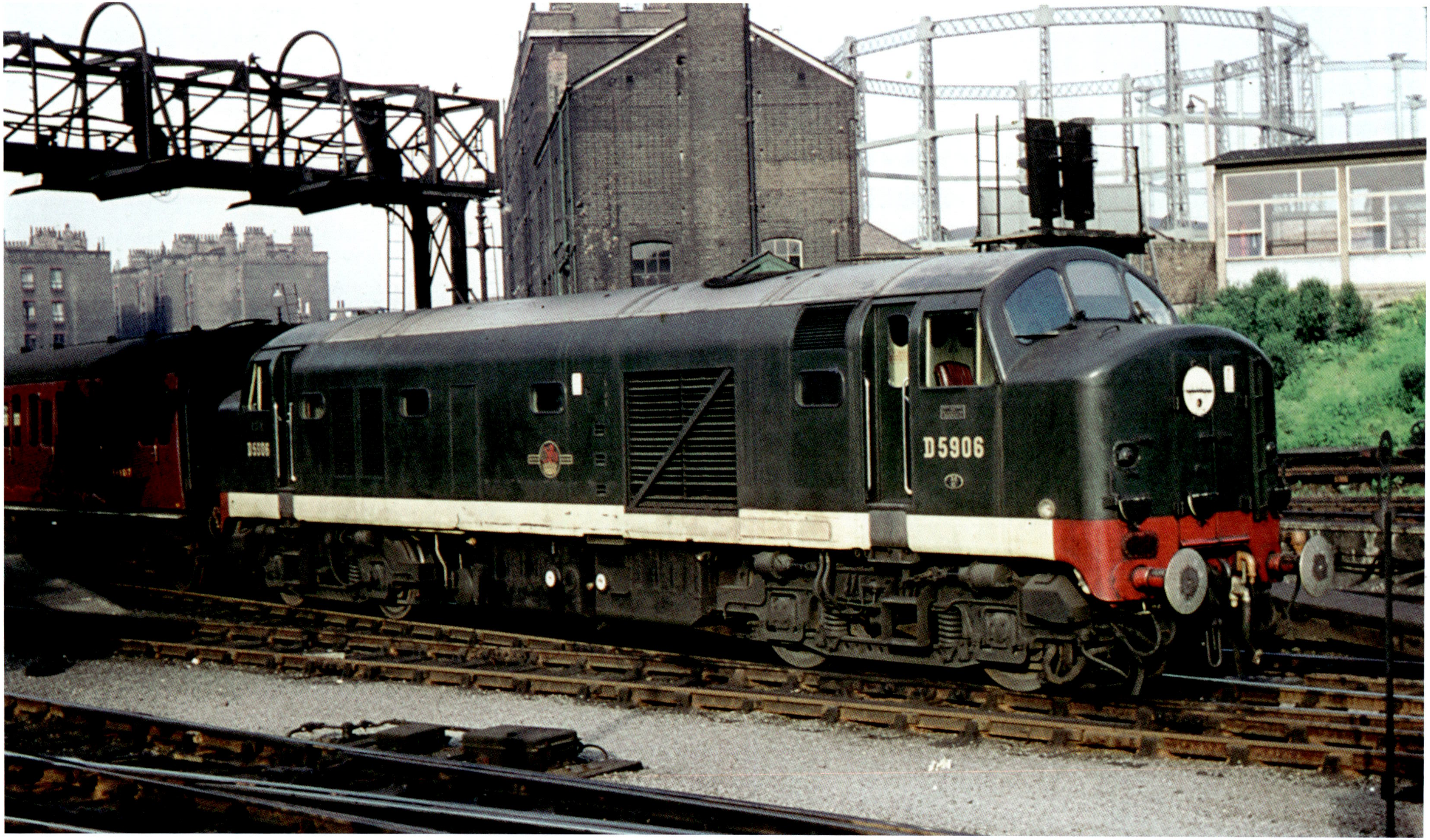

Only our second shot of a Baby Deltic working a train finds D5906 in original condition awaiting the right away from Kings Cross with a rake of British Railways built suburban stock on 13 May 1961. Accepted into service on 8 May 1959, D5906 along with her other class members spent almost two years out of traffic between 1963 and 1965, but it was this example that had the distinction of being the first to be withdrawn on 30 September 1968. For the record it had been stored at Doncaster shed since 6 June where it remained until December 1968 when it was moved within the works complex. In June 1969 it found itself being moved again this time to Kettering to join its sisters and become the sixth to be broken up here during that November. ***D Twibell/Transport Treasury***

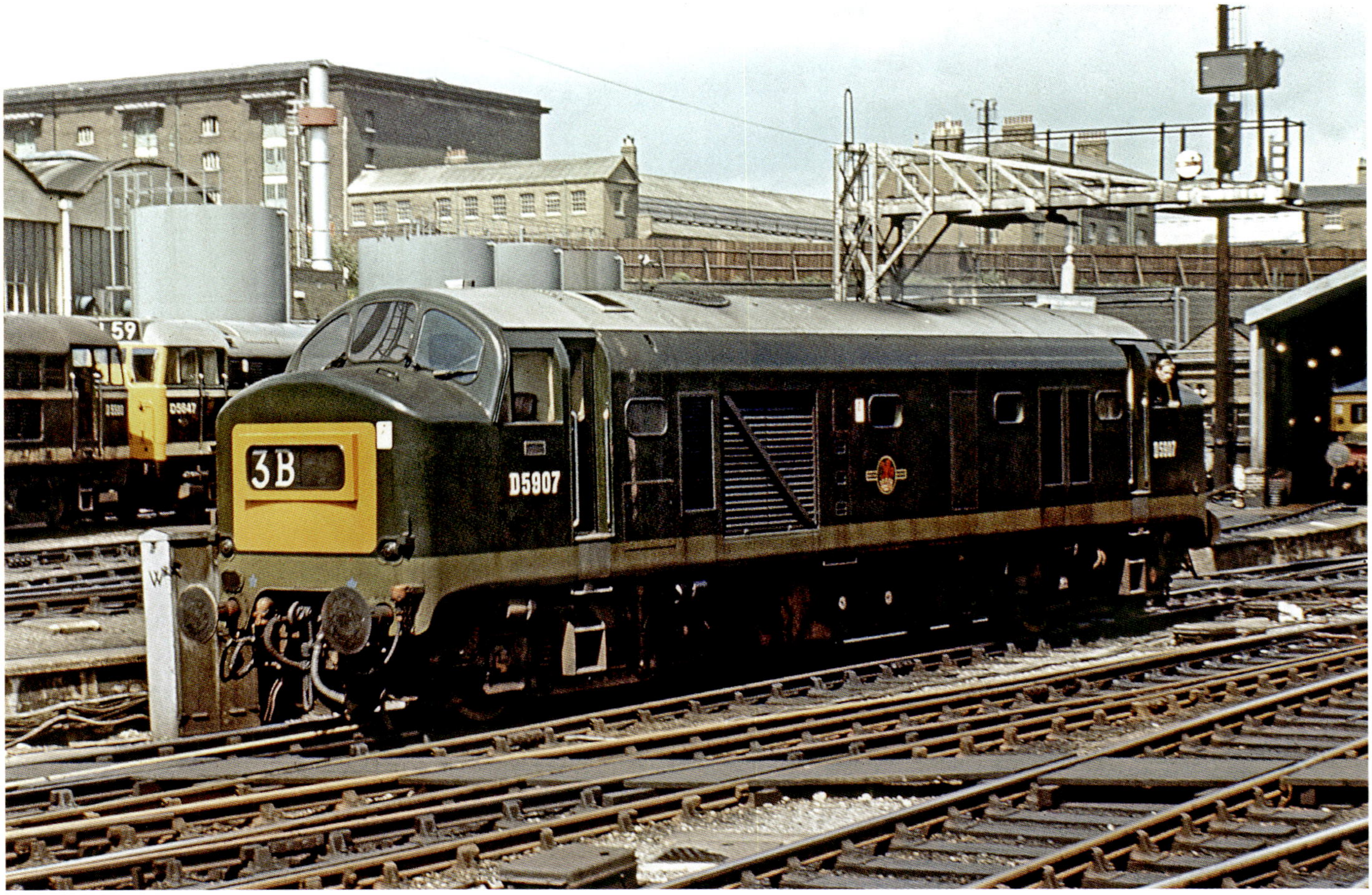

The platform ends at Kings Cross were always a magnet for spotters and cameramen alike to watch the movements around the station throat. This time we find D5907 in respectable condition shuffling around between outer suburban workings during April 1967. Withdrawn on 20 October 1968 this locomotive would be the first to feel the torches of George Cohen's cutters in July 1969. ***Rail Photoprints/Mike Jefferies***

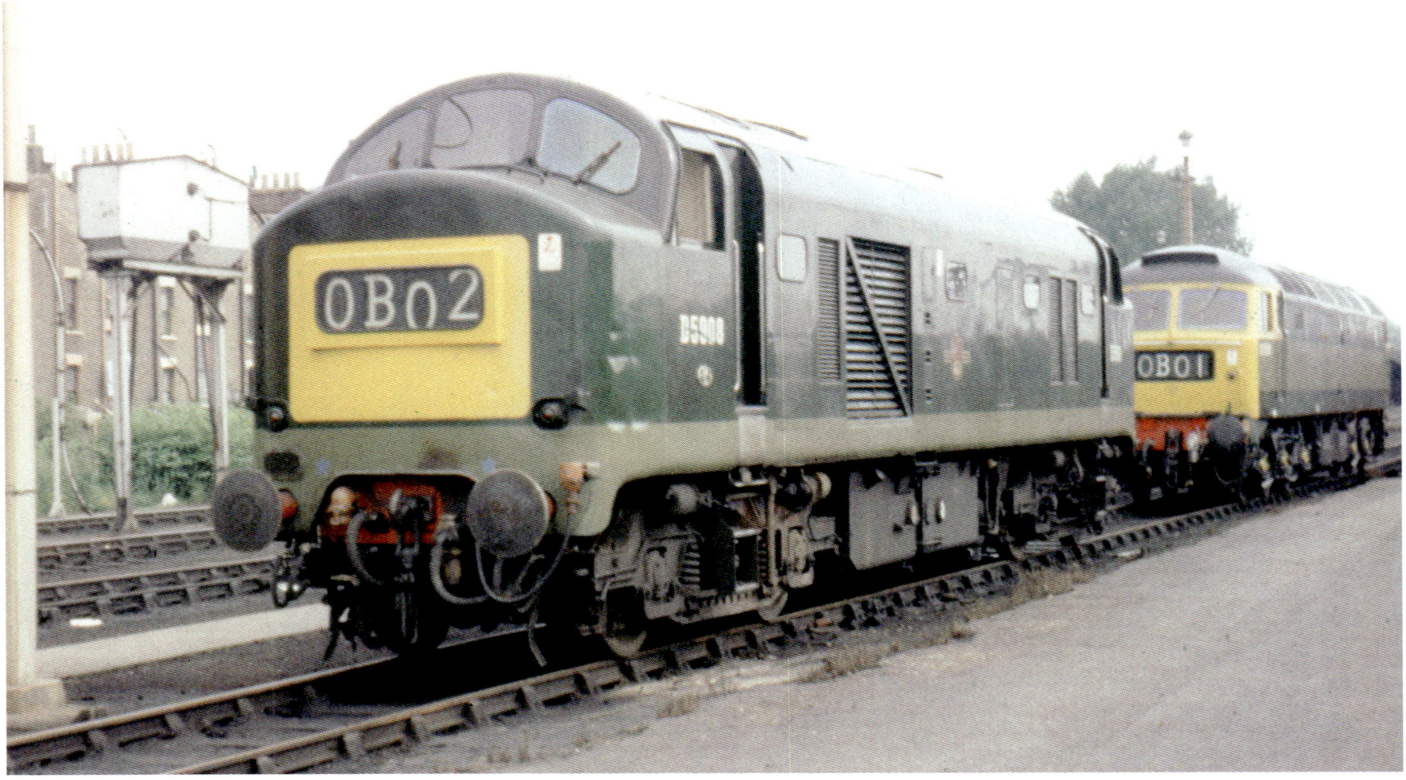

We see D5908 on the depot at 34G Finsbury Park during the summer of 1967. Now termed as Class 23 this had now become their main allocation depot since it opened in the spring of 1960. We are reminded of the modified style of headcode panel placed across the sealed up front access doors that were originally specified for the locomotives. Modellers should note that almost all of the photographs we viewed in selecting shots for this book the second prefix on this four character headcode system was set as B denoting the London area of the Great Northern Secton of the Eastern Region at the time. ***The Late Robert Jenkins, courtesy of the Railway Club of Wales***

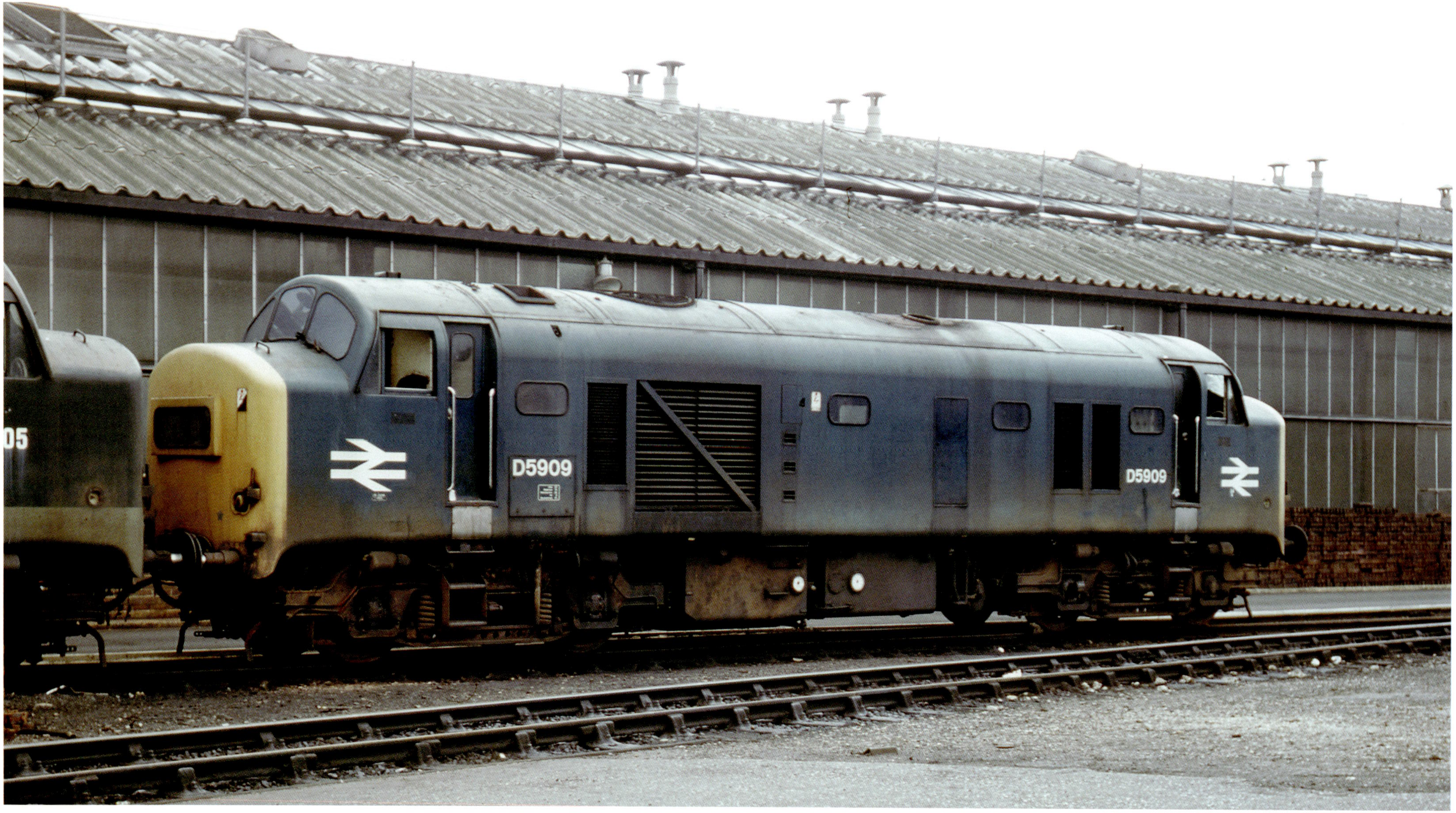

As we have already mentioned D5905 and D5909 worked in tandem during their latter months of service during 1970. On Valentine's Day 1971 D5905 was withdrawn and D5909 which was the only example to make it to a blue repaint and withdrawn officially on 7 March. The pair were reunited once more at Stratford during the summer of 1971, where they remained coupled together again tucked away until May 1973 where we see them here awaiting the move to Kettering a few days later. Both would succumb to the cutters that October. Thus with only D5908 having found its way to John Cashmore's yard at Great Bridge near Bescot in late 1969 it left just D5901 as the last survivor, which as we have already mentioned would be the last to be disposed of during January 1977 bringing this chapter of English Electric history to a close. Or is it, as this book is published, a group are recreating a Baby Deltic with a surviving T9-29 Napier Deltic engine and the much modified body from 37372 which was once D6859! ***Rail Photoprints***

Racehorses & Regiments

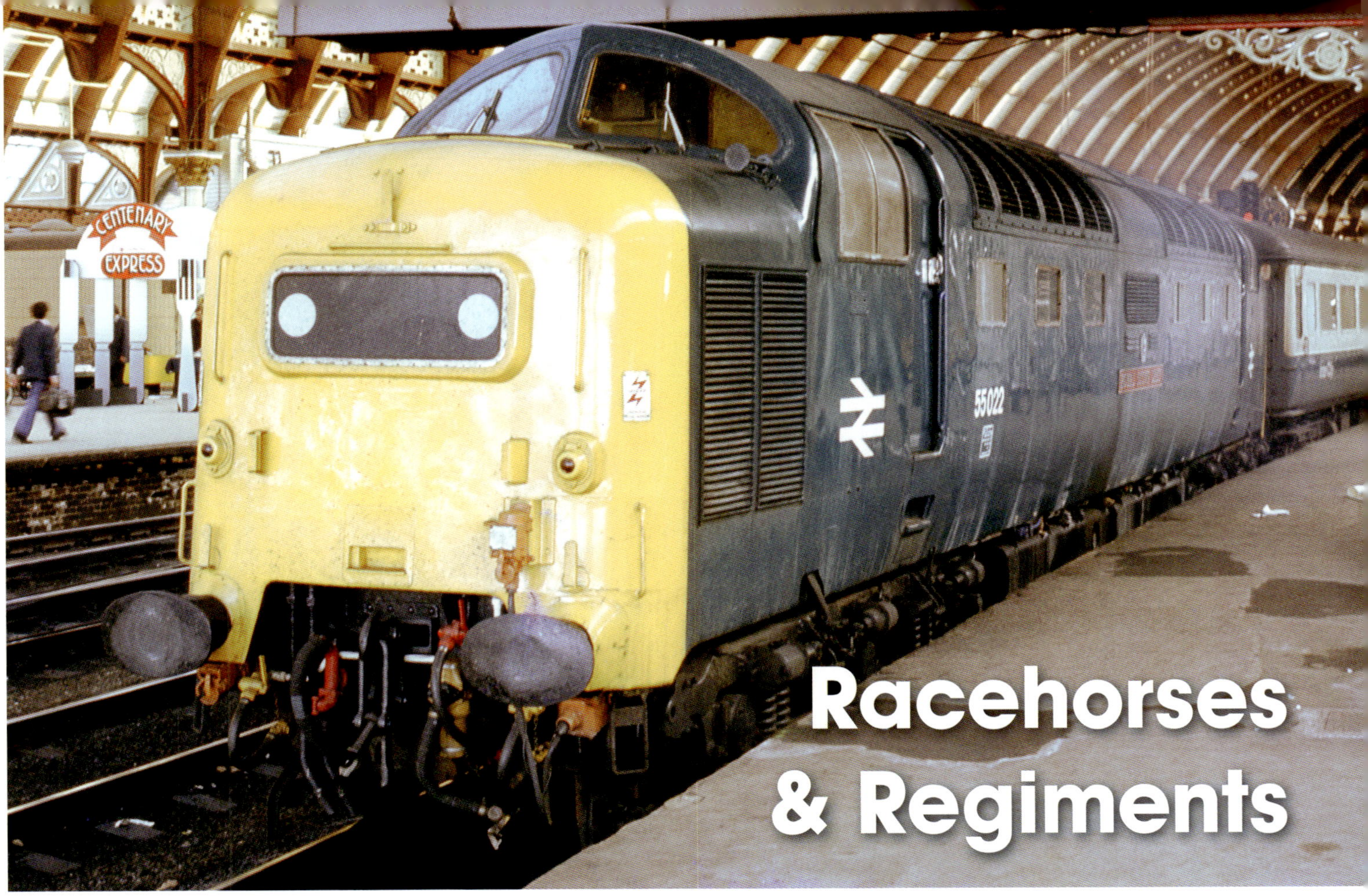

The 14.05 Kings Cross to York has just arrived at its destination behind 55022 Royal Scots Grey on 28 September 1979. Six days beforehand the locomotive had just been released from Doncastaer Works after its final Intermediate repairs. ***Len Ball***

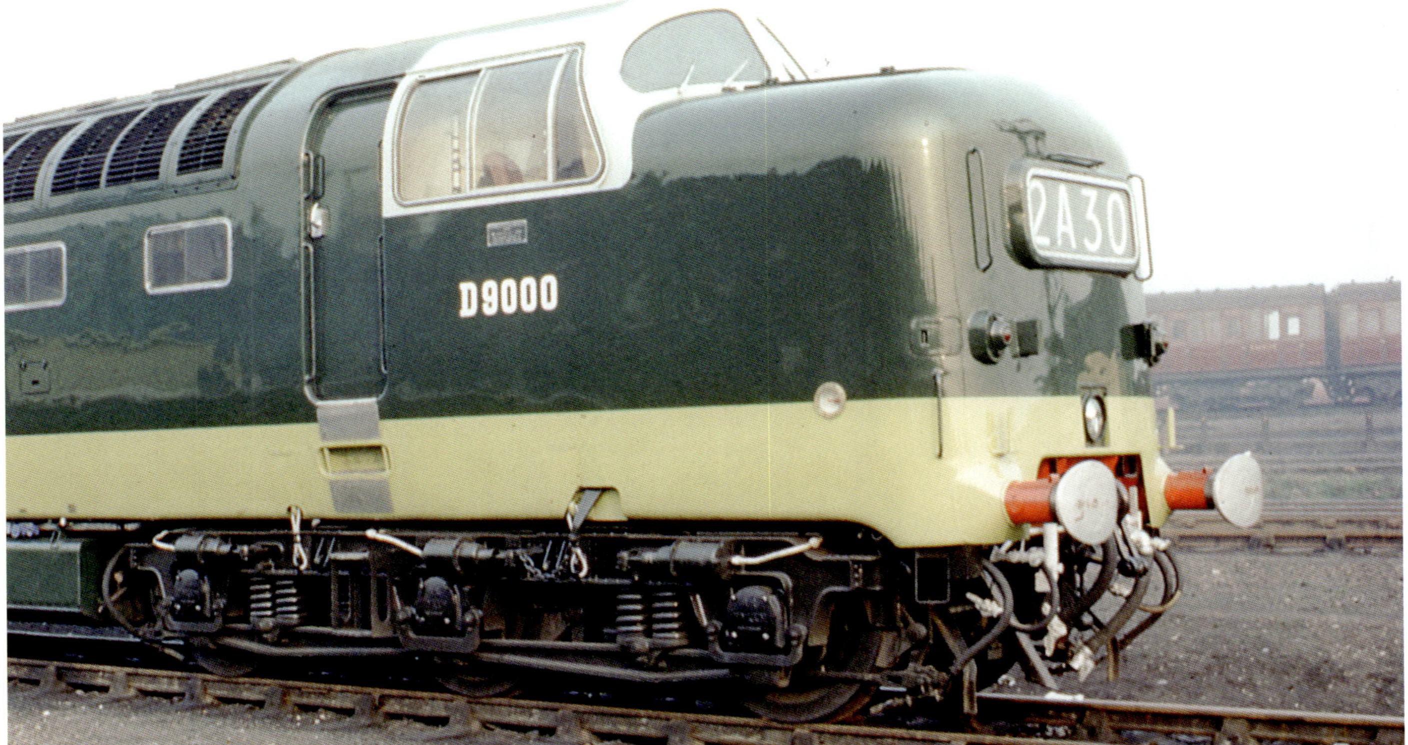

This close up view of the as yet un-named D9000 is thought to have been taken on 28 February 1961 when the locomotive was first delivered and shows one of the reasons for the locomotives delayed introduction due to the installation of an experimental flashing headlight fitted to both ends above the buffer beams. The locomotive was noted with the flashing light on test around the Hadley Wood area on the 10 March whilst running light engine from Finsbury Park to Doncaster. Experiments were however abandoned and the lights were later removed during August 1961. ***Strathwood Library Collection***

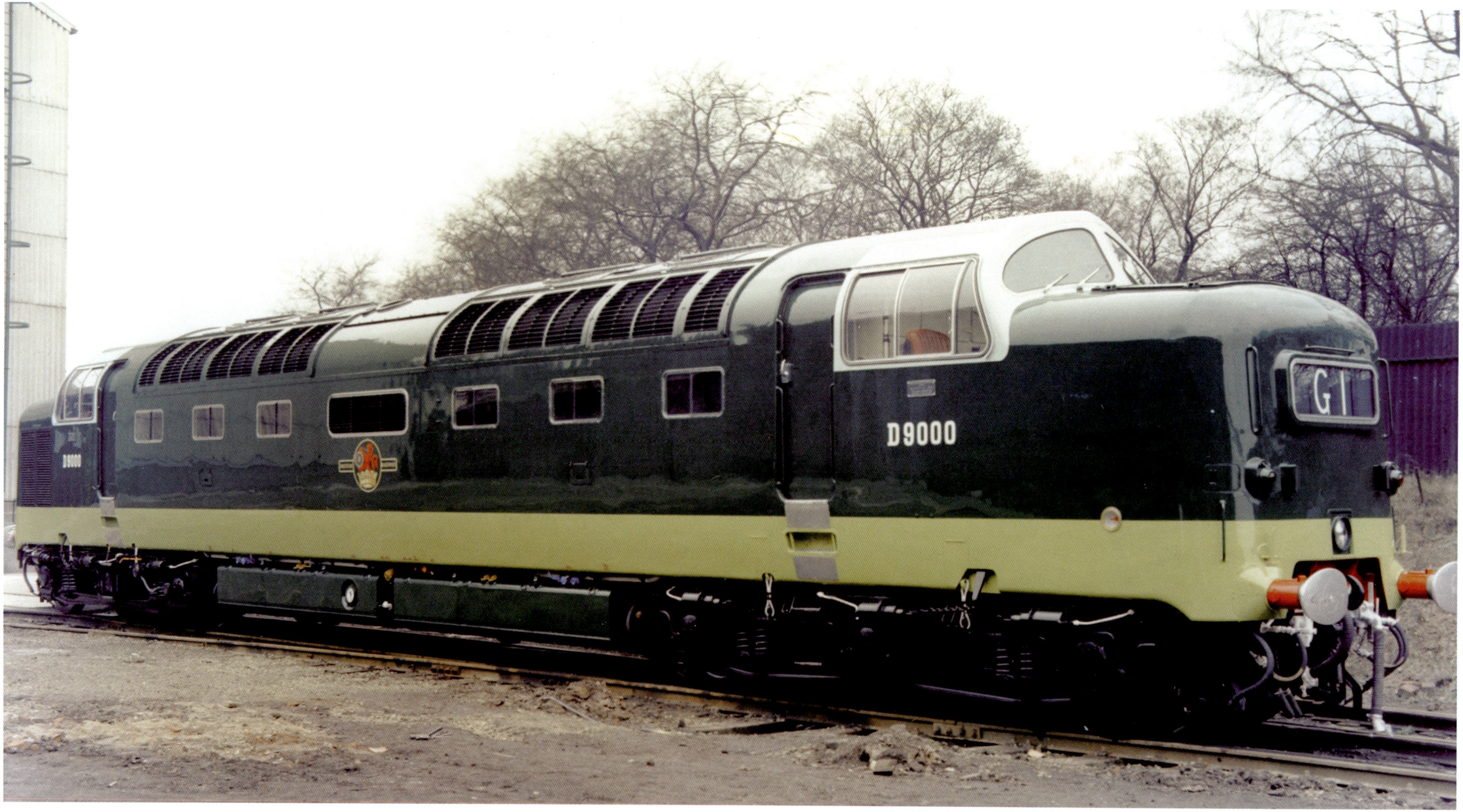

This was the scene a few days earlier in February 1961 as D9000 stands posed outside the workshops of English Electric's Vulcan Foundry near Newton le Willows. As can be seen the underslung fuel tanks were originally painted in the darker green to match the upper panels of the locomotive. It is reported that consideration was given to painting the whole locomotive in the lighter shade of green which was not dissimilar to the London North Eastern Railway's Apple Green. Now that might have been influenced by DELTIC's light blue scheme reminiscent of both the pre-war streamlined A4s and the rival London Midland & Scottish Railway's Coronation. As the locomotives were destined for the prestige services of the East Coast Main Line it is not unreasonable to suggest that the Eastern Region management who had been apprenticed to the former LNER might have favoured this option. However the British Railways Board at Marylebone clearly did not want to see any reversion to former livery styles for the Eastern or Scottish Regions. Meanwhile the Western Region was dabbling with colour variations of their own for the early builds of Westerns on their prestige trains. ***Strathwood Library Collection***

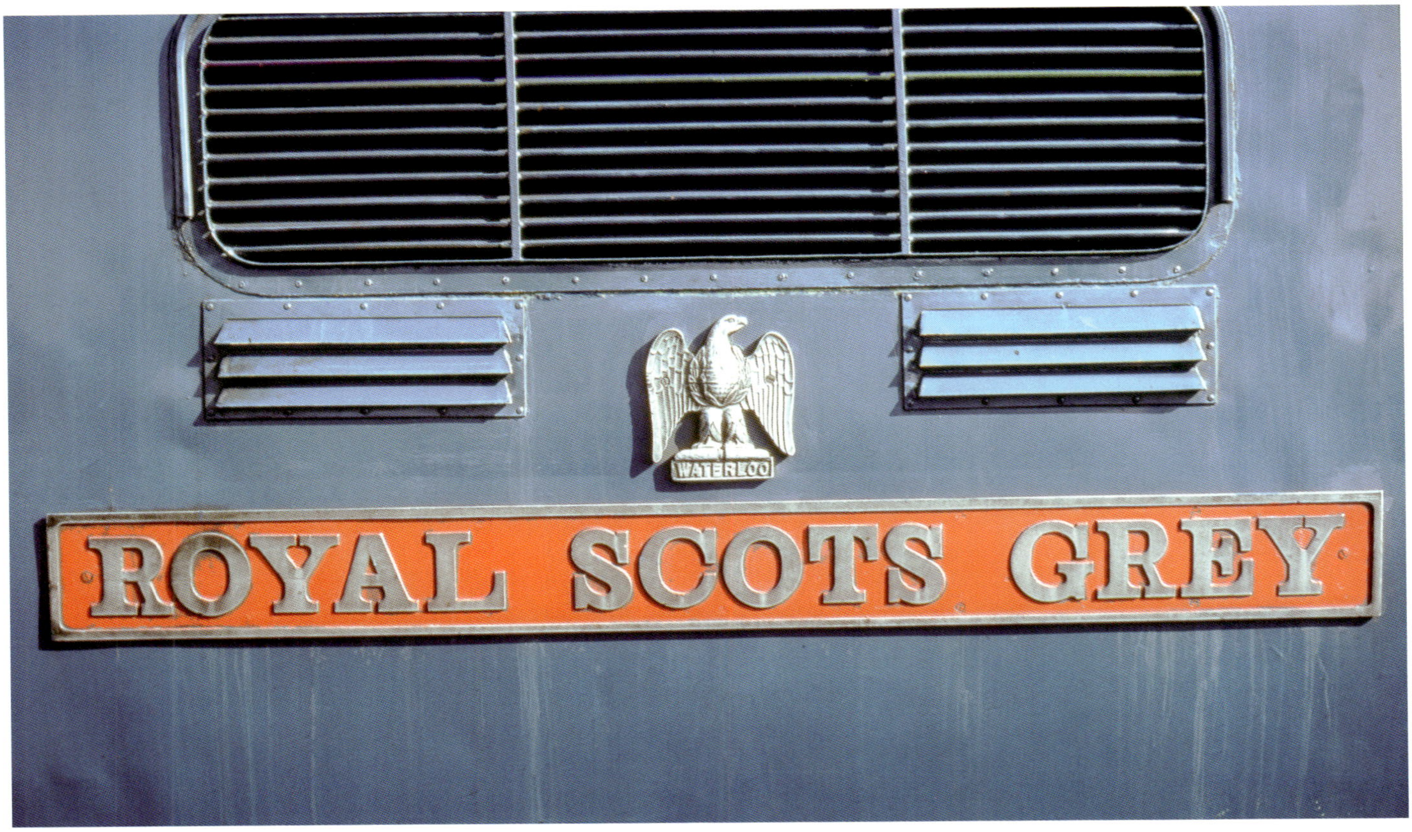

Following completion of the delivery of all of the class into service a full Deltic diagrammed timetable was introduced from the 18 June 1962 at the start of the new summer timetable. This date also coincided with the centenary of The Flying Scotsman service and D9020 Nimbus was specially prepared at Finsbury Park to haul the down centenary Flying Scotsman whilst Haymarket produced D9000 for the up service. Prior to departure from Edinburgh Waverley D9000 was named Royal Scots Grey during a ceremony performed by Brigadier J.E. Swetenham D.S.O., Colonel of The Royal Scots Greys. By June 1977 when this photograph was taken the locomotive had been renumbered as 55022 since 10 April 1974. ***Sid Steadman***

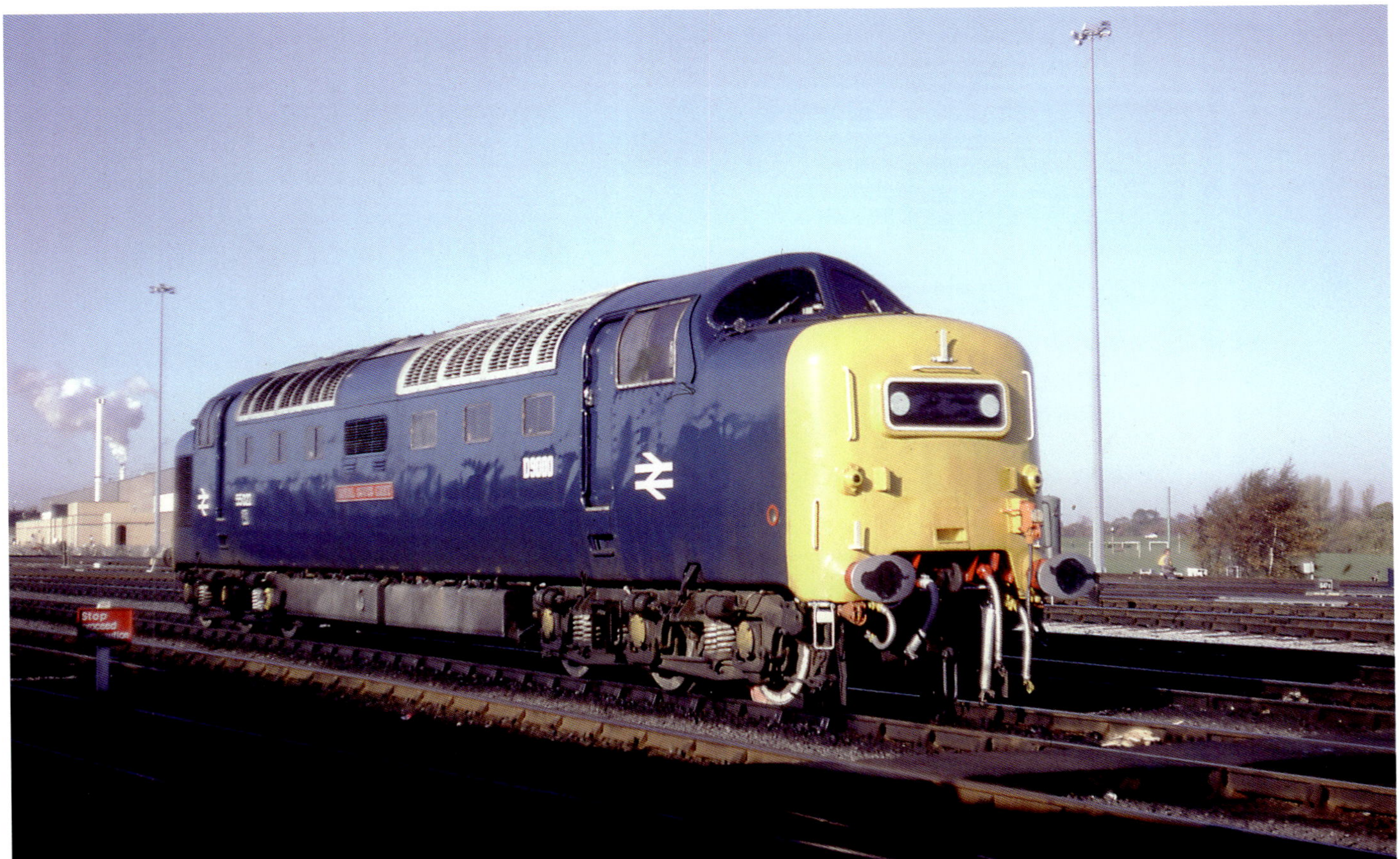

Towards the very end of Deltic running and 55022 Royal Scots Grey also sported D9000 numbers together with painted white roof grills, wheel rims and other details as seen here at York in the afternoon before Bonfire Night 1981. ***Strathwood Library Collection***

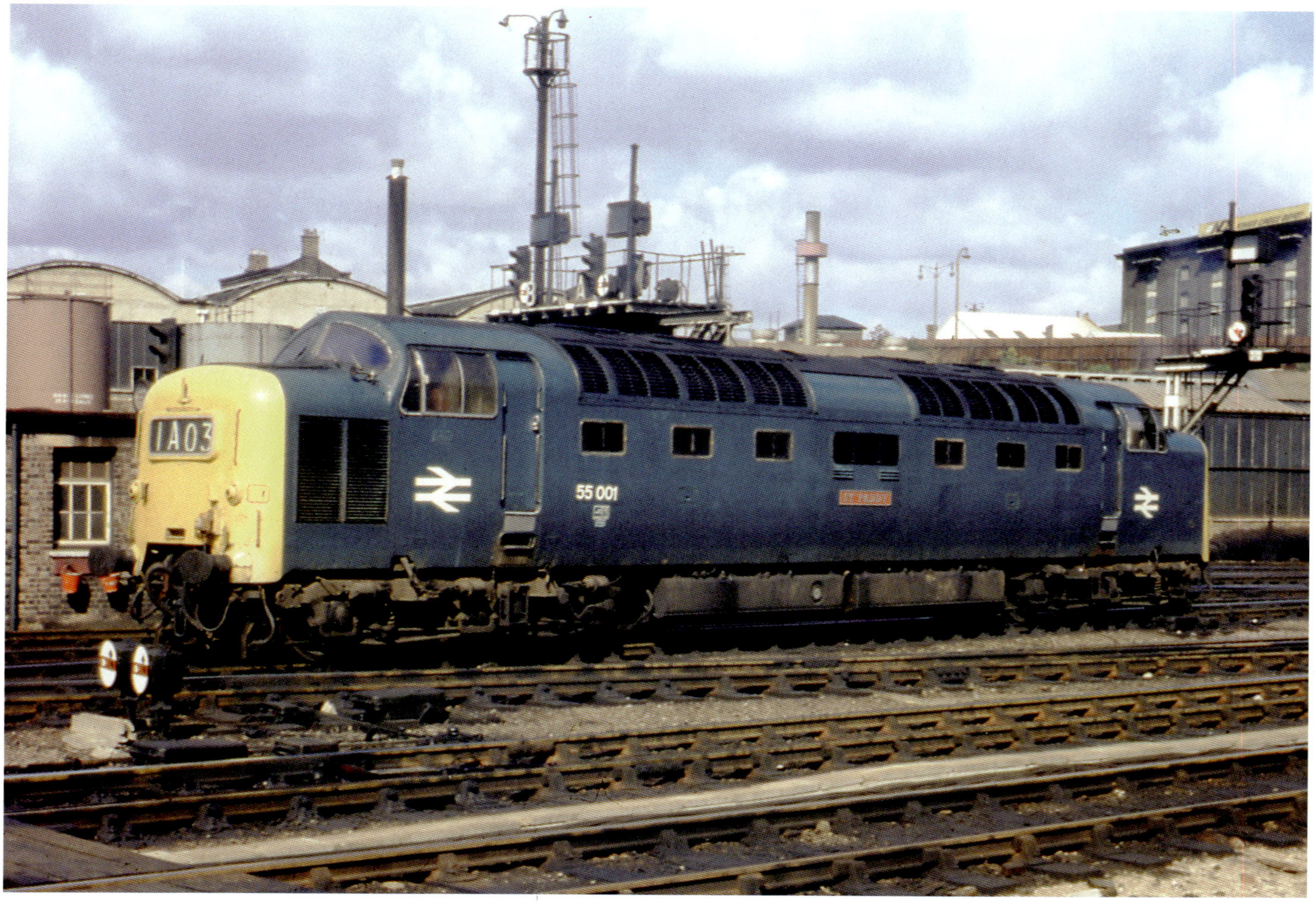

The up Moorgate platform at Kings Cross has always been a popular spot for watching the departures and arrivals together with the once inevitable light engine movements to the stabling point. Here in 1974 55001 St. Paddy performs just such an exercise with her home depot of Finsbury Park being just a few miles away. ***Les Byatt***

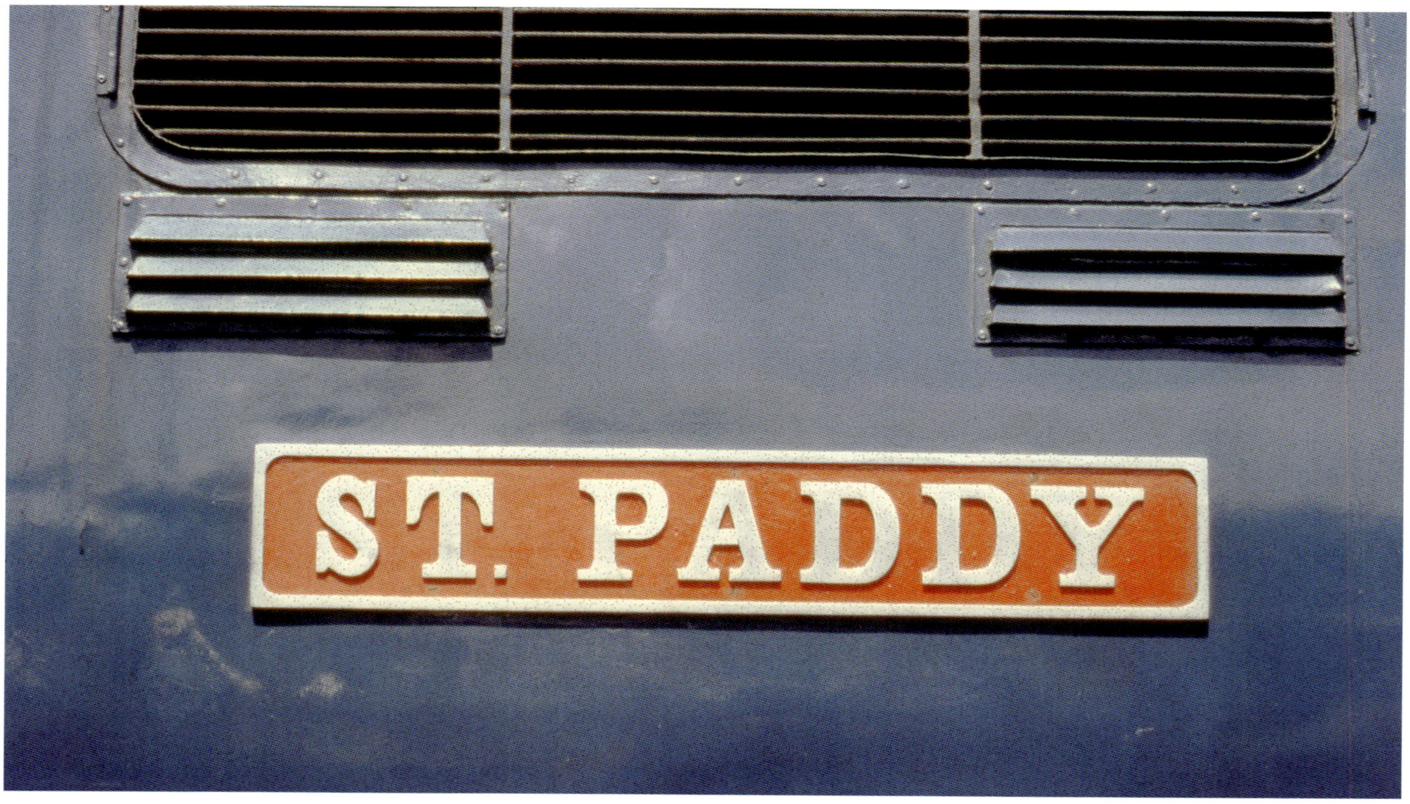

Just over four months after D9001 entered service the locomotive was fitted with these nameplates on 7 July 1961 at Doncaster Works without ceremony, this was in honour of the racehorse owned by Sir Victor Sassoon, winner of the Derby, St. Leger, 2,000 Guineas and a notable racehorse of the time. ***Steve Scott***

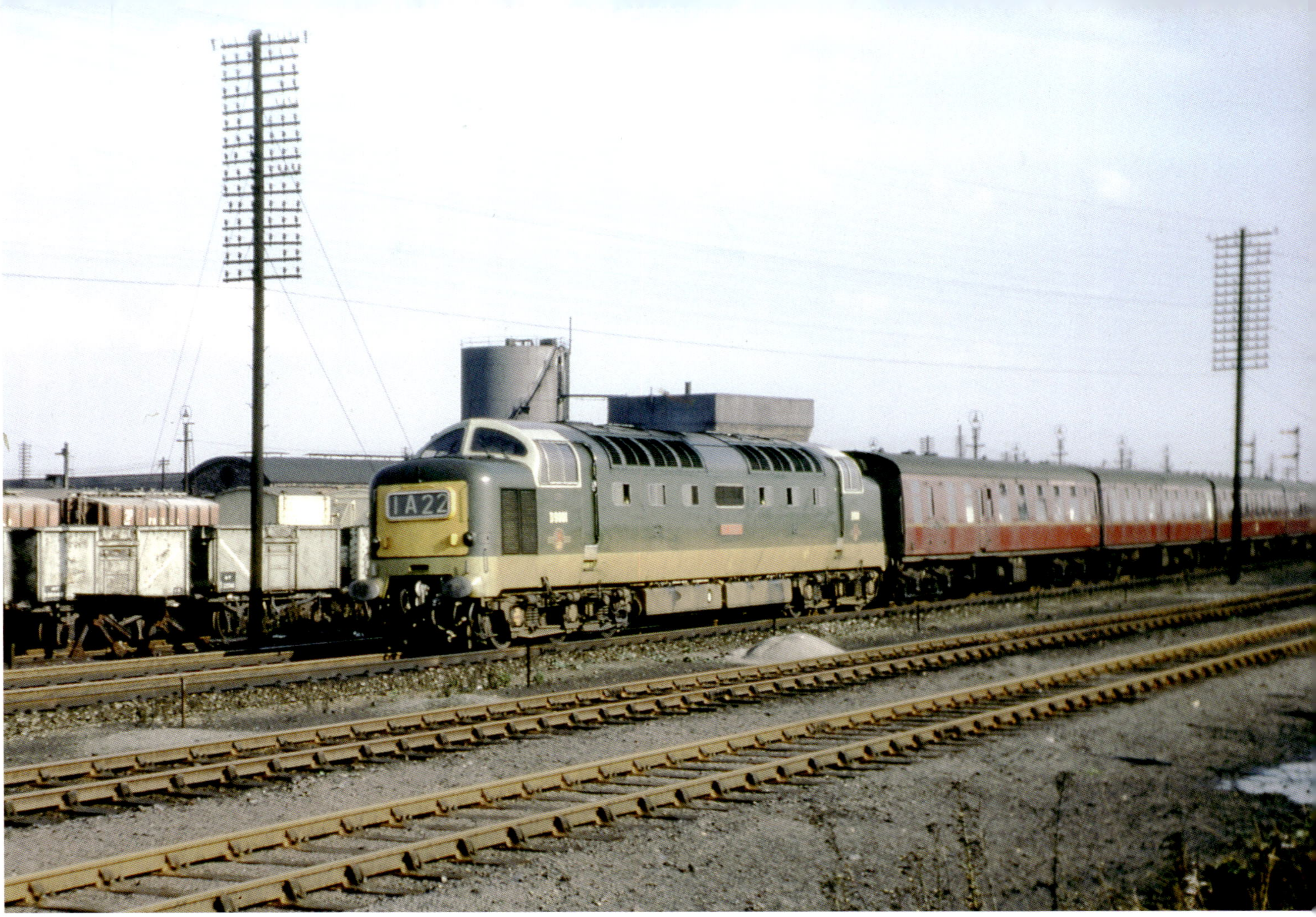

As can be seen from these two views Finsbury Park could not always keep its front line locomotives spotlessly clean in service as we witnessed by D9001 St. Paddy passing through Doncaster in 1962. ***John Rowe***

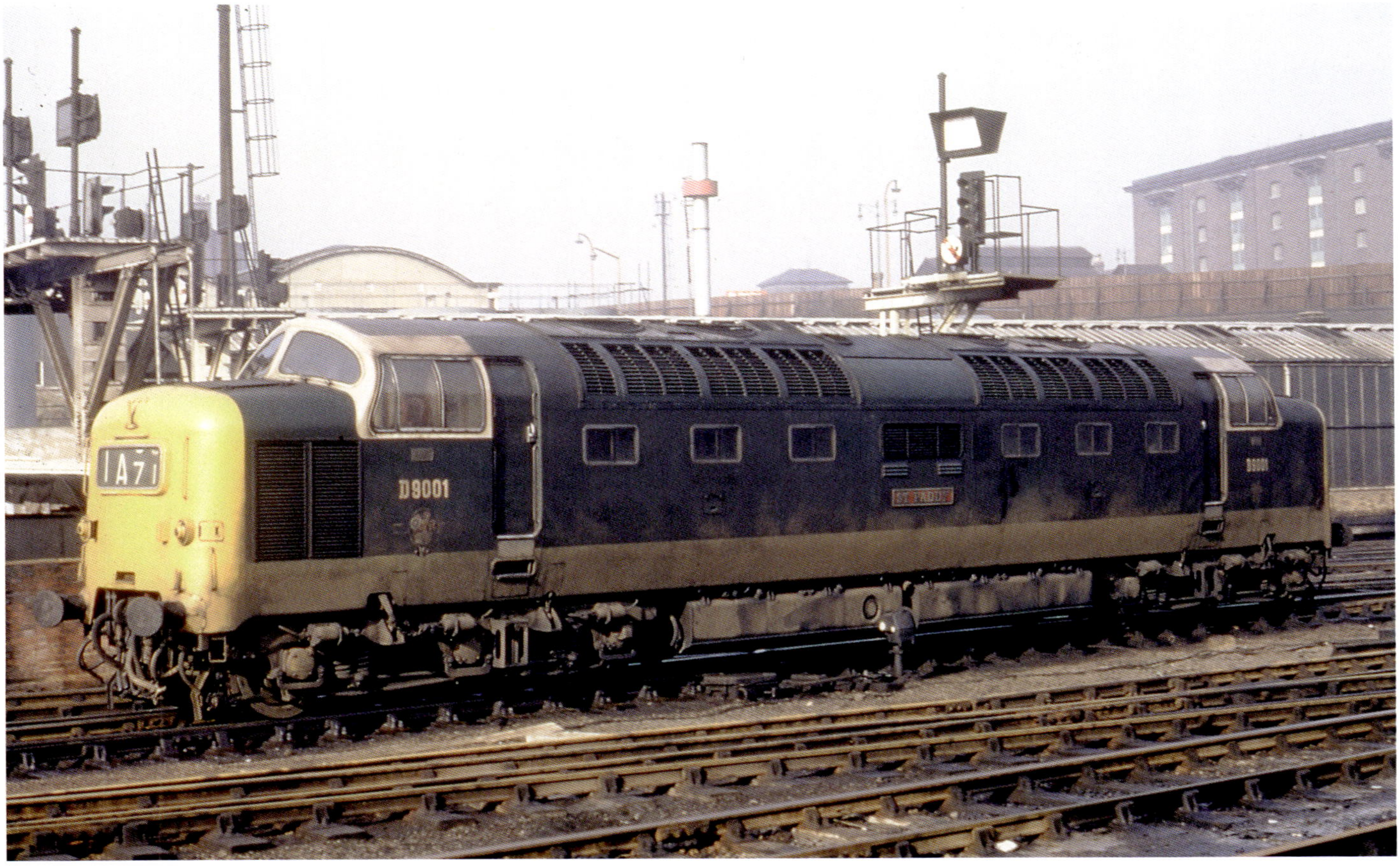

By the start of 1968 D9001 St.Paddy had started a spell lasting just over six months allocated to 64B Haymarket on their rosters whilst the class were undergoing fitment of dual braking. This example had already long clocked up over one million miles along the ECML when we see it early the following year at Kings Cross. ***Strathwood Library Collection***

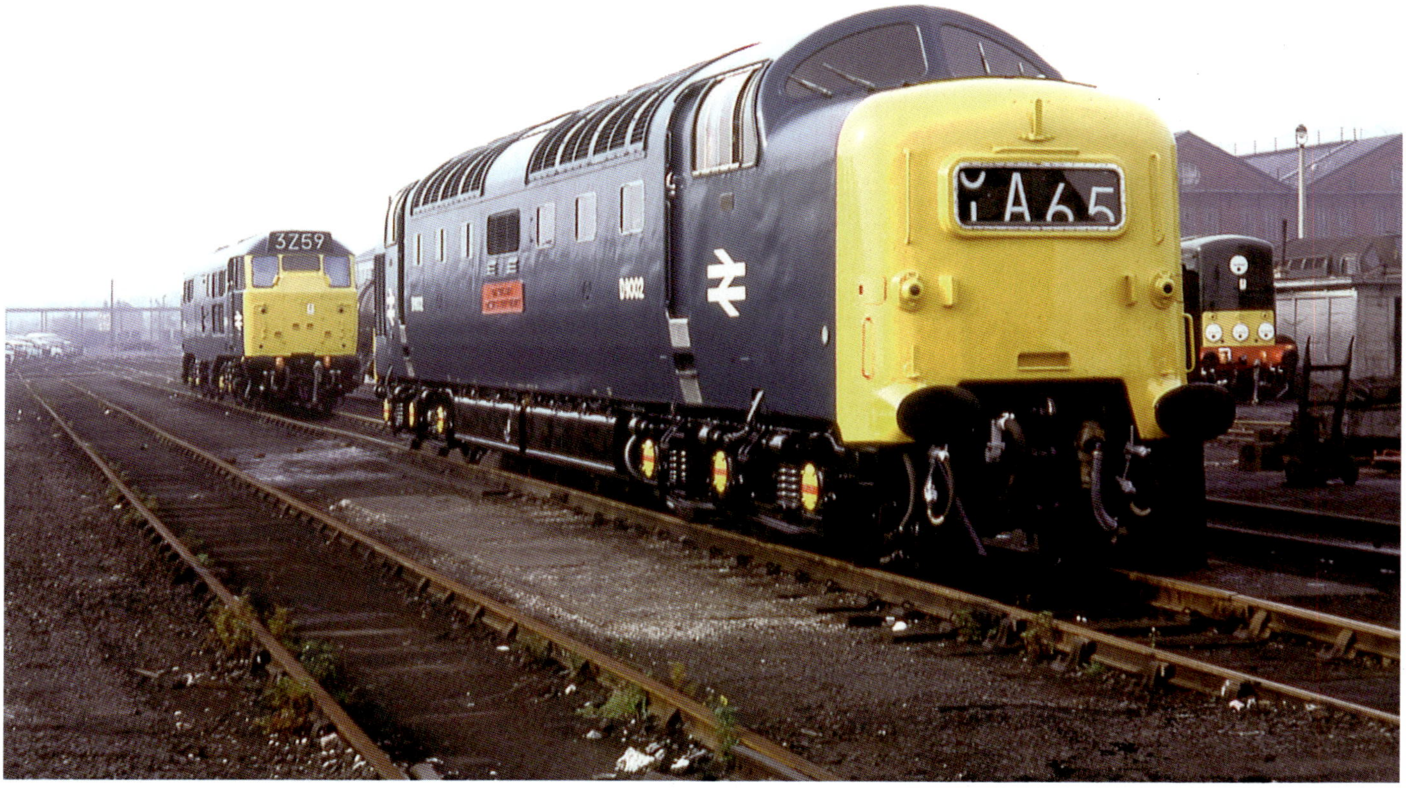

The first of the production Deltics into blue would be D9002 The King's Own Yorkshire Light Infantry seen here ready for release from Doncaster Works on 18 October 1966. It would return to the works again a year later to be equipped with dual brakes. ***Grahame Wareham***

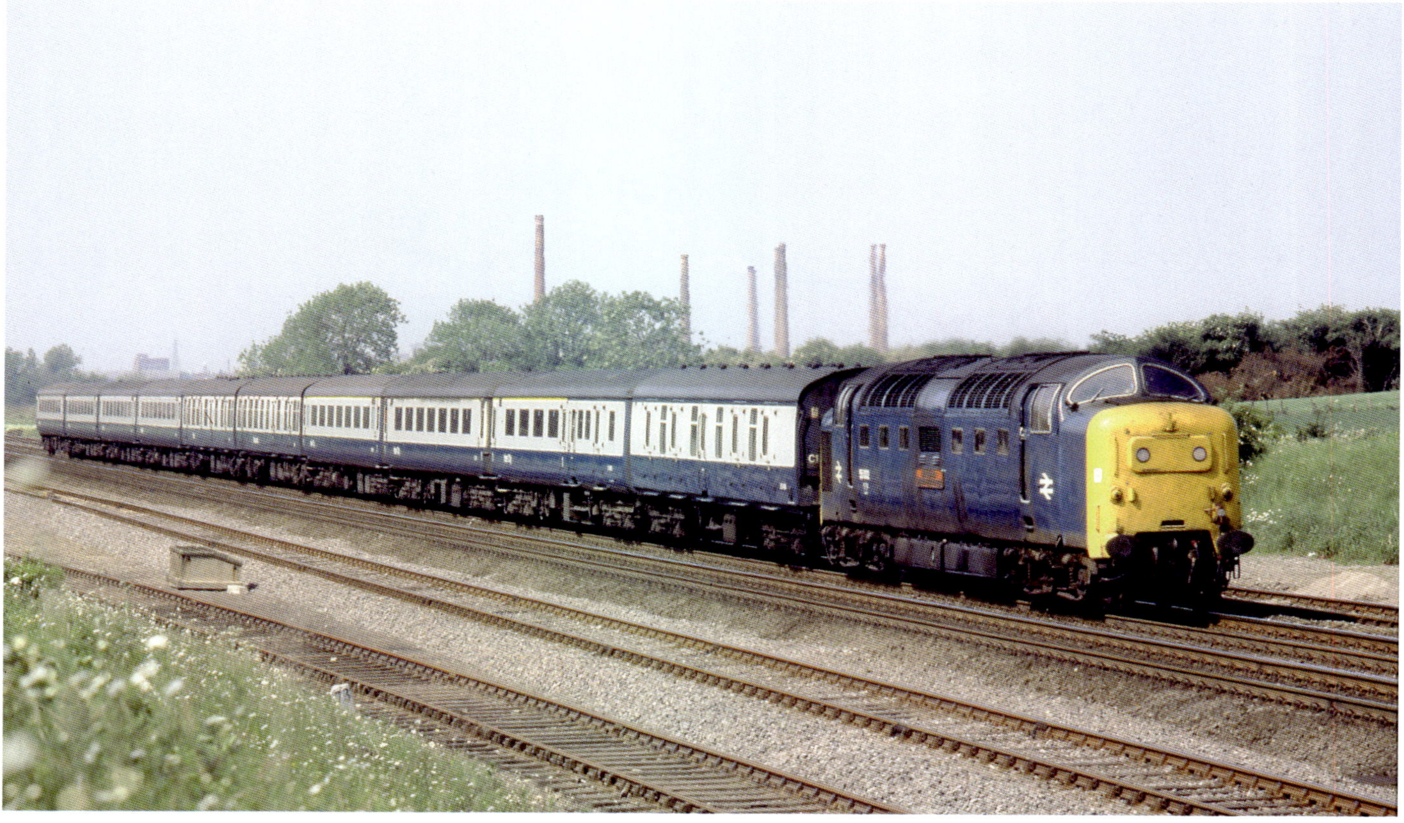

The once familiar tall chimneys of the many brickworks around Peterborough can be seen in the distance as 55002 The King's Own Yorkshire Light Infantry makes speedy progress on 3 June 1978. Another visit to Doncaster Works for a Heavy General Repair two years before this photograph was taken had included the plating over of route indicators, sand-box fillers and the cab quarter light windows. ***Aldo Delicata***

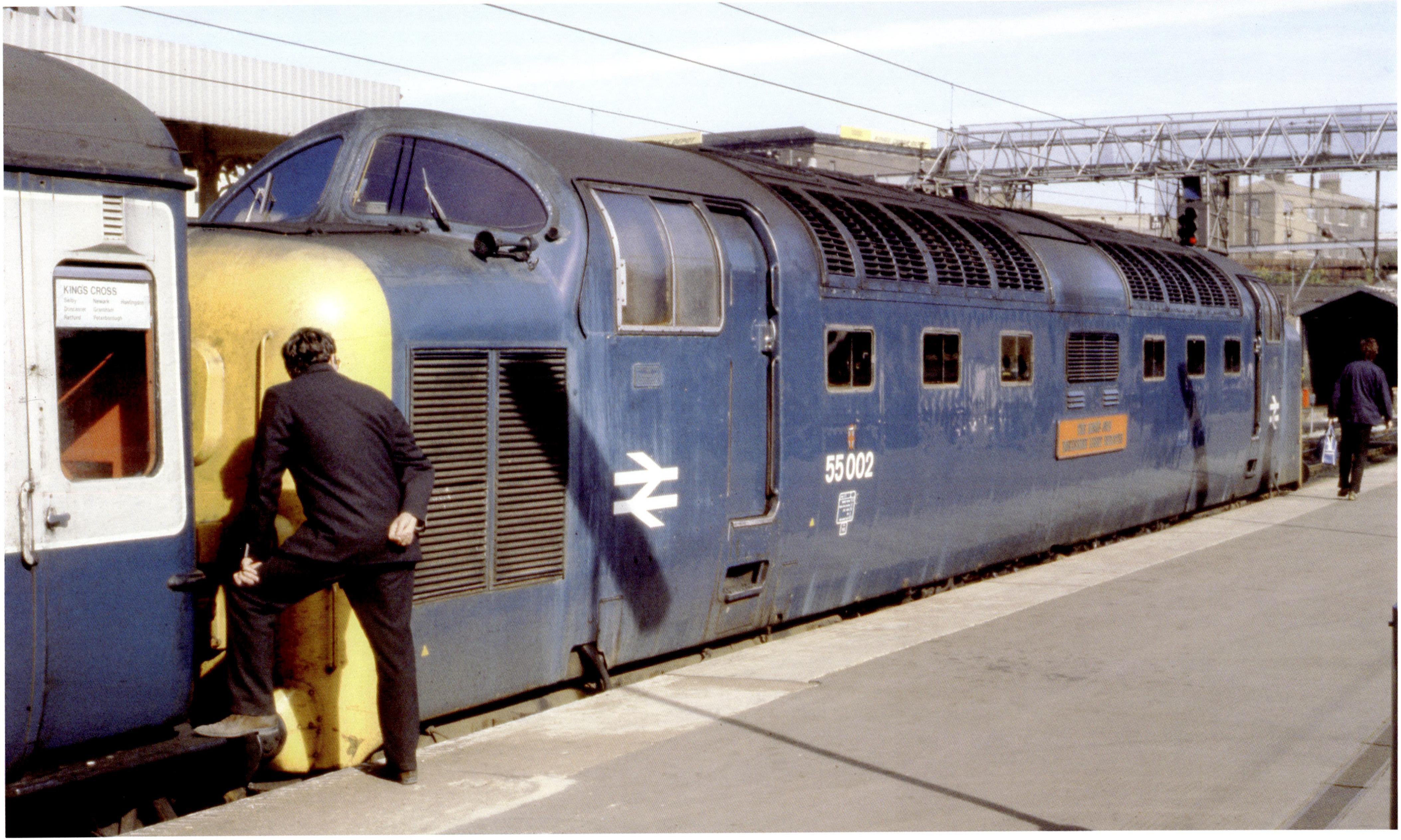

The following year sees the crew of 55002 The King's Own Yorkshire Light Infantry prepare for depature from Kings Cross on 15 September 1979 with the 10.05 service for York. The crests for the City of York have been affixed just above the locomotive number as since new this example had previously been a Gateshead machine until May 1979, an association it would keep beyond withdrawal on 2 January 1982 as the locomotive joined the National Railway Museum's collection for a life in preservation. It is also worth noting the placement of the locomotives horns since the shot opposite when ex-works at Doncaster thirteen years previously. ***Len Ball***

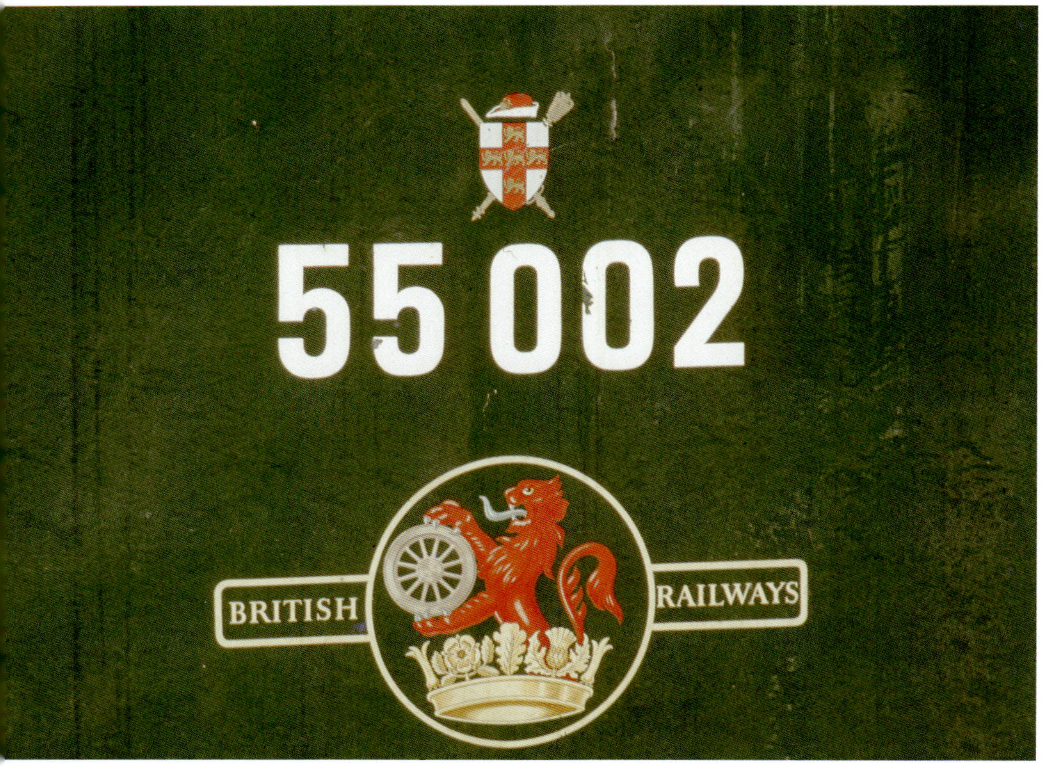

Ironically as the first of her class in blue livery she would also become the first back into two tone green when Doncaster Works released the locomotive back into traffic following its final Intermediate repair on 11 December 1980. The earlier style of numbers were applied with the official TOPS identity of 55002. ***Bruce Smetham***

As a celebrity locomotive it would be often selected for specials but could also be found on what had become the Deltics now staple diet of secondary express workings such as here at Scarborough to take over the 08.54 Filey to Newcastle on 5 September 1981. ***Bernard Mills***

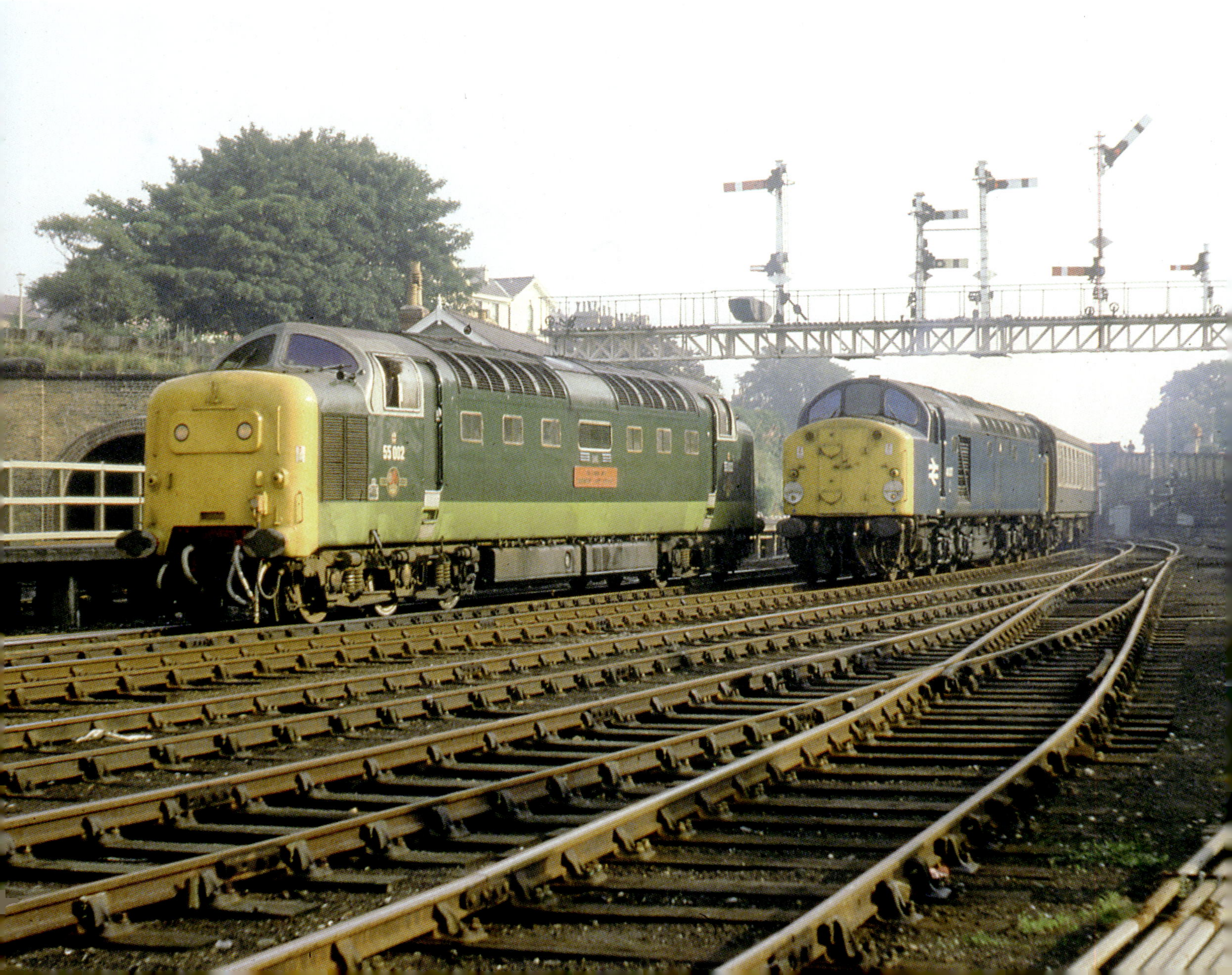

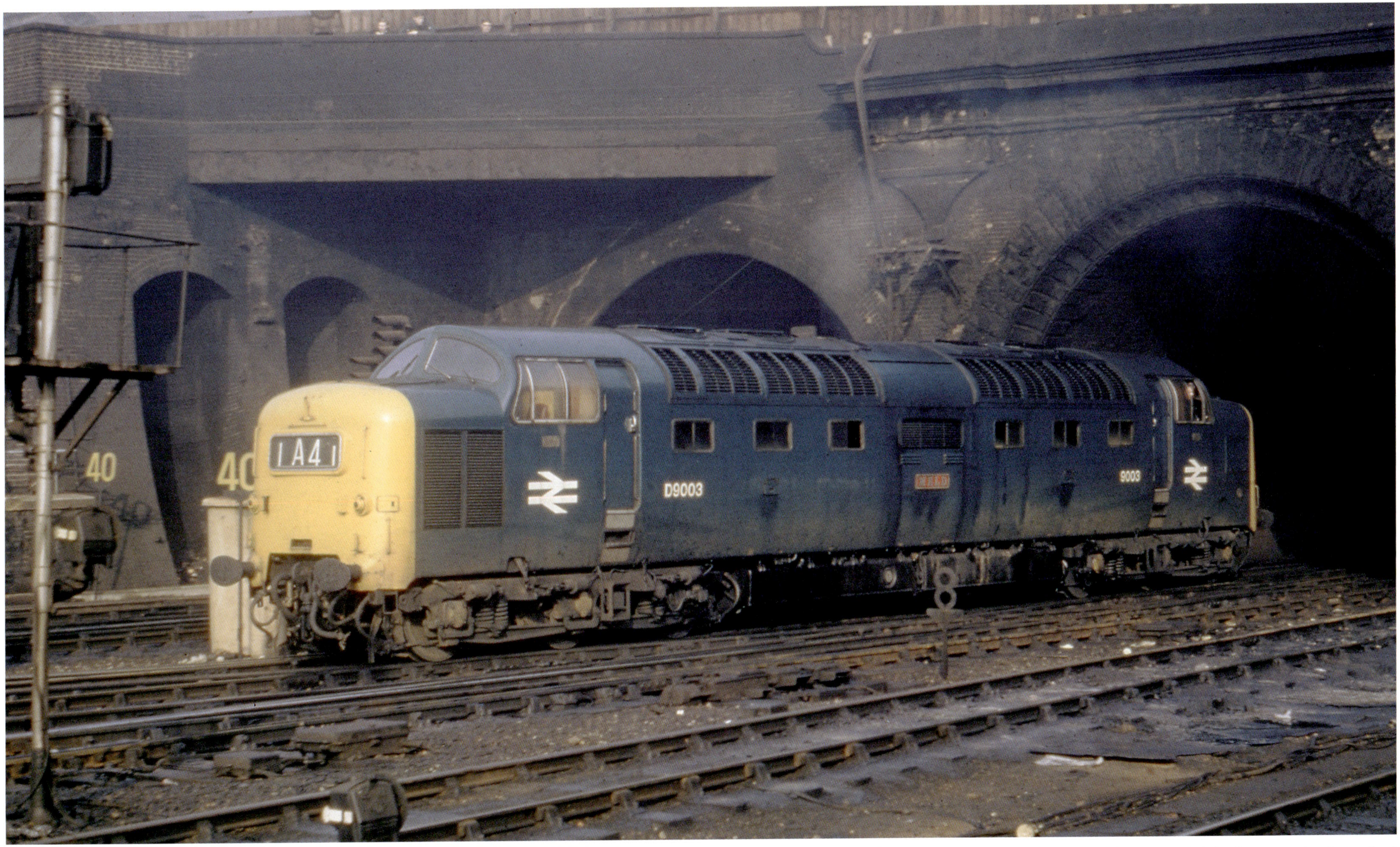

A sight and sound to quicken the pulse of many enthusiasts at Kings Cross was the swift acceleration around the station throat in and out of the tunnels when running light engine such as here with D9003 Meld early in 1969. On Valentine's Day the previous year the engine had been released from Doncaster Works, after a General repair, repainted into blue livery and equipped for dual braking. Aside from a short spell at Haymarket during the dual braking programme in late 1967 and early 1968, Meld would always be allocated to Finsbury Park. ***Strathwood Library Collection***

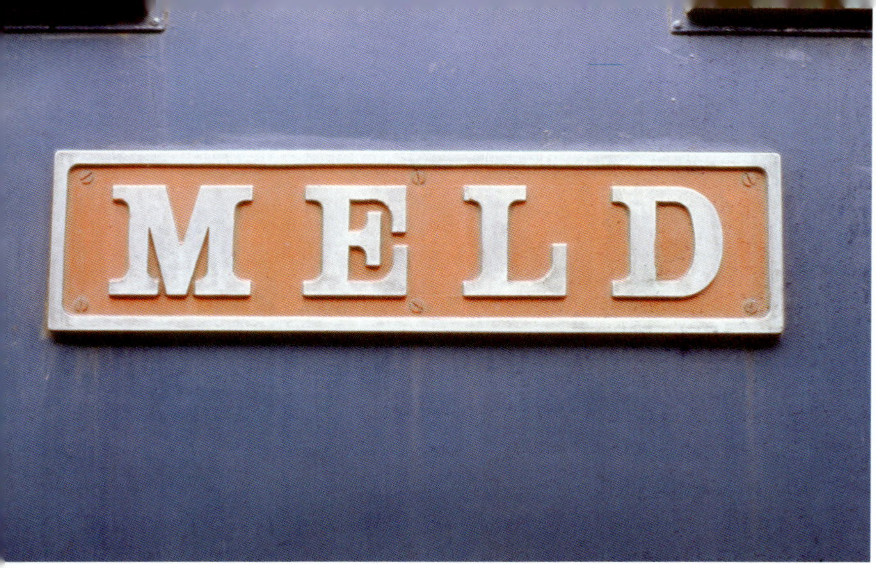

She would also be named on 7 July 1961 at Doncaster Works without any course to ceremony but in honour of the racehorse owned by Lady Zia Wernher. The racehorse being a winner of The Oaks, 1,000 Guineas, Coronation Stakes and the St. Leger, she was also the only filly to be commemorated by a Deltic. ***Len Ball***

Finsbury Park's trademark white window surrounds frame the driver on-board 55003 Meld at Peterborough on 24 September 1979 as he awaits the off with the 13.05 Kings Cross to Cleethorpes service. ***Stuart Broughton***

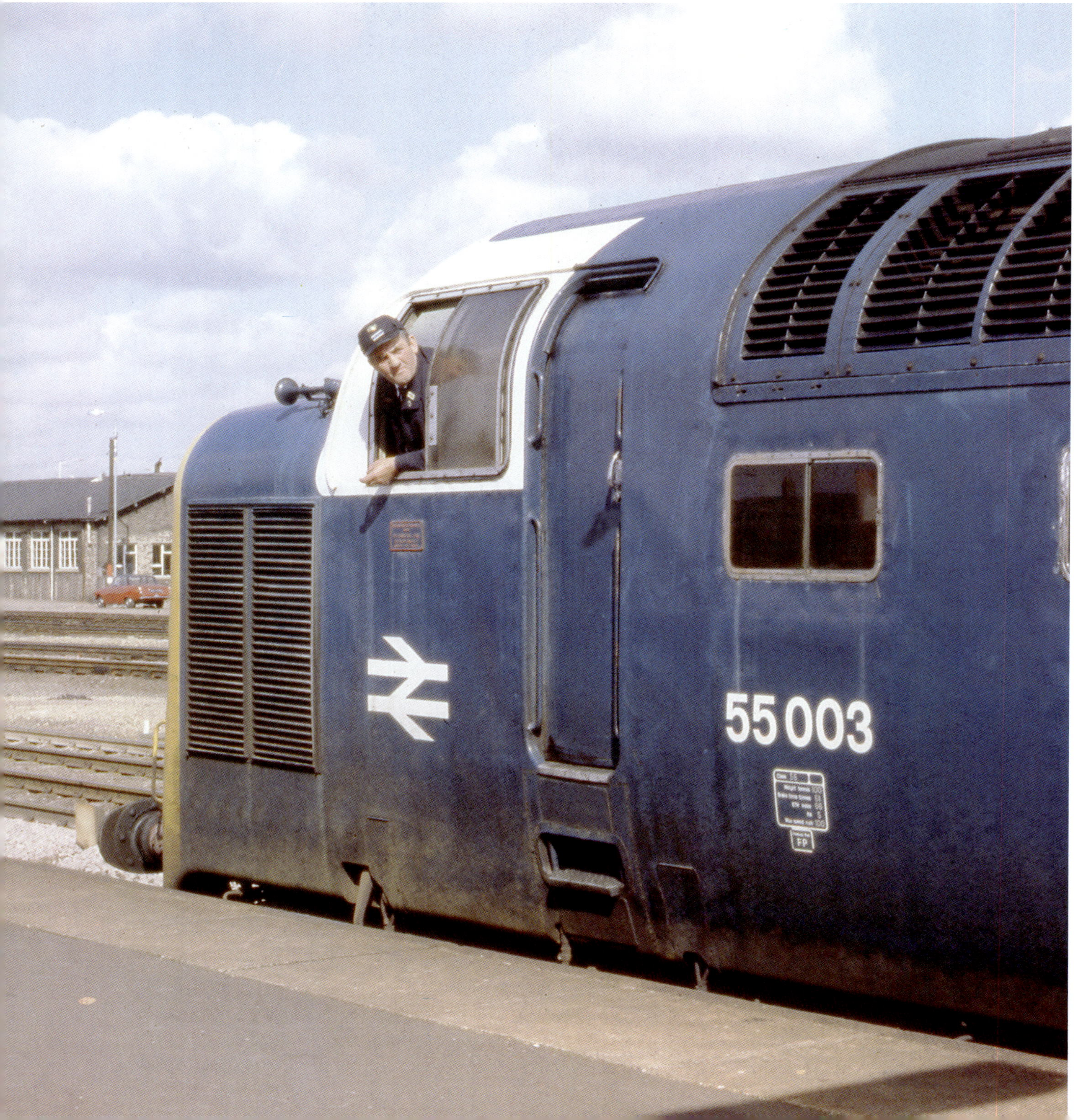

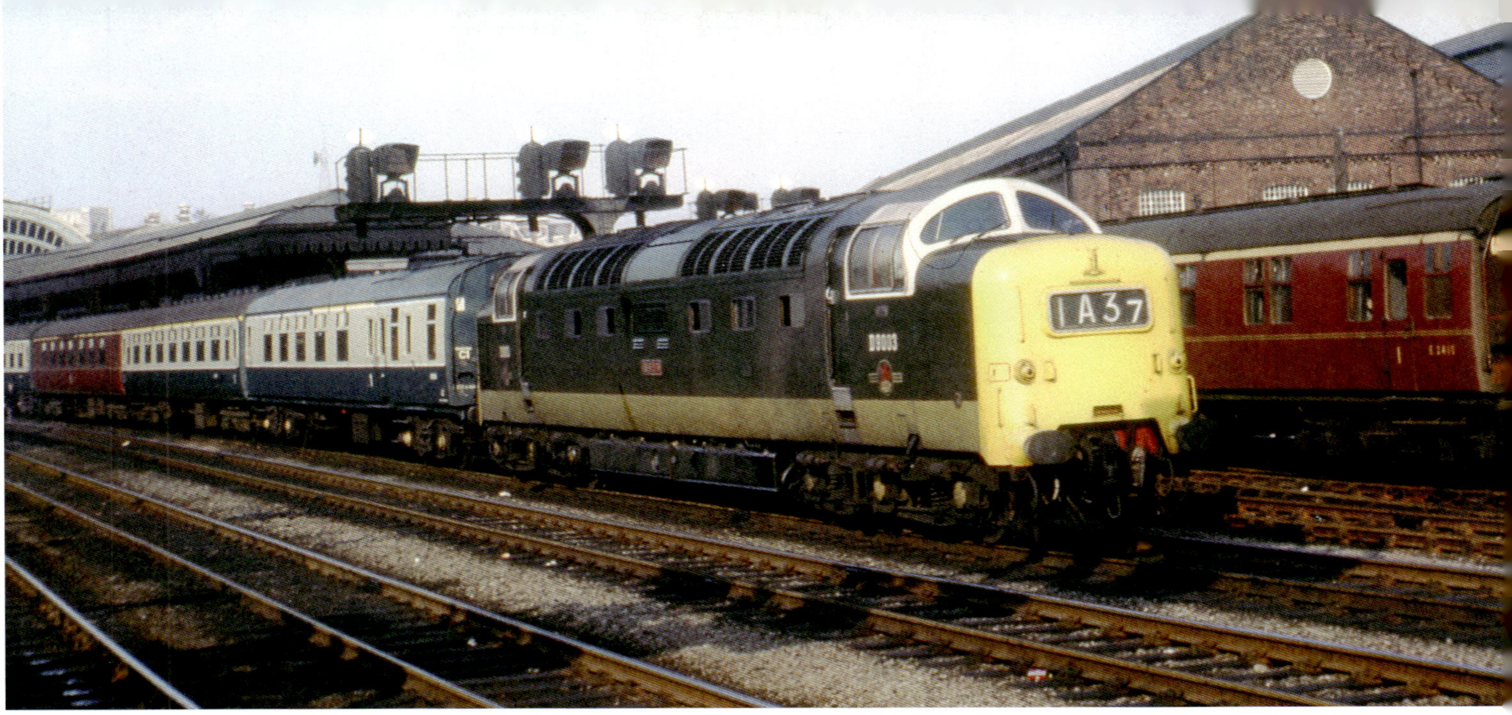

Meld would only run for just on a year in two tone green with full yellow ends, here we see her taking the up Heart of Midlothian out of York on 3 May 1967. ***Mick Farrer***

On the 26 April 1963 D9003 Meld would be entrusted with the up Queen of Scots Pullman service seen here at Berwick-on-Tweed, she had at least two reported engine failures both at Grantham in the preceeding two months resulting in A3s 60112 St. Simon and 60106 Flying Fox coming to her rescue. ***Strathwood Library Collection***

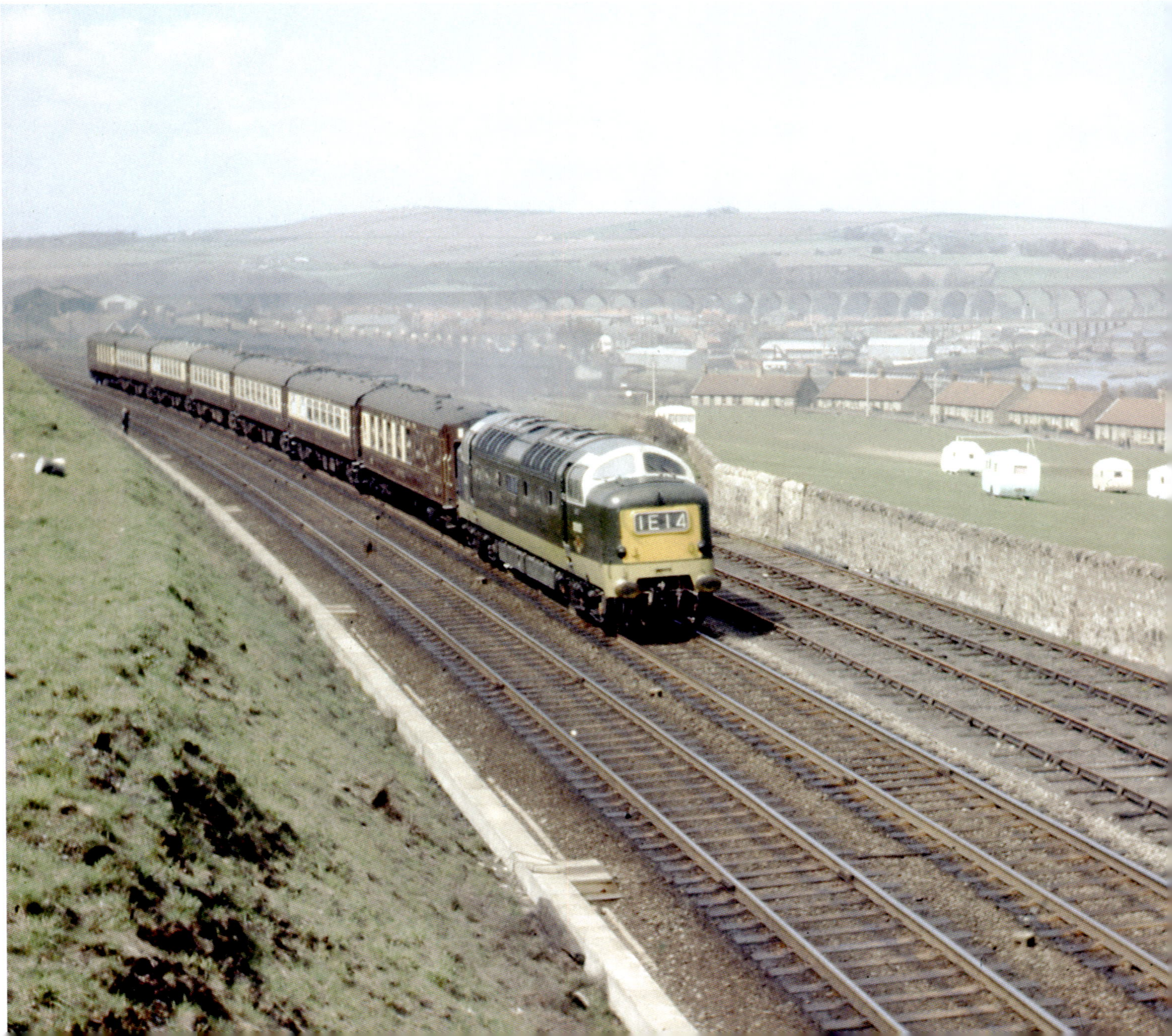

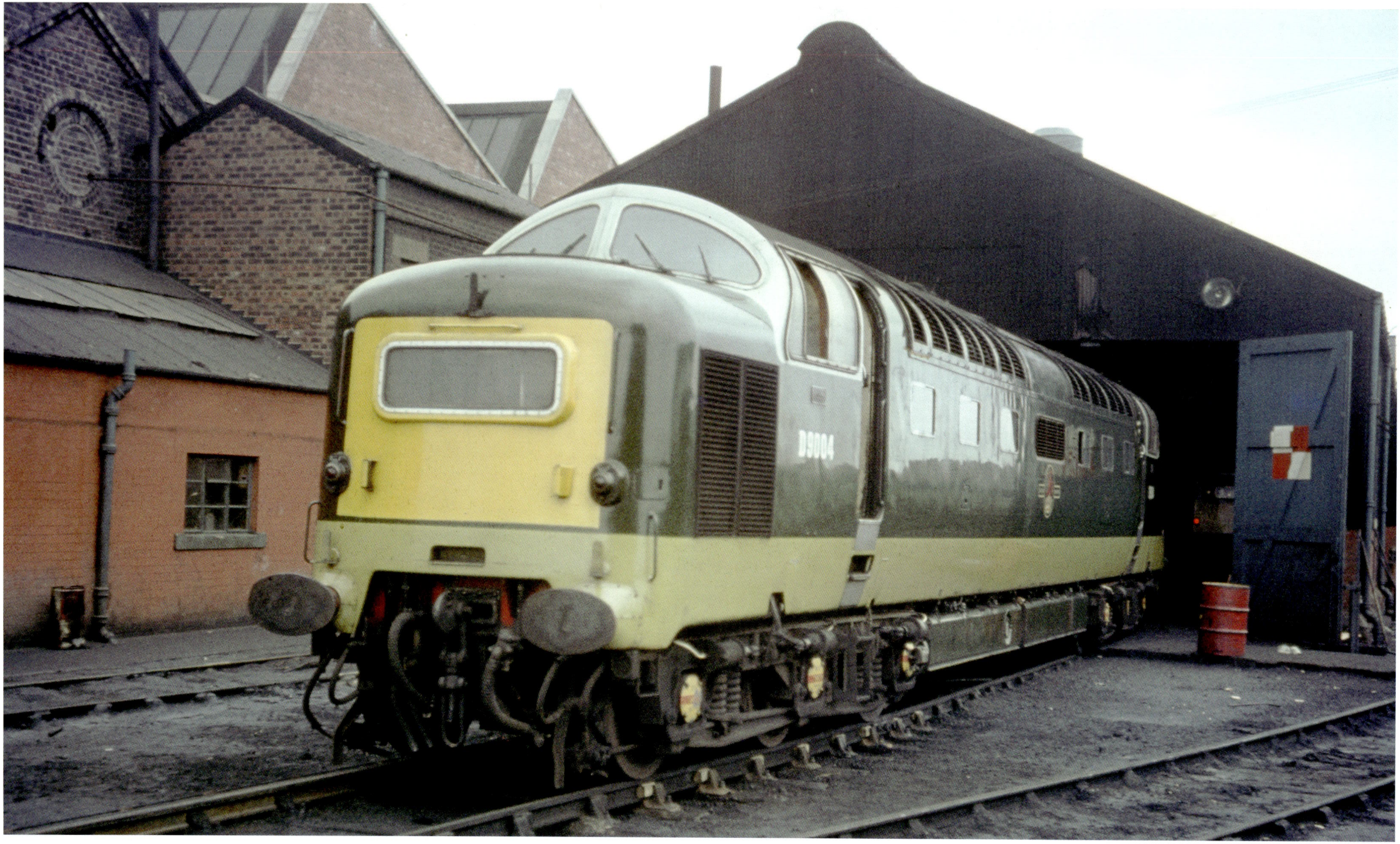

Entering into service on 18 May 1961 D9004 would make the journey light engine from Vulcan Foundry, Newton-le-Willows, to Doncaster Works for acceptance into British Railways service and was allocated to 64B Haymarket depot in Edinburgh. By early 1964 when we see the locomotive on its home shed it had gained a yellow warning panel but was yet to find a name. This would come a few weeks later on 23 May with a ceremony at Inverness to become the Queen's Own Highlander. After naming the engine was rostered to head back south at the head of the 17.45 Inverness to Euston known as The Royal Highlander service as far as Perth where it was taken off. ***Richard Sinclair Collection***

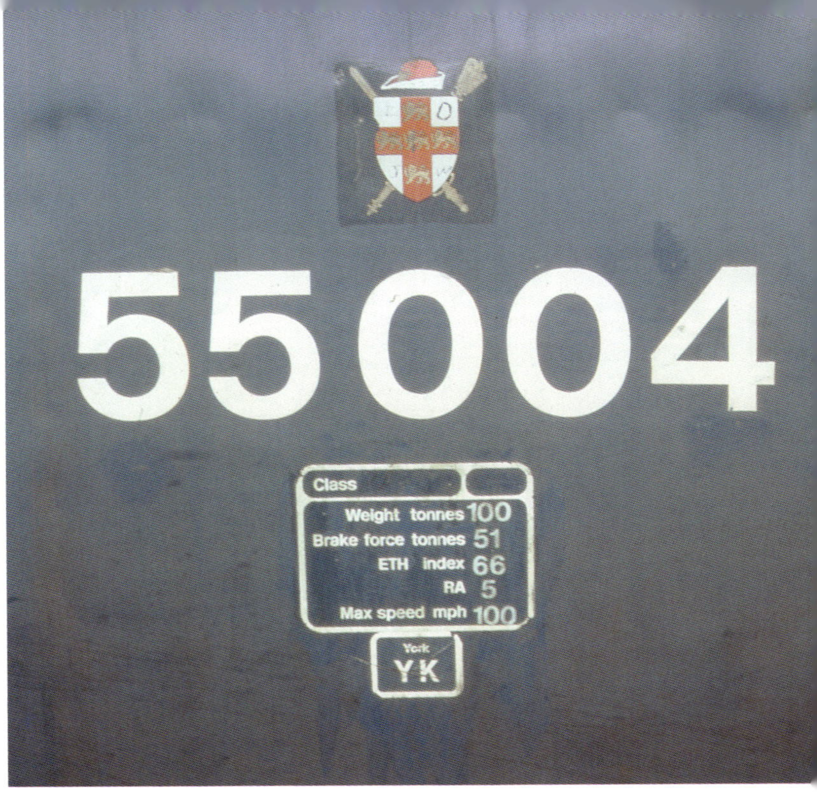

Another glimpse of the crest motif transfers applied to York based engines towards the end of the Deltic's careers with number and data panel seen in August 1980. We also see the handsome nameplate and badge fitted. ***Photos; Graham Courts & Nev Sloper***

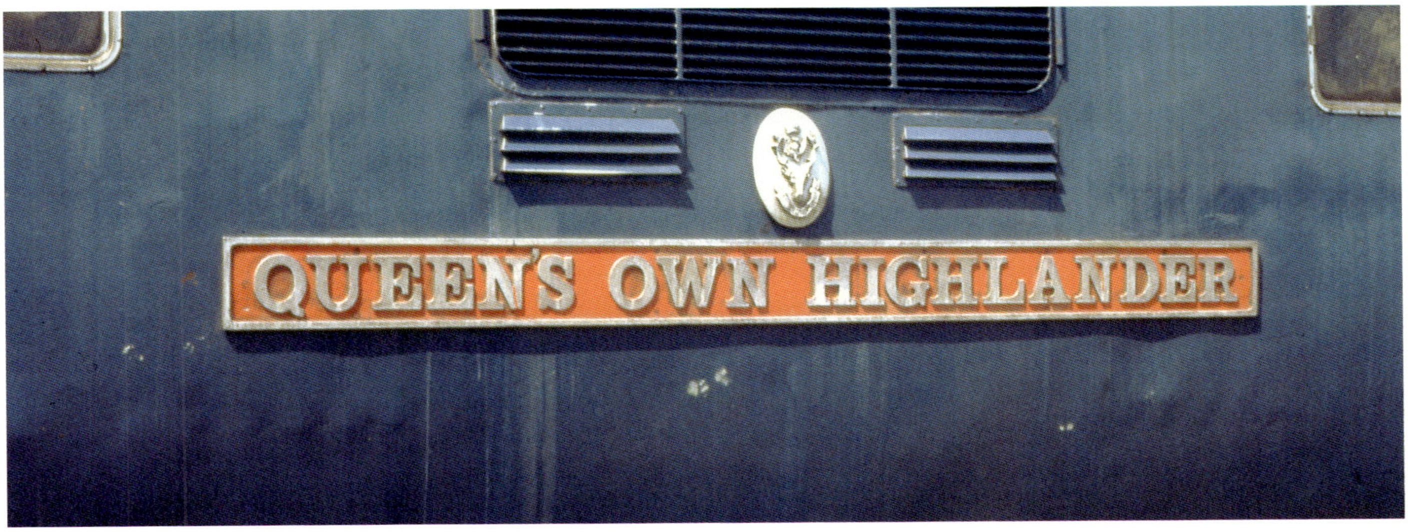

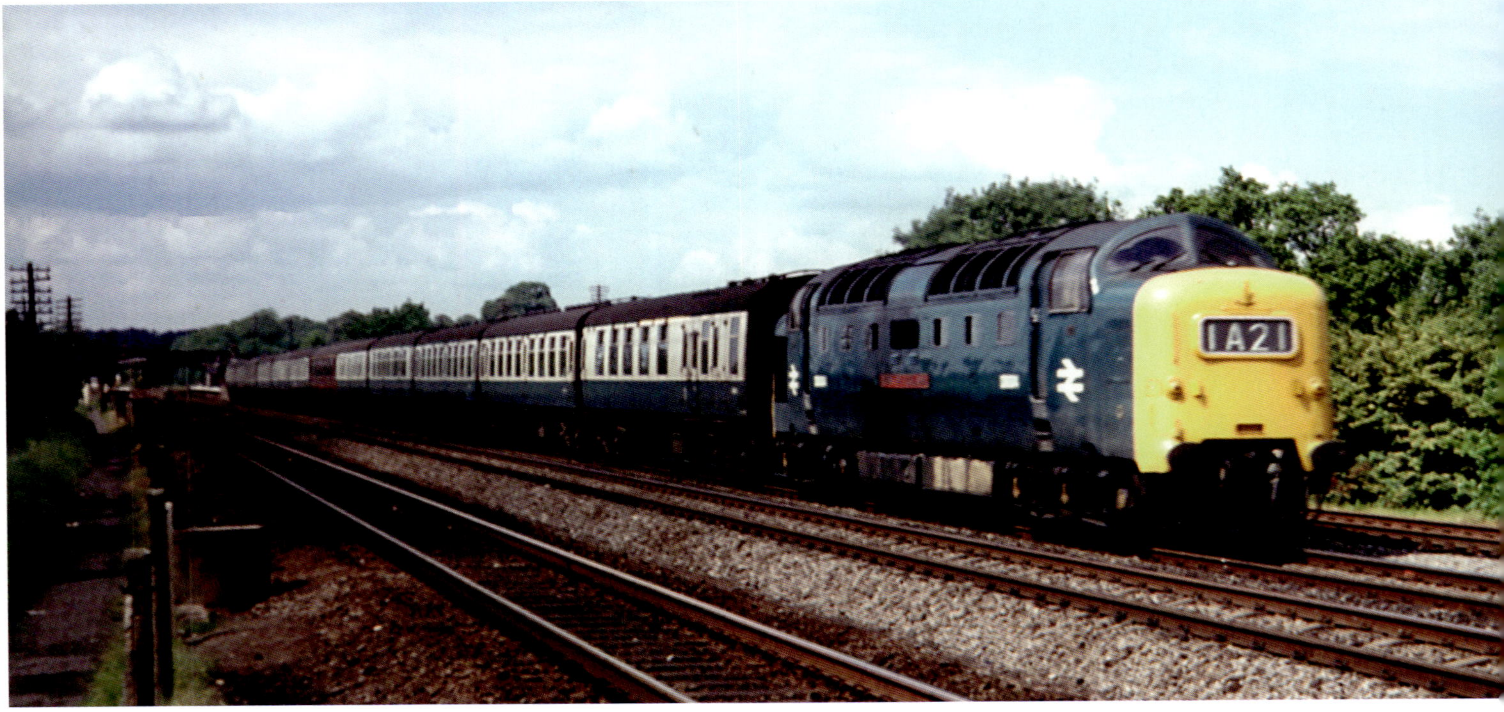

On 6 June 1968 running as D9004 Queen's Own Highlander thundered past Brookmans Park with an express from Newcastle, fifteen years later she would be the last Deltic to be cut up in July of 1983. ***D Twibell/Transport Treasury***

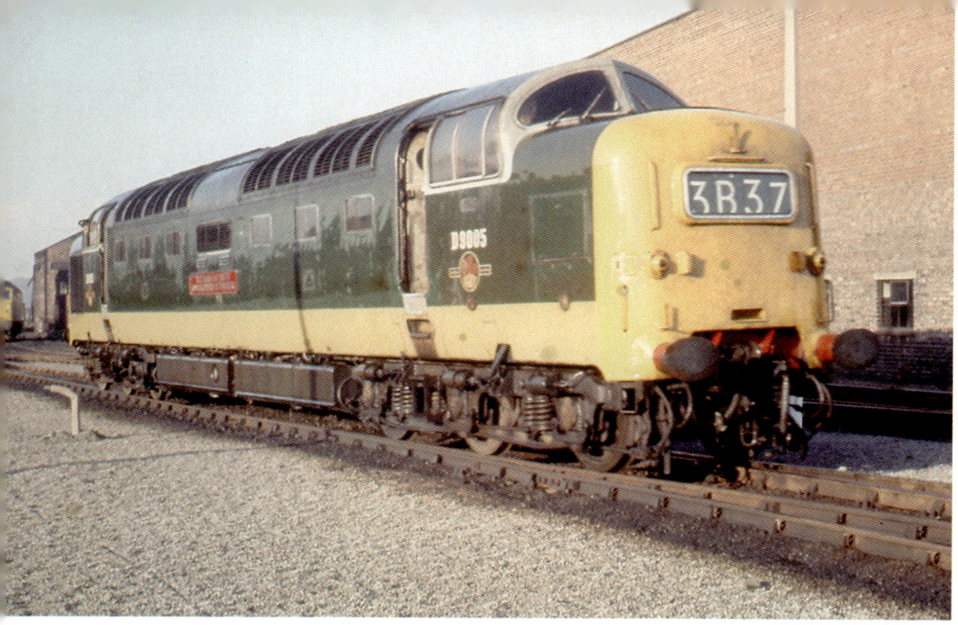

Outside in the sunshine at its home depot of Gateshead in October 1967 was D9005 The Prince of Wales's Own Regiment of Yorkshire. ***Strathwood Library Collection***

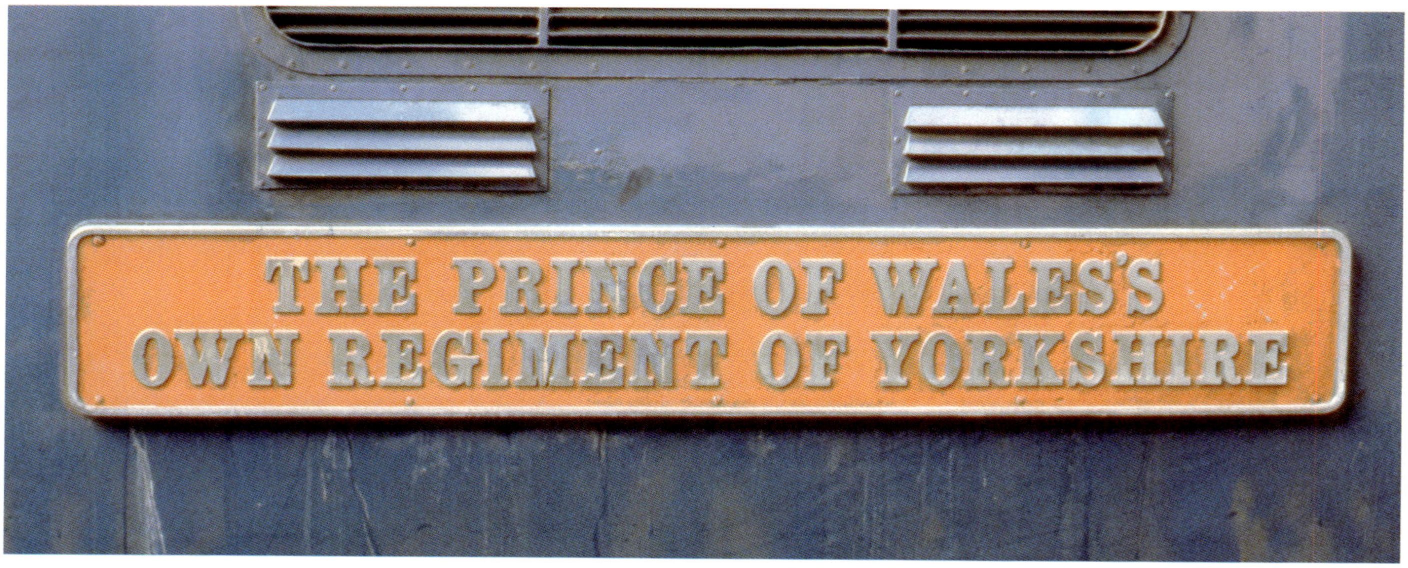

Another impressive nameplate is seen for this Deltic in 1980 and below in 1974 covered with oil at Kings Cross. ***Photos: Colin Whitbread & Les Byatt***

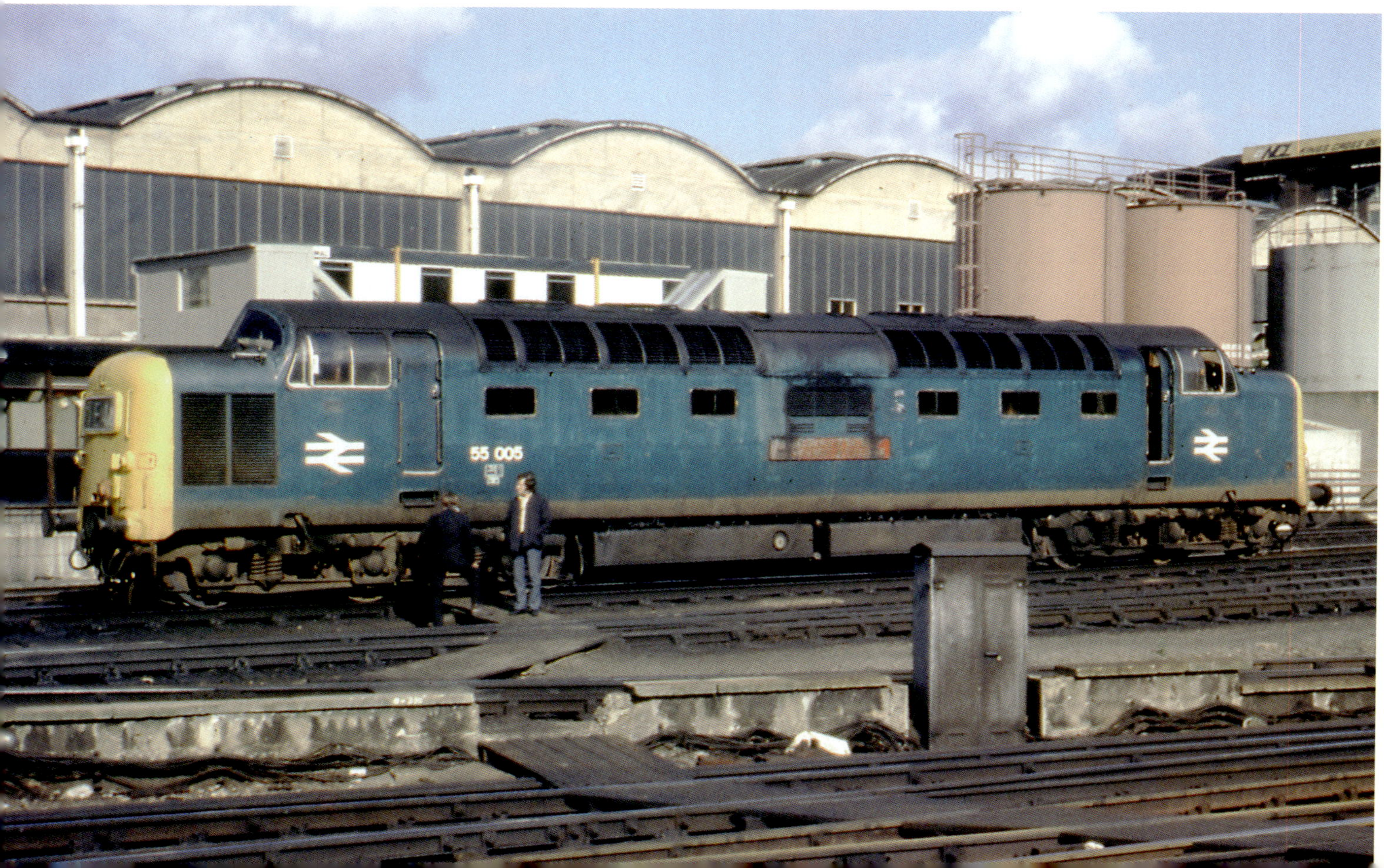

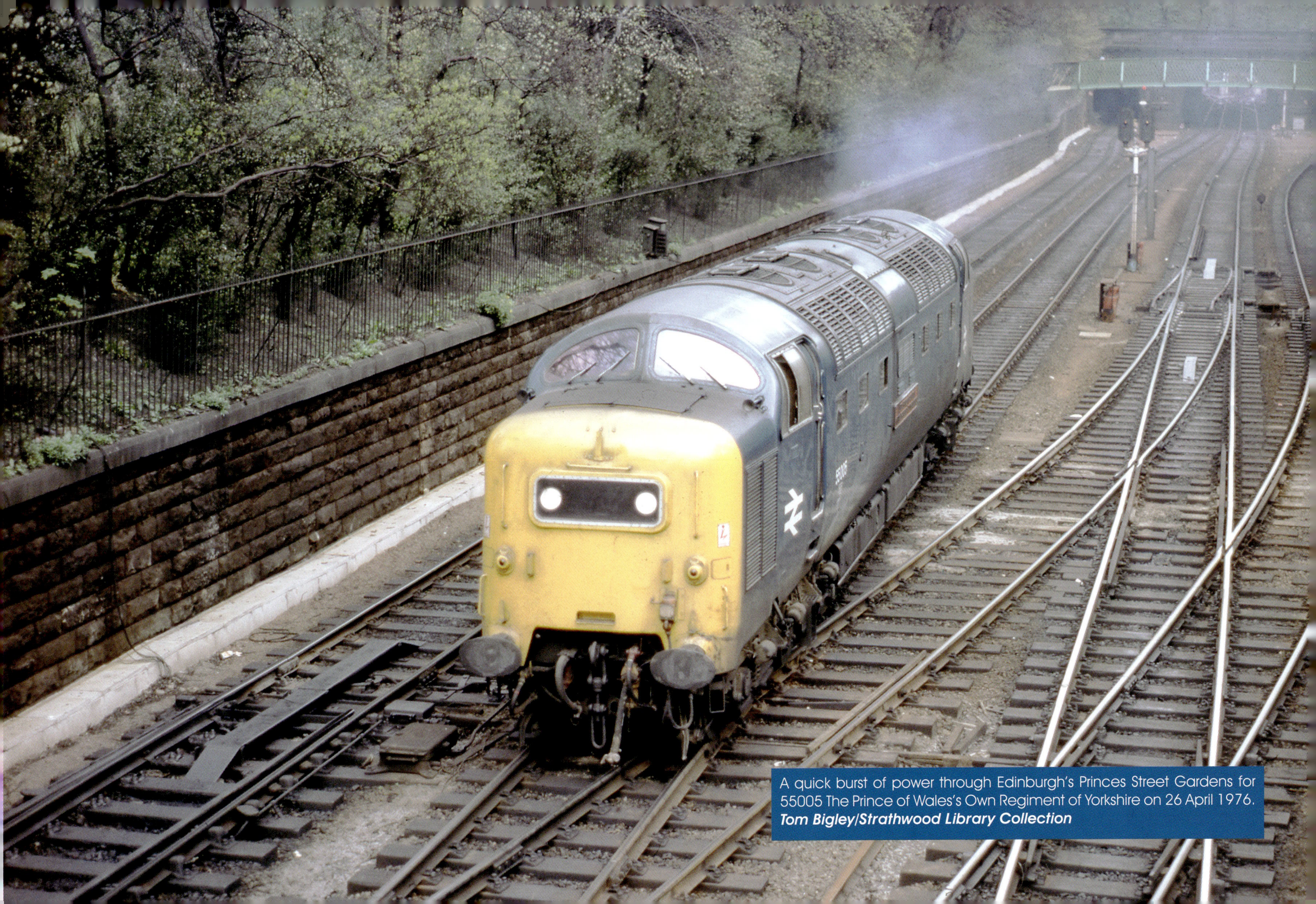

A quick burst of power through Edinburgh's Princes Street Gardens for 55005 The Prince of Wales's Own Regiment of Yorkshire on 26 April 1976.
Tom Bigley/Strathwood Library Collection

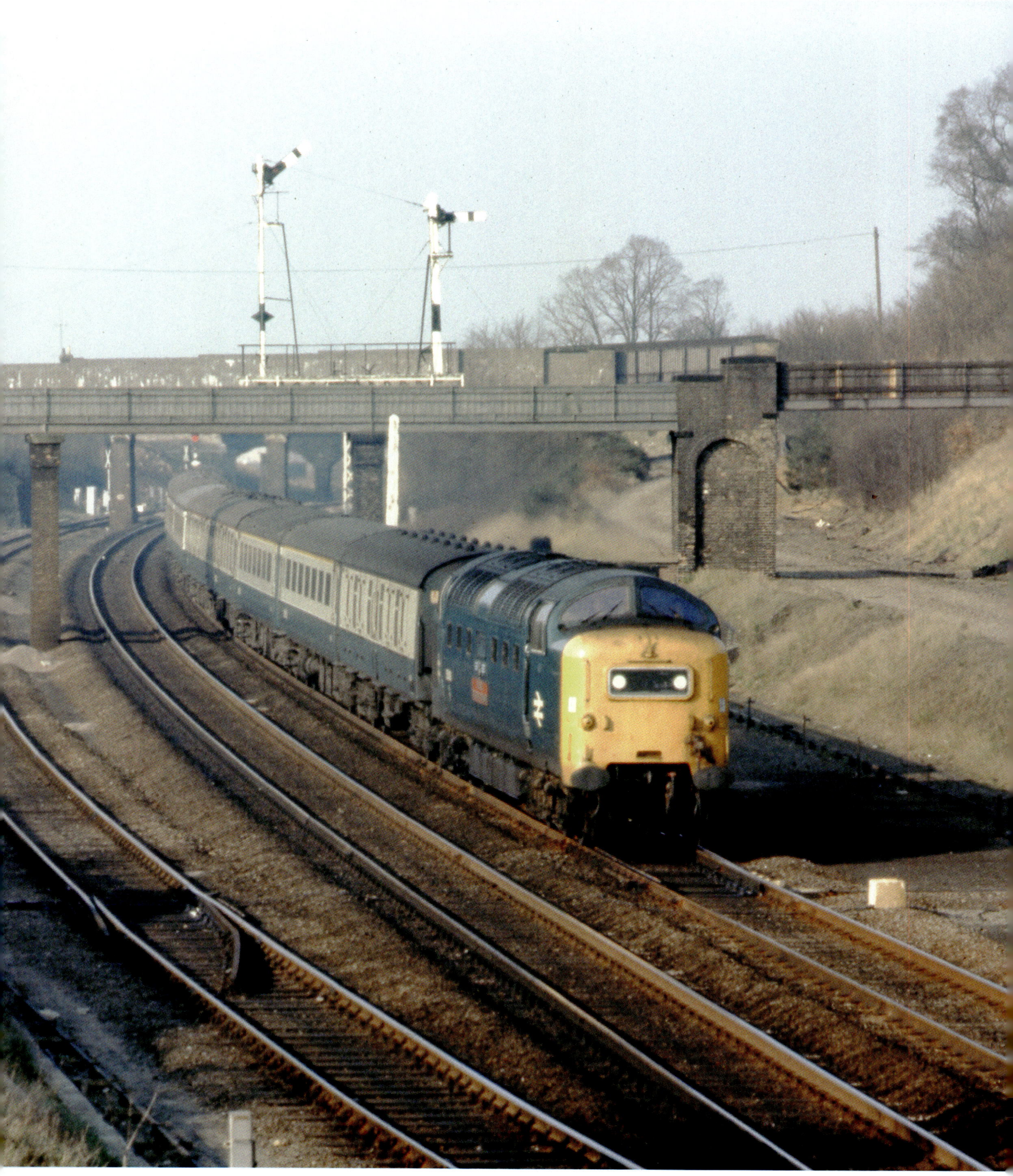

Going well under an exhaust haze at Sandy on 6 March 1976 was 55005 The Prince of Wales's Own Regiment of Yorkshire at the head of the up Flying Scotsman. On withdrawal on 8 February 1981 the locomotive was stored at Doncaster Works just in case something happened to the National Railway Museum's first choice for preservation which was 55002 The King's Own Yorkshire Light Infantry as they both carried Yorkshire within their names. In the event 55005 was not to survive after February 1983 when the cutting staff at Doncaster Works finally set about their task. ***John Dawson***

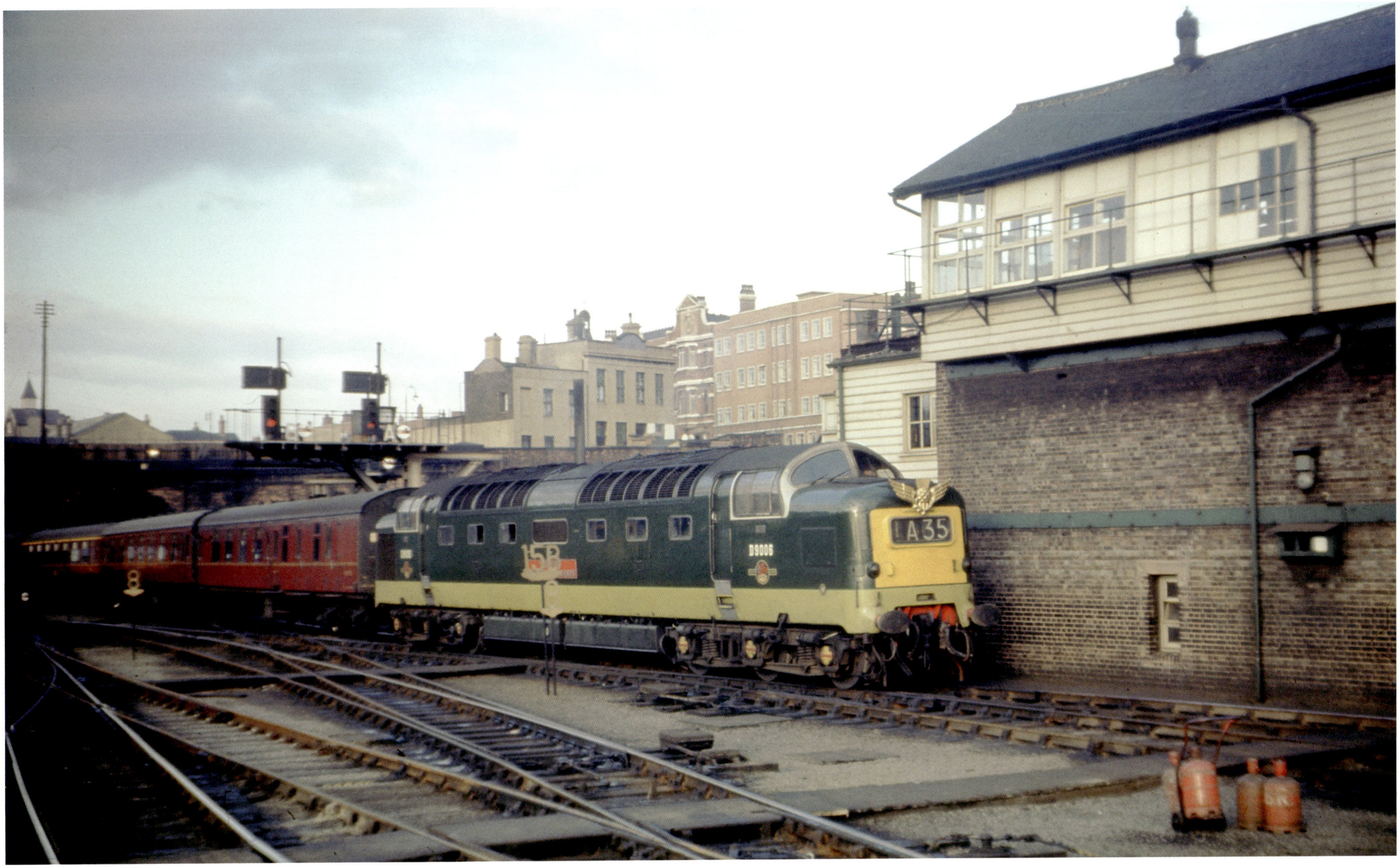

As appropriate for another of Haymarket's Deltics a suitable Scottish regiment was chosen and on 5 December 1964 D9006 was bestowed the name The Fife & Forfar Yeomanry in a ceremony at Cupar in the Kingdom of Fife. In 1966 dressed with the wonderful winged thistle headboard for the Flying Scotsman the up service arrives at the capital. ***Len Smith***

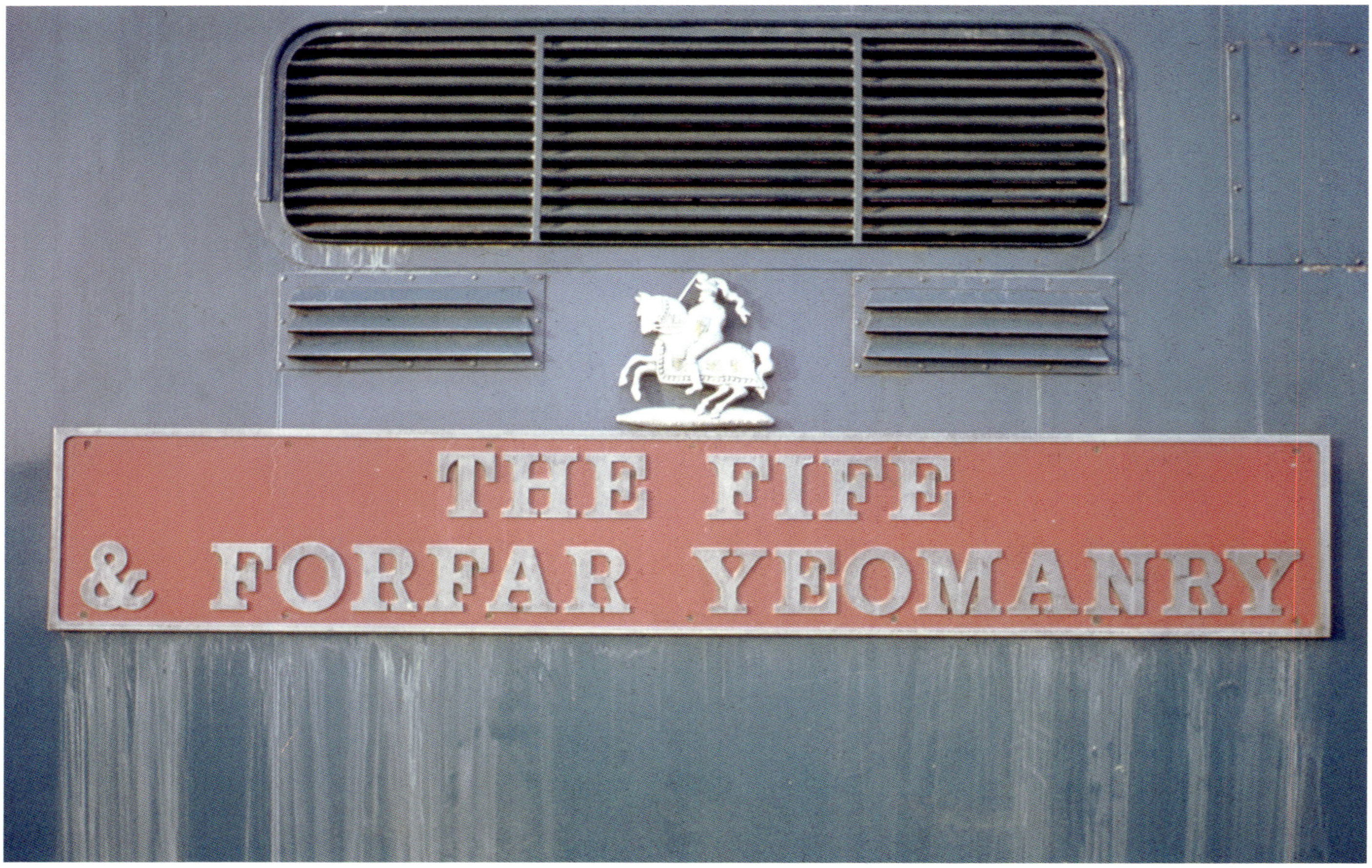

Showing the effects of the cleaning solutions and water on the unprotected rear of the nameplates and the resultant paintwork streaking that occurs was 55006 The Fife & Forfar Yeomanry complete with the splendid badge. ***Jeffrey Lane***

The scene of the tragically horrific 1876 Abbots Ripton crash in which thirteen passengers lost their lives when the Flying Scotsman express ran into a coal train in a blizzard is past in brilliant sunshine a century later by 55006 The Fife & Forfar Yeomanry running at speed with an afternoon Kings Cross to Bradford train. ***John Harrup***

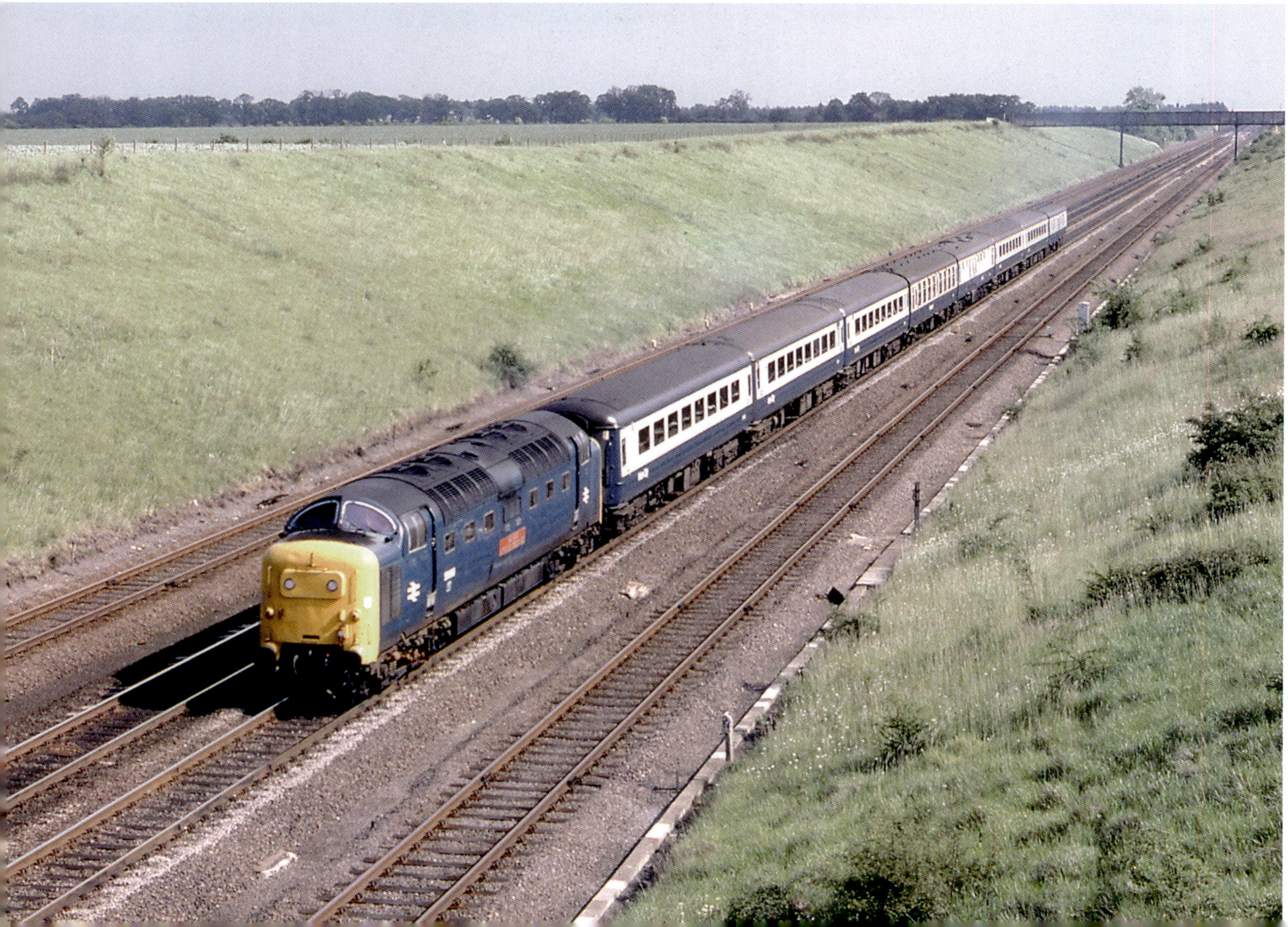

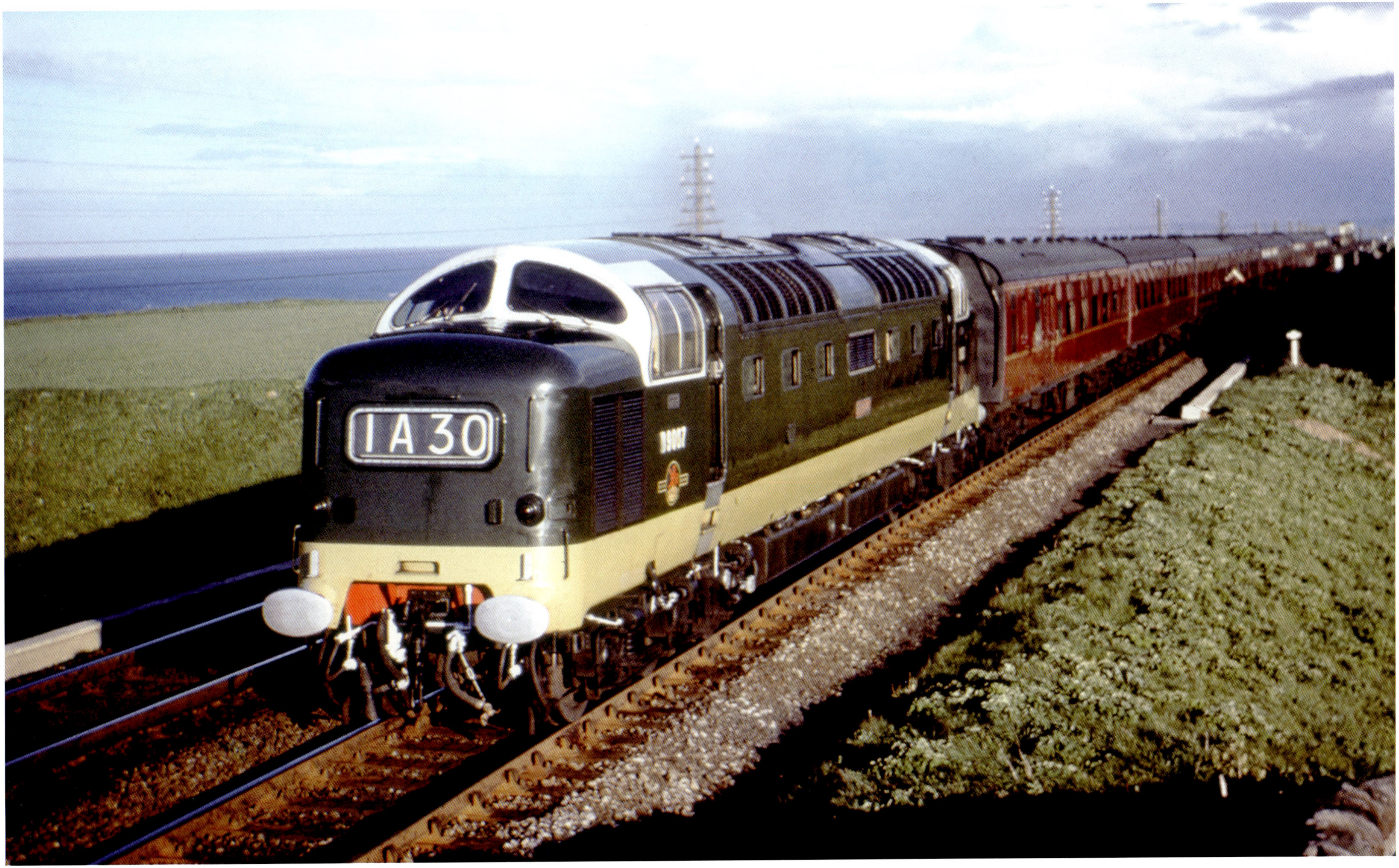

With what has to be one of the most delightful earliest shots of a Deltic in original livery with two British Railways crests per side and named from entry into service, the photographer has captured D9007 Pinza running along the scenic stretch of the East Coast Main Line skirting the North Sea where England borders Scotland in the summer of 1961. ***Michael Mensing***

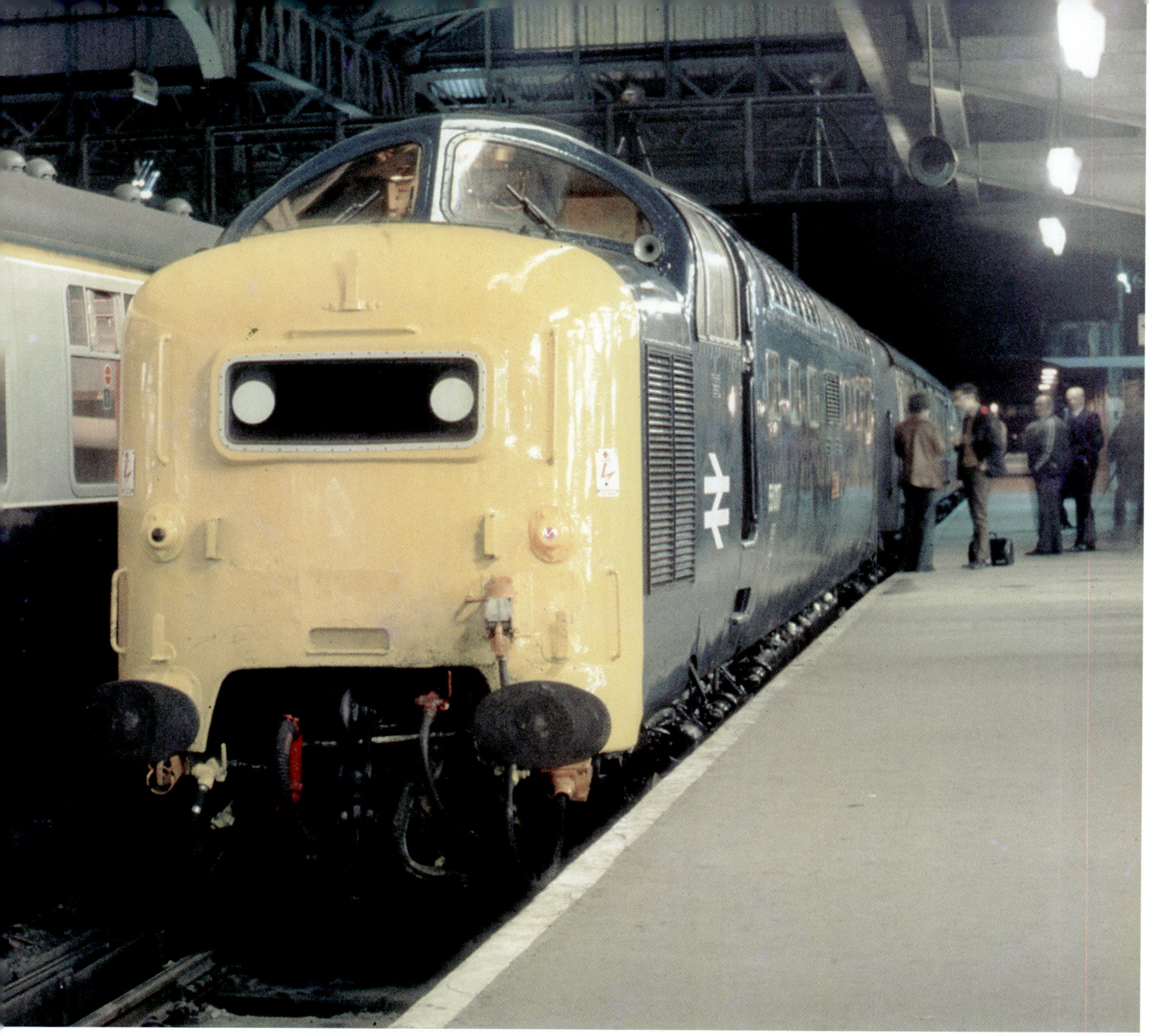

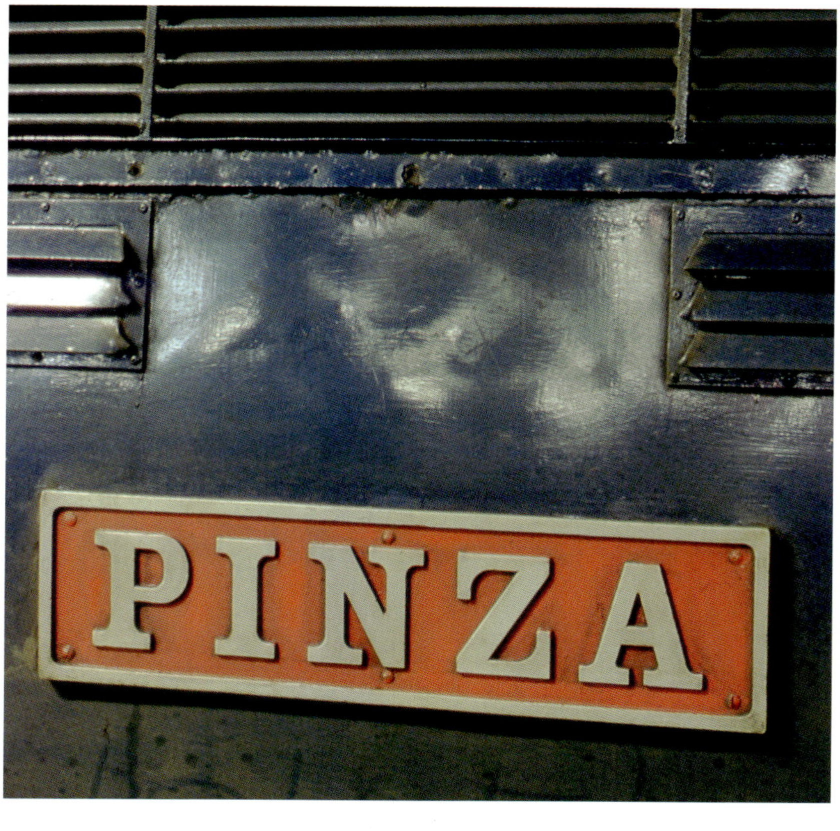

Among the modifications since Pinza entered traffic almost seventeen years before we can see evidence of electric train heating, external horns, single windscreen wipers as well as the now redundant four character headcode with the Eastern Region's favoured marker dots in place, as 55007 stands on arrival at London's Victoria station after working The Man of Kent railtour of 26 March 1978.
Photos: Bruce Smetham & Colin Whitbread

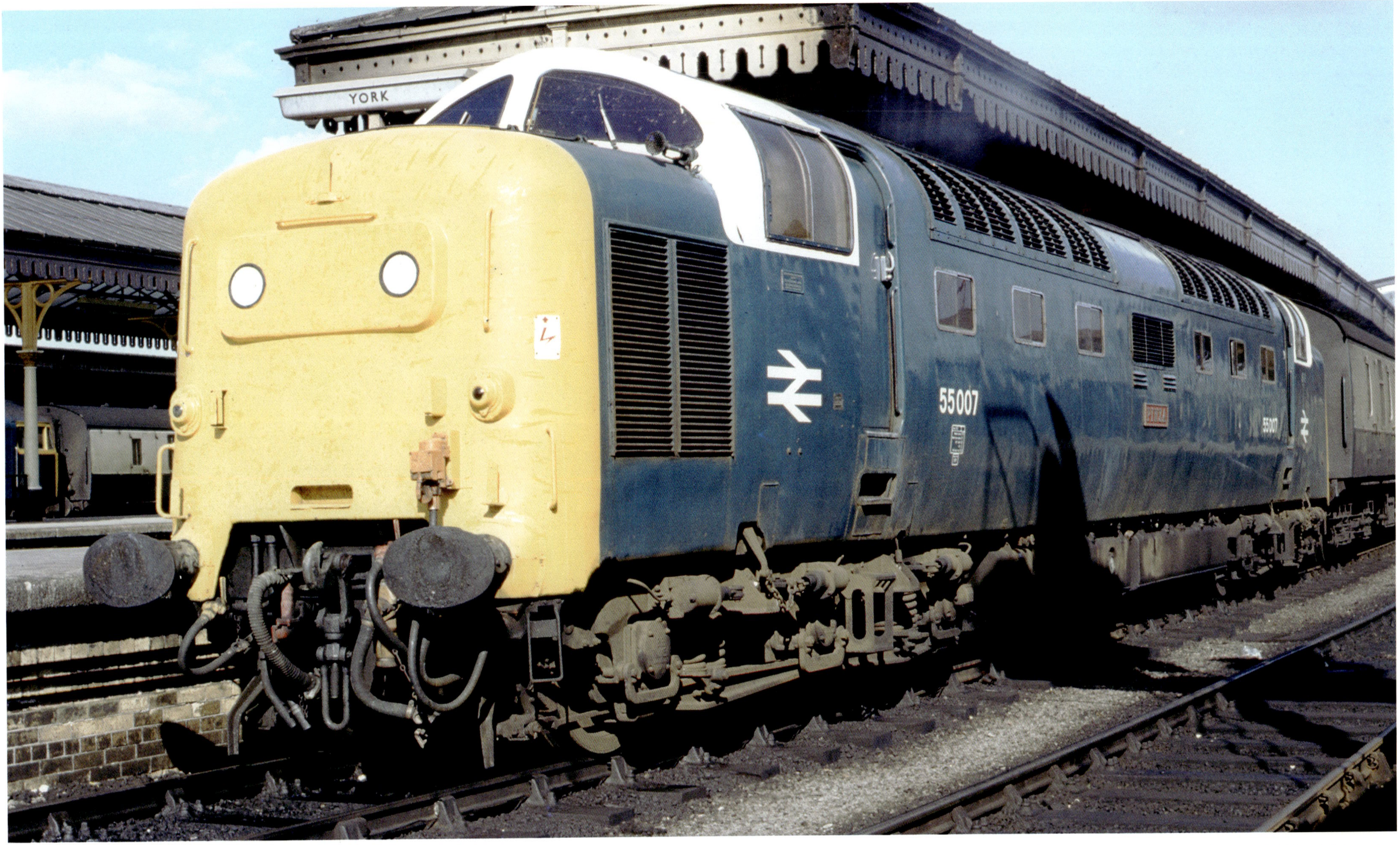

A year later and 55007 Pinza sports the colours of Finsbury Park's painters with white window surrounds and has had her headcodes plated over with marker lights fitted when seen standing at York ready to work the 14.11 service for Kings Cross on 28 September 1979. Pinza foaled in 1950 and was owned, like Crepello, by Sir Victor Sassoon. The horse went on to win the Derby in 1953 ridden by Sir Gordon Richards. Put out to stud Pinza's bloodline has sired two further Derby winners in 1979 and 1983, Pinza himself died in 1977. ***Len Ball***

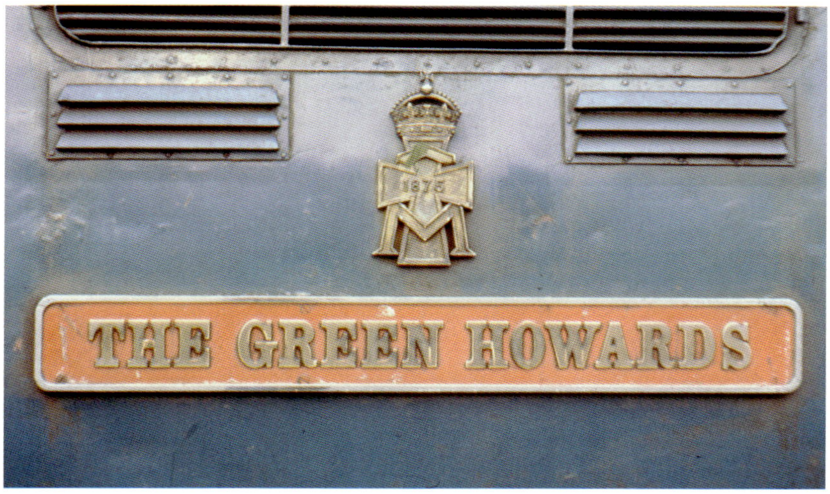

A long term Gateshead locomotive from new in July 1961 until the concentration of the Deltics at York from May 1979. Naming took place on 30 September 1963 at Darlington with a ceremony, performed by Brigadier G.W. Edin. ***Mathew Hall***

On 6 March 1976 the 14.00 Kings Cross to Aberdeen was being worked very fast through Sandy behind 55008 The Green Howards. ***John Dawson***

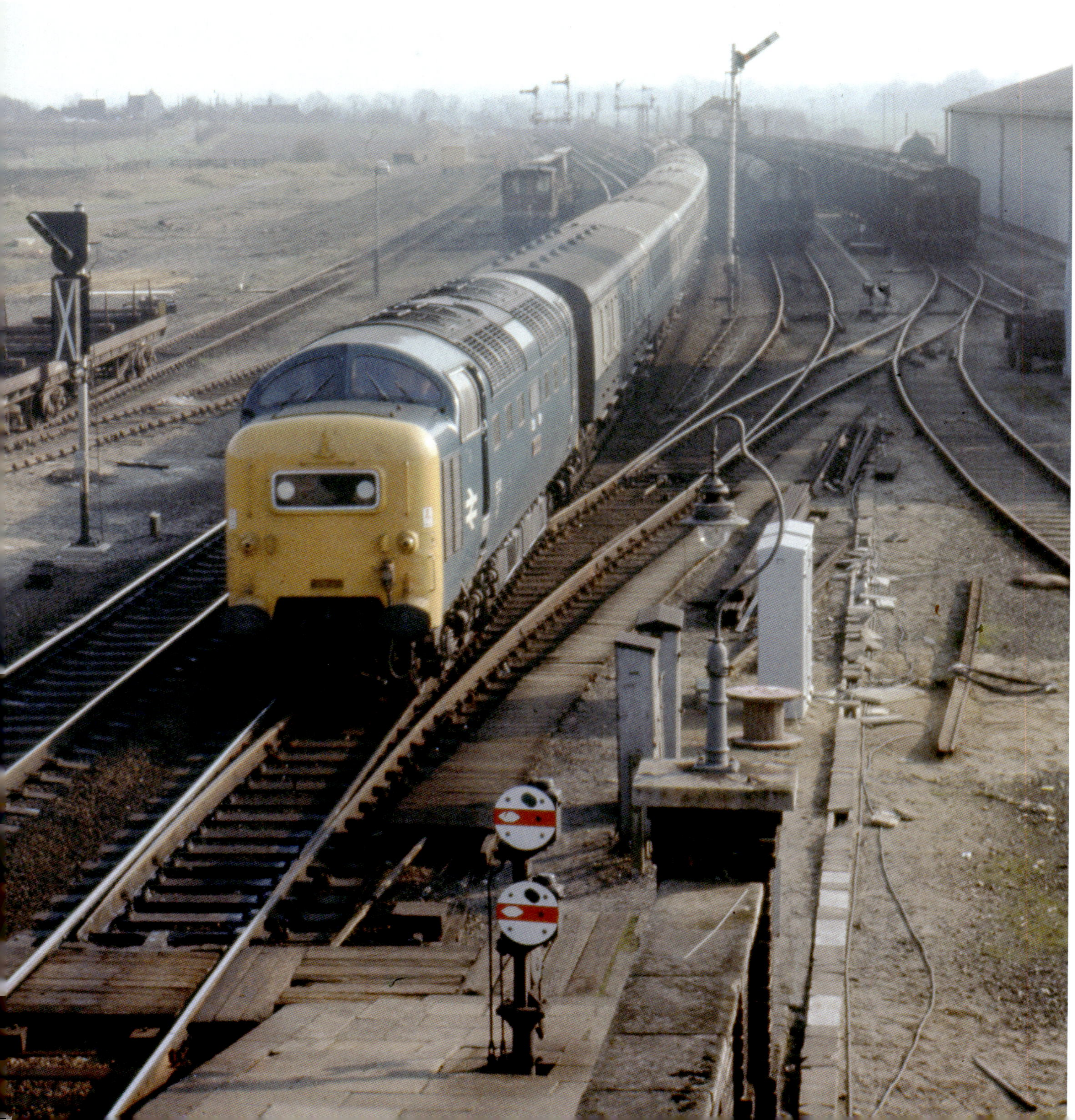

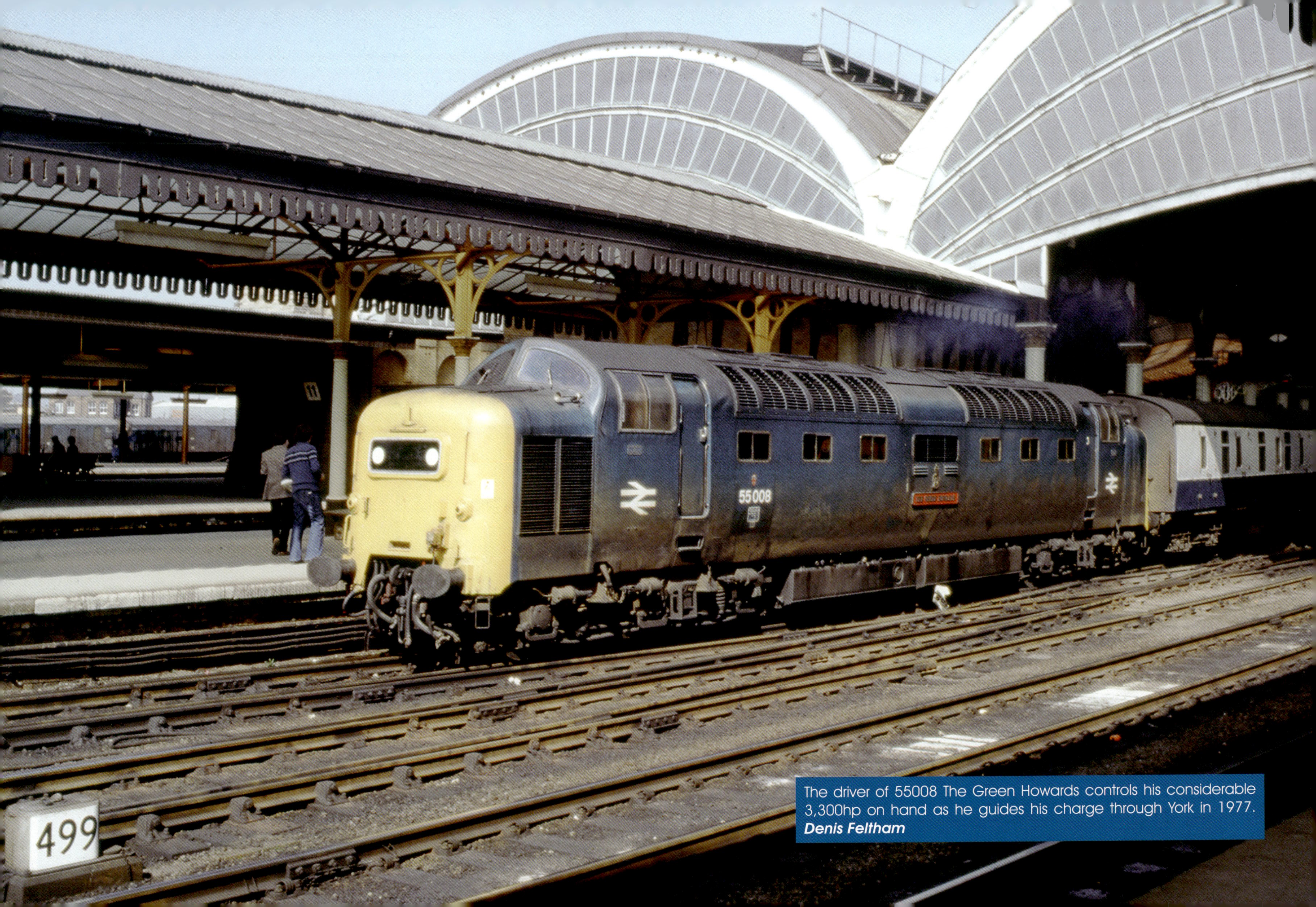

The driver of 55008 The Green Howards controls his considerable 3,300hp on hand as he guides his charge through York in 1977. ***Denis Feltham***

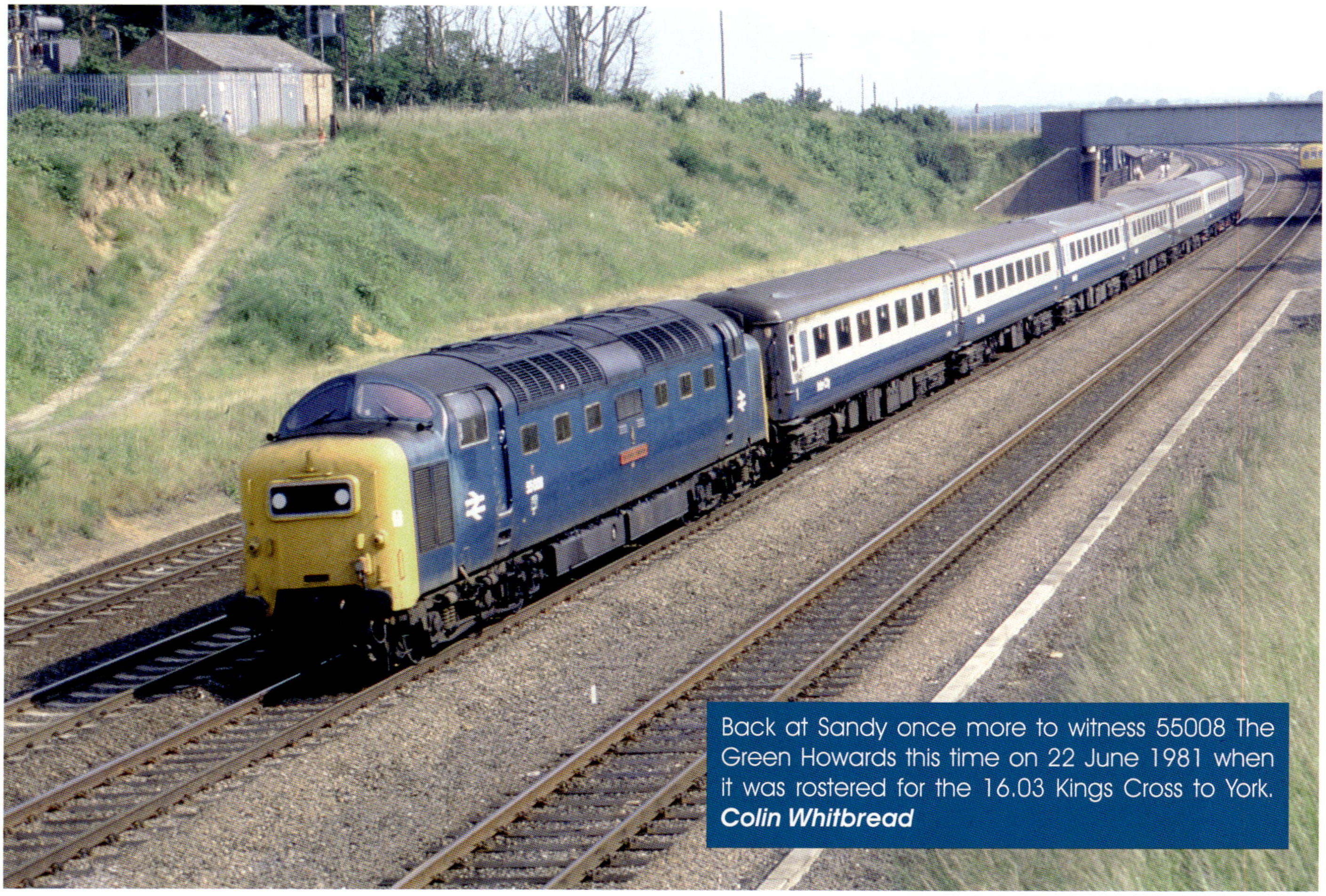

Back at Sandy once more to witness 55008 The Green Howards this time on 22 June 1981 when it was rostered for the 16.03 Kings Cross to York. ***Colin Whitbread***

This time at York the driver of 55008 The Green Howards turns up the power as his train sweeps past York North Yard on 14 July 1981 having taken over a Plymouth to Edinburgh service. ***Strathwood Library Collection***

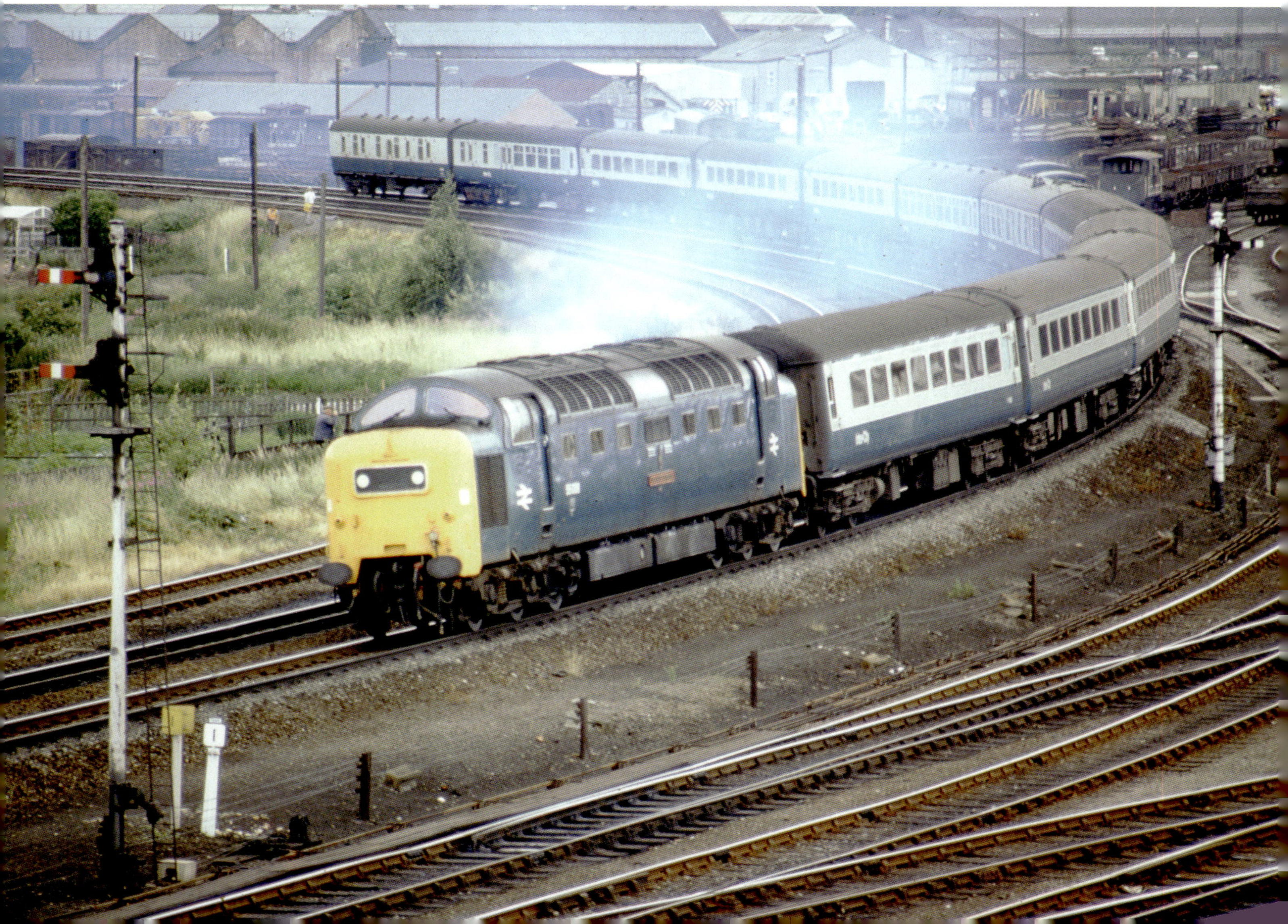

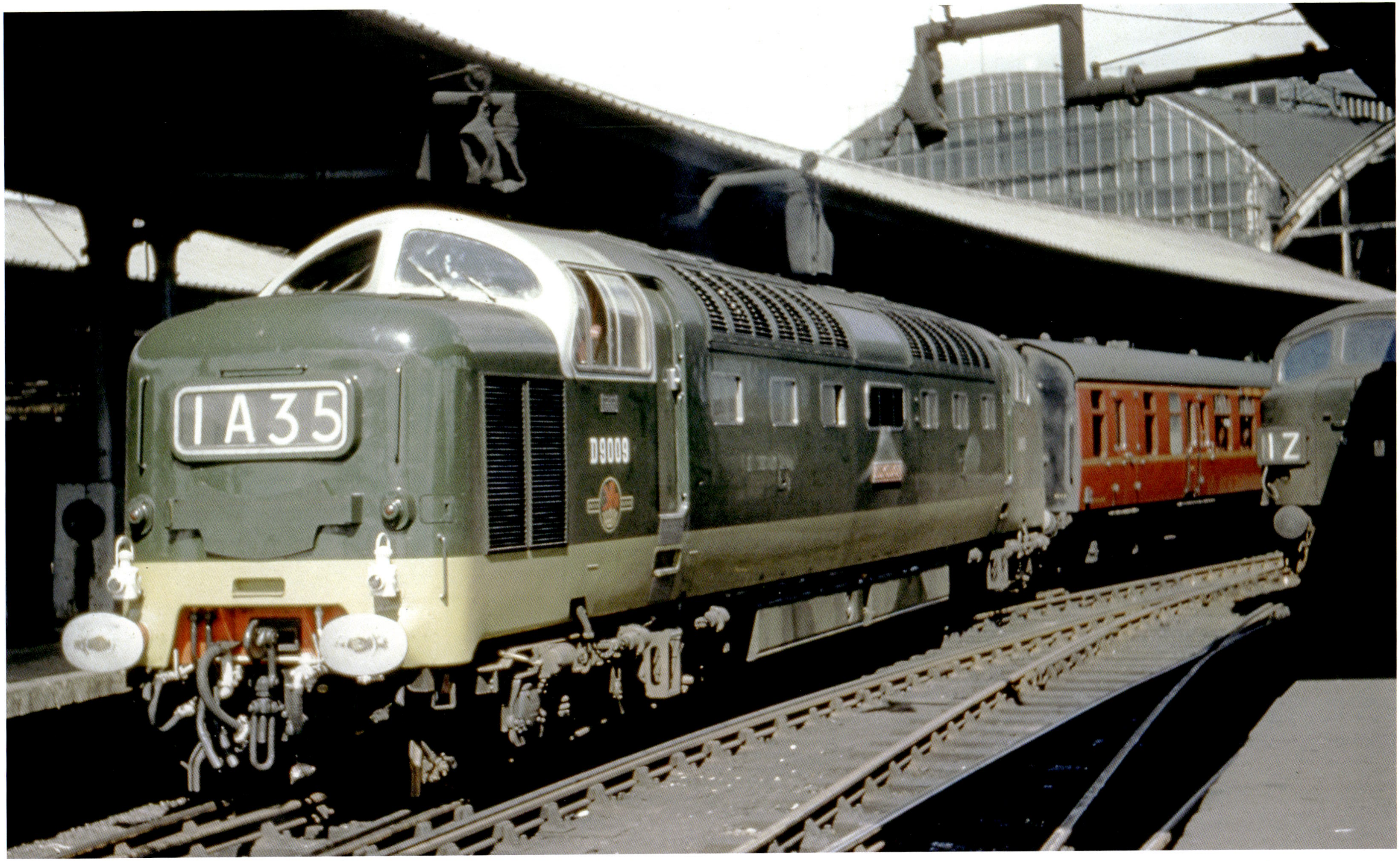

Another racehorse Deltic that was named from new was Finsbury Park's D9009 Alycidon. Entering service in early August 1961 where we see this new locomotive in charge of the up Flying Scotsman at Newcastle Central. The naming was carried out at Doncaster Works without any ceremony on 21 July 1961 in honour of the racehorse owned by 17th Earl of Derby, having won The Ascot Gold Cup, Goodwood Cup, Corporation Stakes and Doncaster Cup. As an aside Alycidon was sire to Meld. ***Hugh Ramsey***

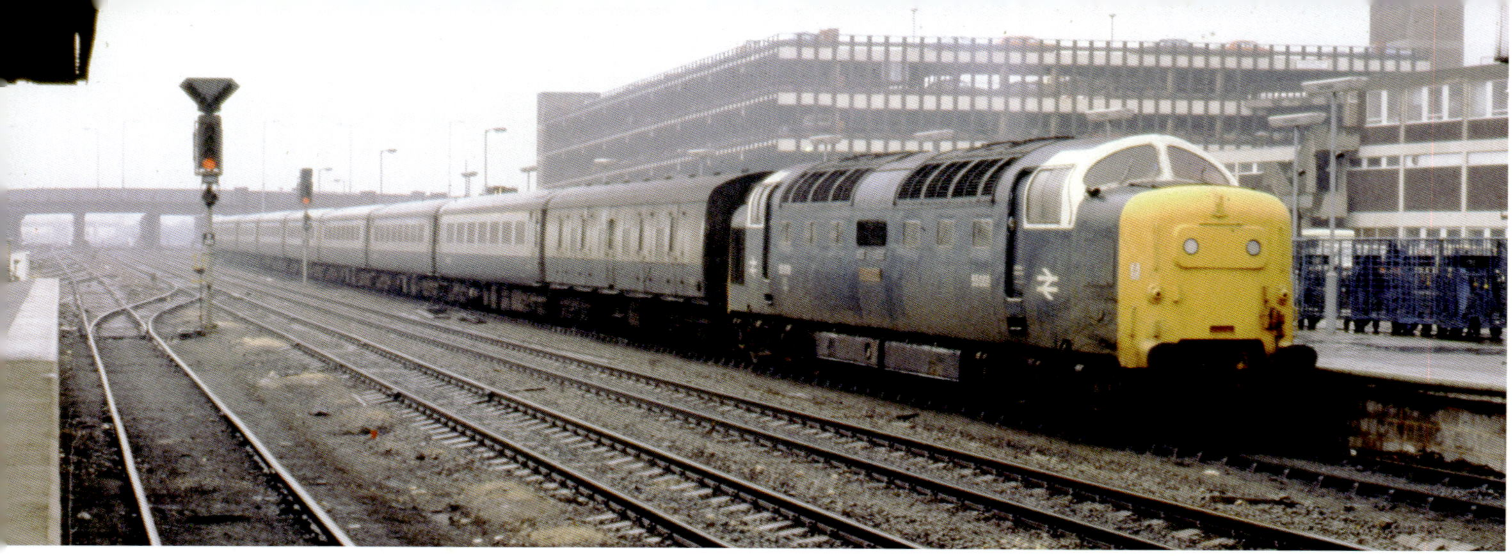

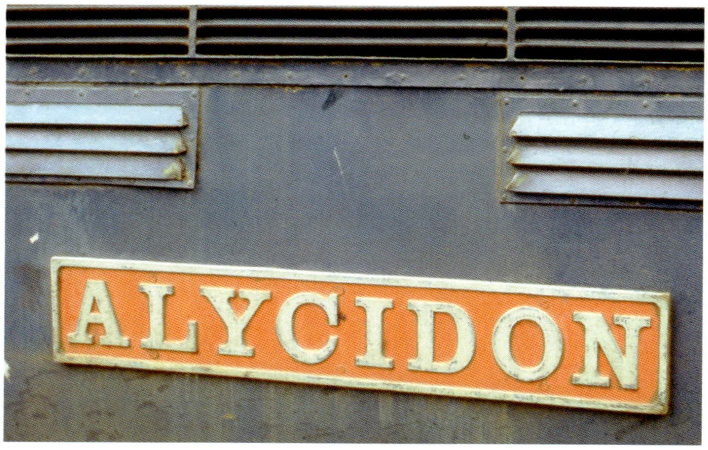

Three shots of 55009 Alycidon in 1979 firstly filthy at Doncaster in the rain, and finally at Kings Cross on 31 August awaiting clearance from the platform roads. ***Photos: Strathwood Library Collection, Colin Whitbread and Jeffrey Lane***

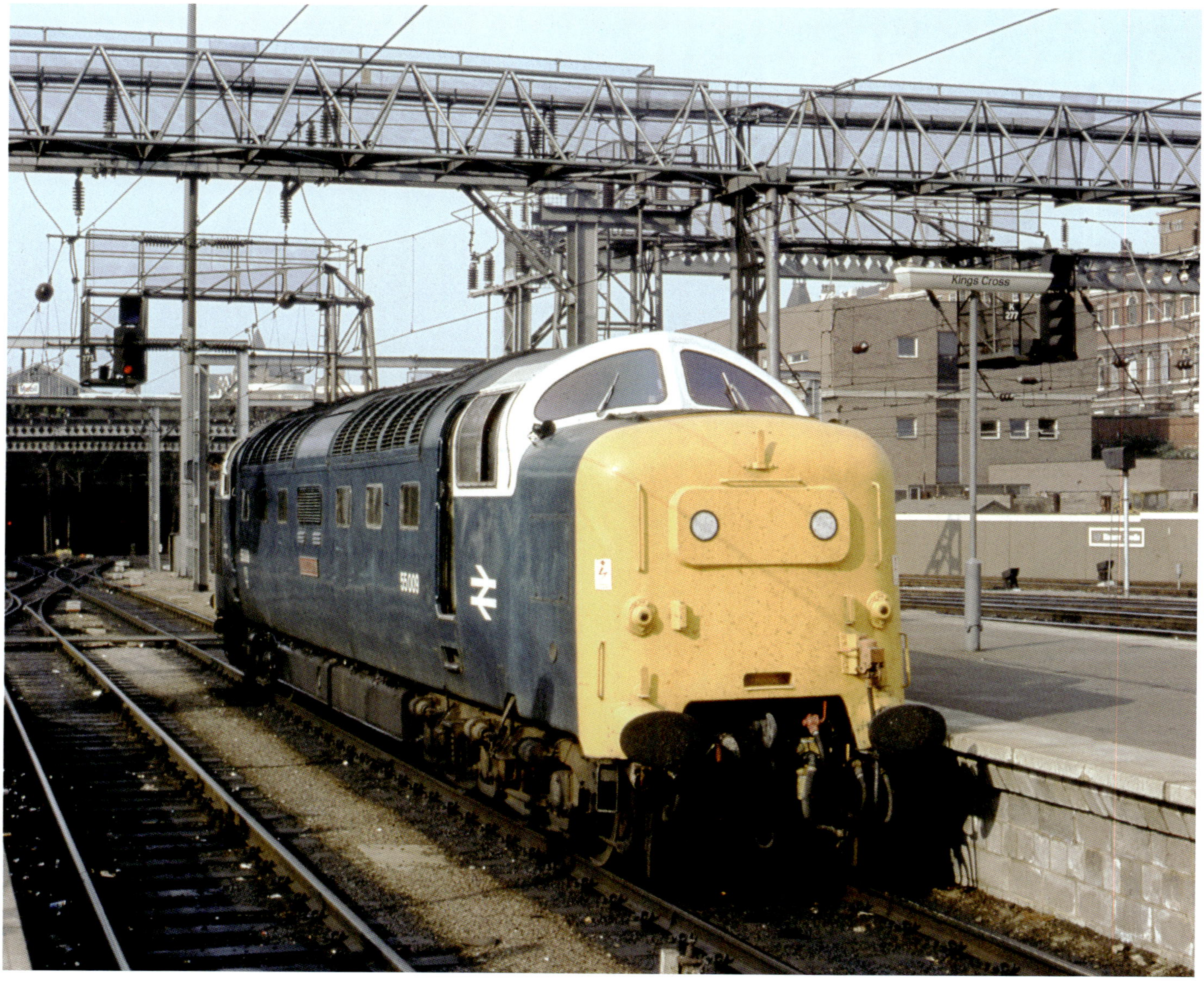

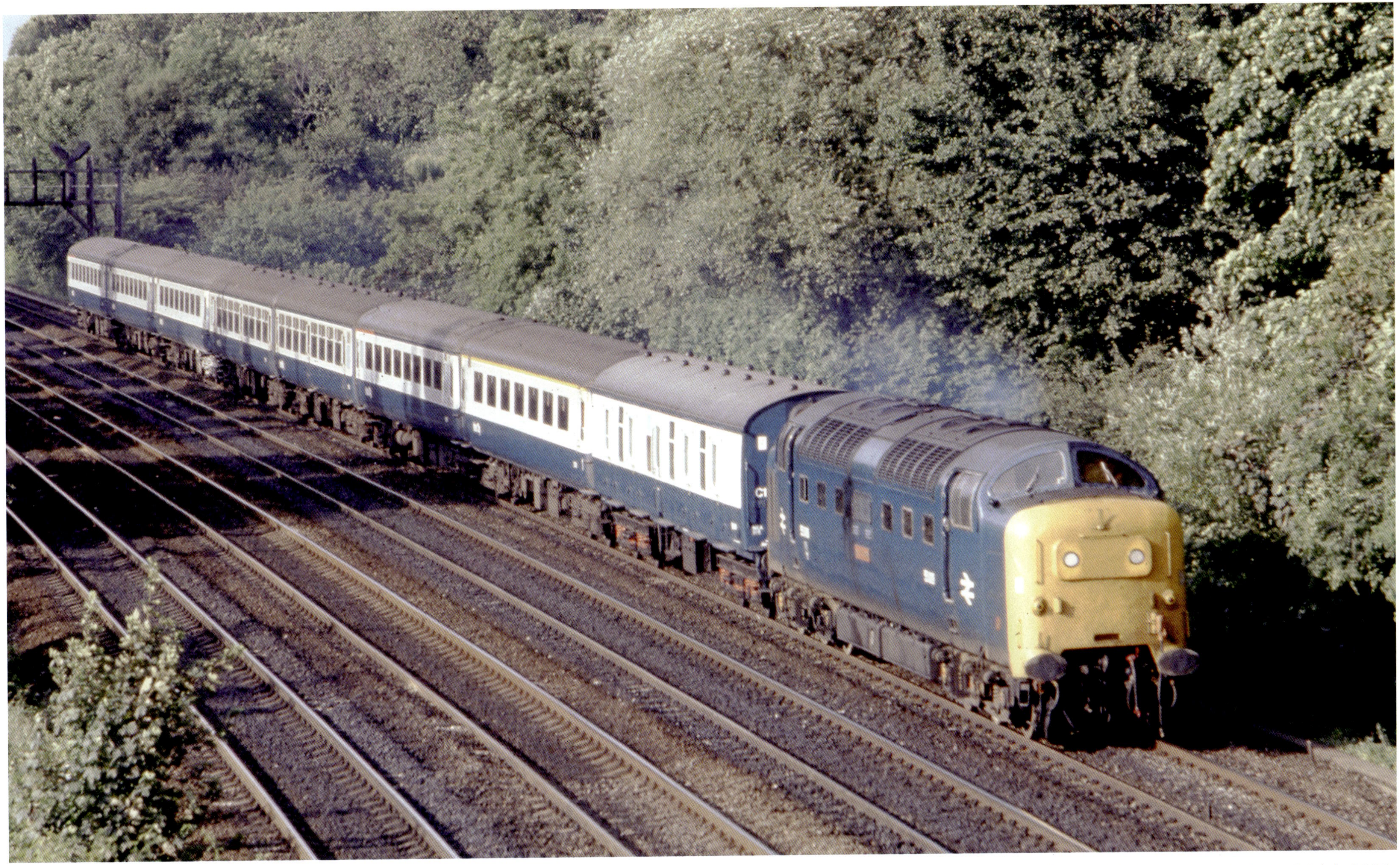

During the last summer of regular Deltic operations along the East Coast Main Line and now transferred away from Finsbury Park sees 55009 Alycidon running now having lost those attractive white painted surrounds. We see the locomotive powering past Chaloners Whin Junction with a York to Kings Cross train on 14 July 1981. ***John Arthur Bennett/Strathwood Library Collection***

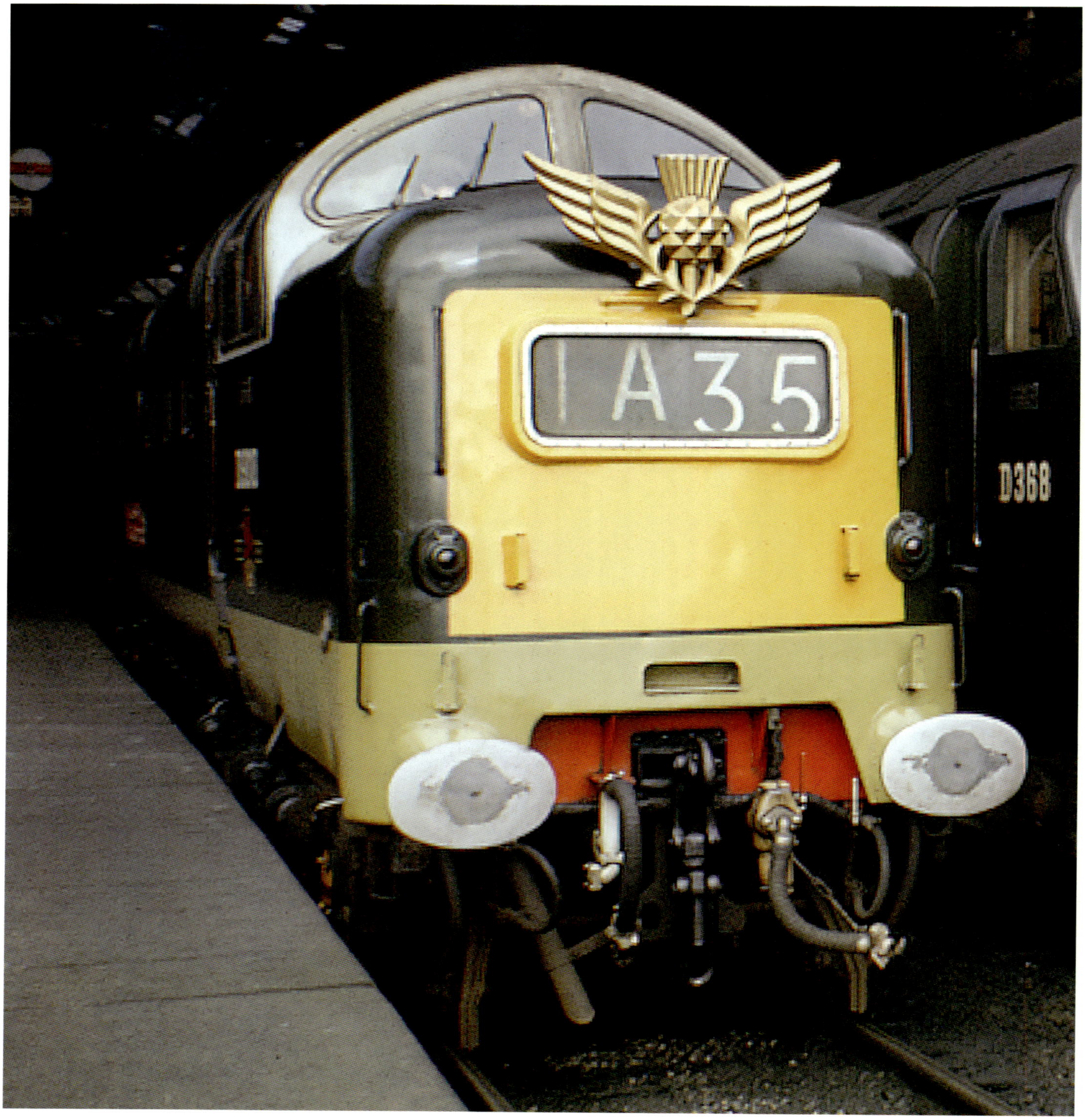
1A35
D368

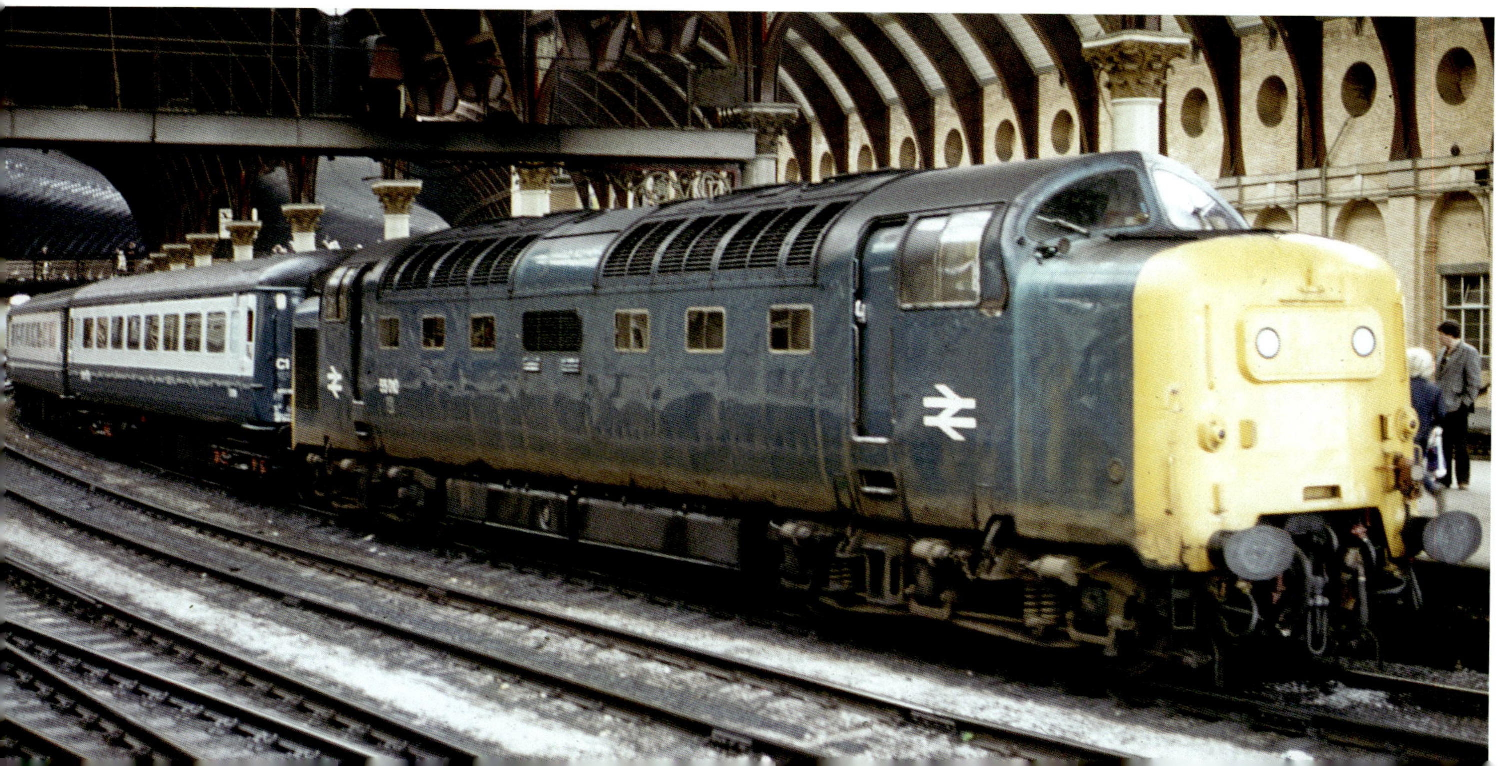

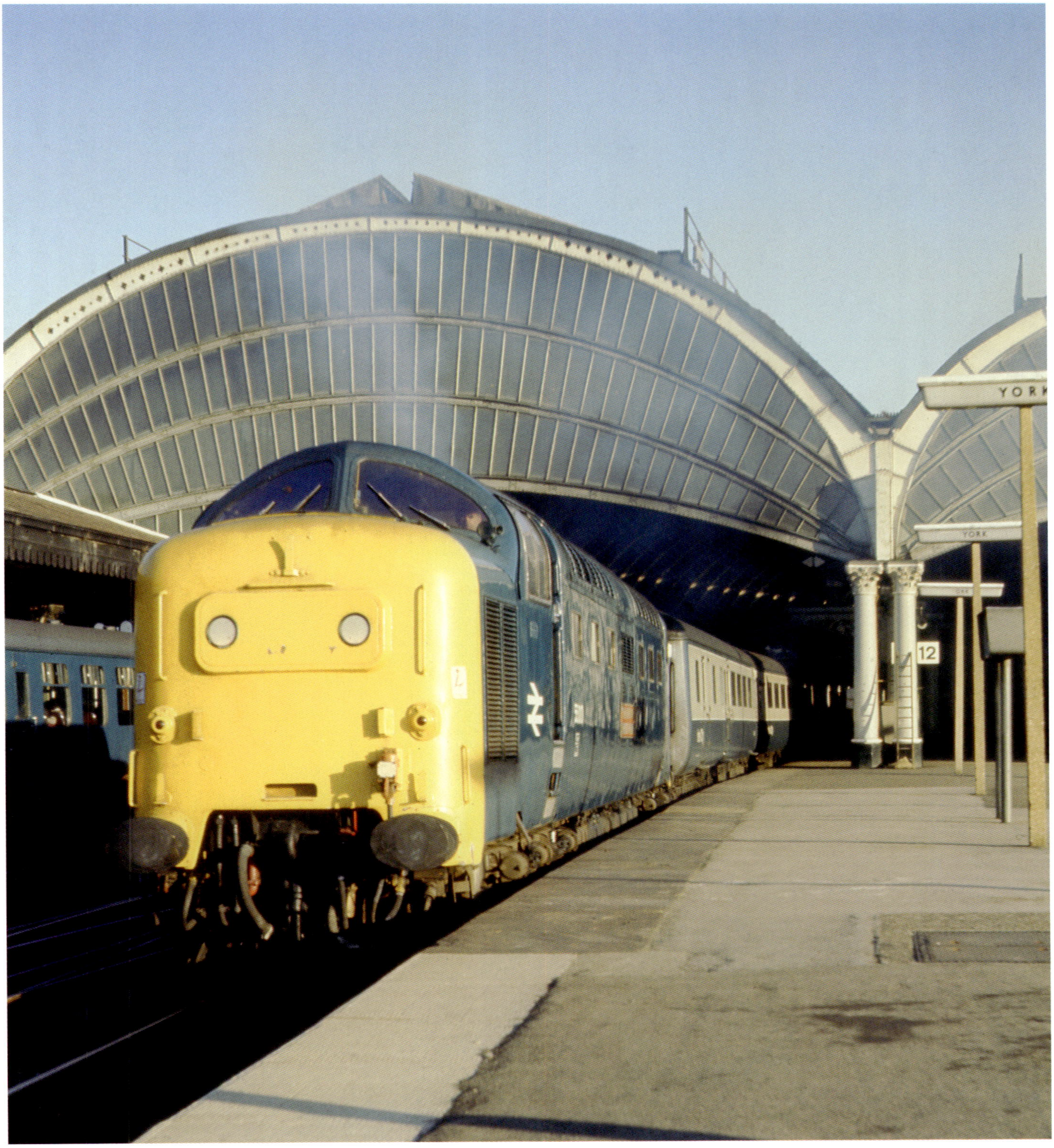

Page opposite: Surely the most attractive of headboards ever was the gold winged thistle designed for use with the Deltics rostered for the Flying Scotsman services. In 1966, D9010 The King's Own Scottish Borderer shows off this magnificent embellishment at Edinburgh Waverley.When the locomotive was painted with full yellow fronts in December 1966, with the locomotive still in green, it gained Inter City arrows in place of the original emblems, this rare livery variant remained until very early 1968 when a full repaint into blue took place. ***Strathwood Library Collection***

Page opposite: It was during December 1979 55010 The King's Own Scottish Borderer was taken into Doncaster Works for an Unclassified repair, which included the removal of one nameplate for inspection and repair following damage, and the nameplate was never replaced. Withdrawal would come on Christmas Eve a few months later but this was the scene at York on 19 September 1981. ***Strathwood Library Collection***

Above: All looks to be in splendid order as 55010 The King's Own Scottish Borderer gets away from York in 1979. This Deltic's naming ceremony took place on 8 May 1965 almost four years into its service career held at Dumfries. The nameplates from the withdrawn Royal Scot 46104 Scottish Borderer were handed over to officers of the Regiment during the proceedings. After which the Deltic took out an Inverness bound troop special carrying King's Own Scottish Borderer's territorial's to their annual camp. Travelling via Dalry as far as Perth with a train bound for Inverness. Most likely making this the first Deltic over the Glasgow & South Western route. ***Sid Steadman***

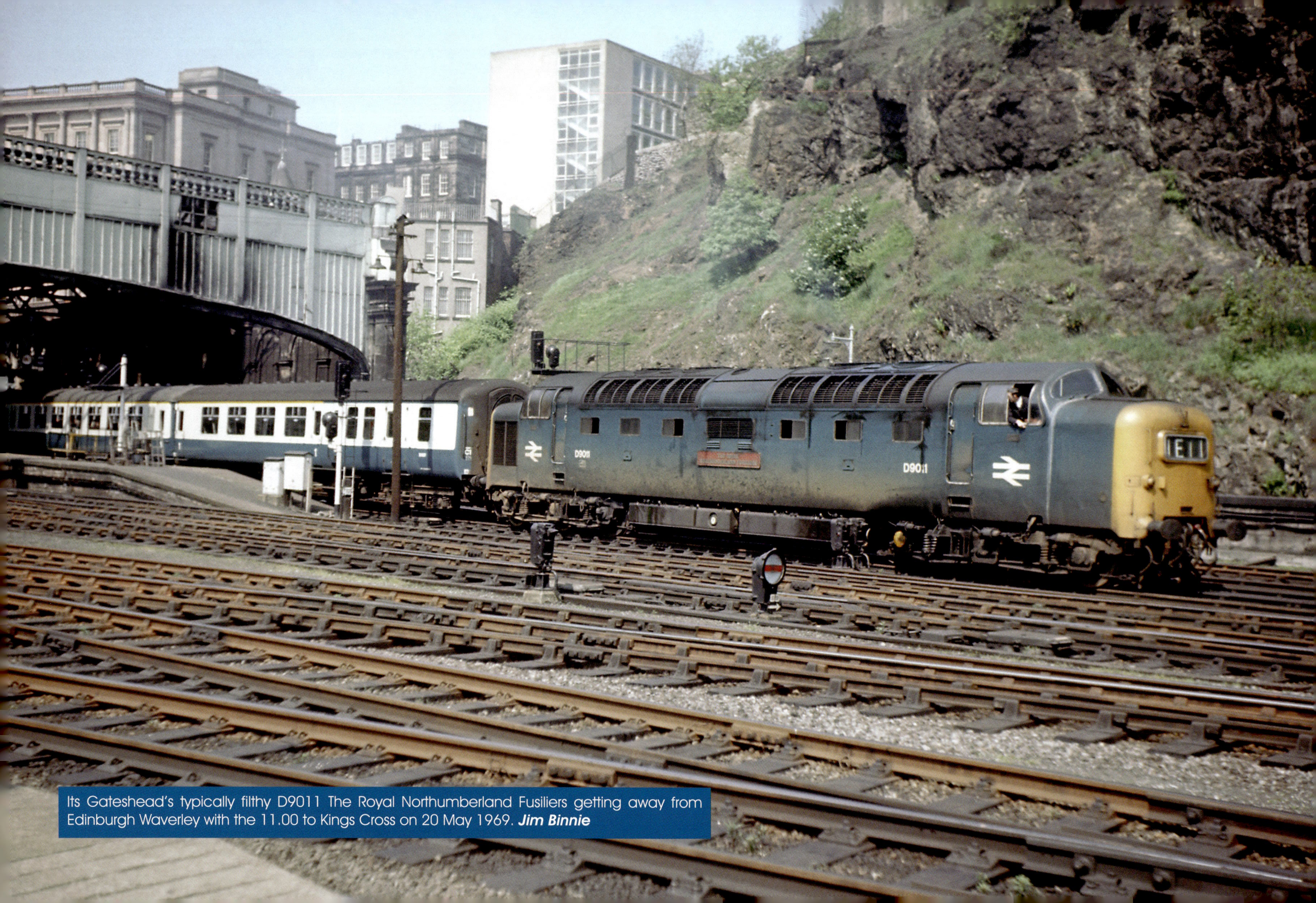

Its Gateshead's typically filthy D9011 The Royal Northumberland Fusiliers getting away from Edinburgh Waverley with the 11.00 to Kings Cross on 20 May 1969. ***Jim Binnie***

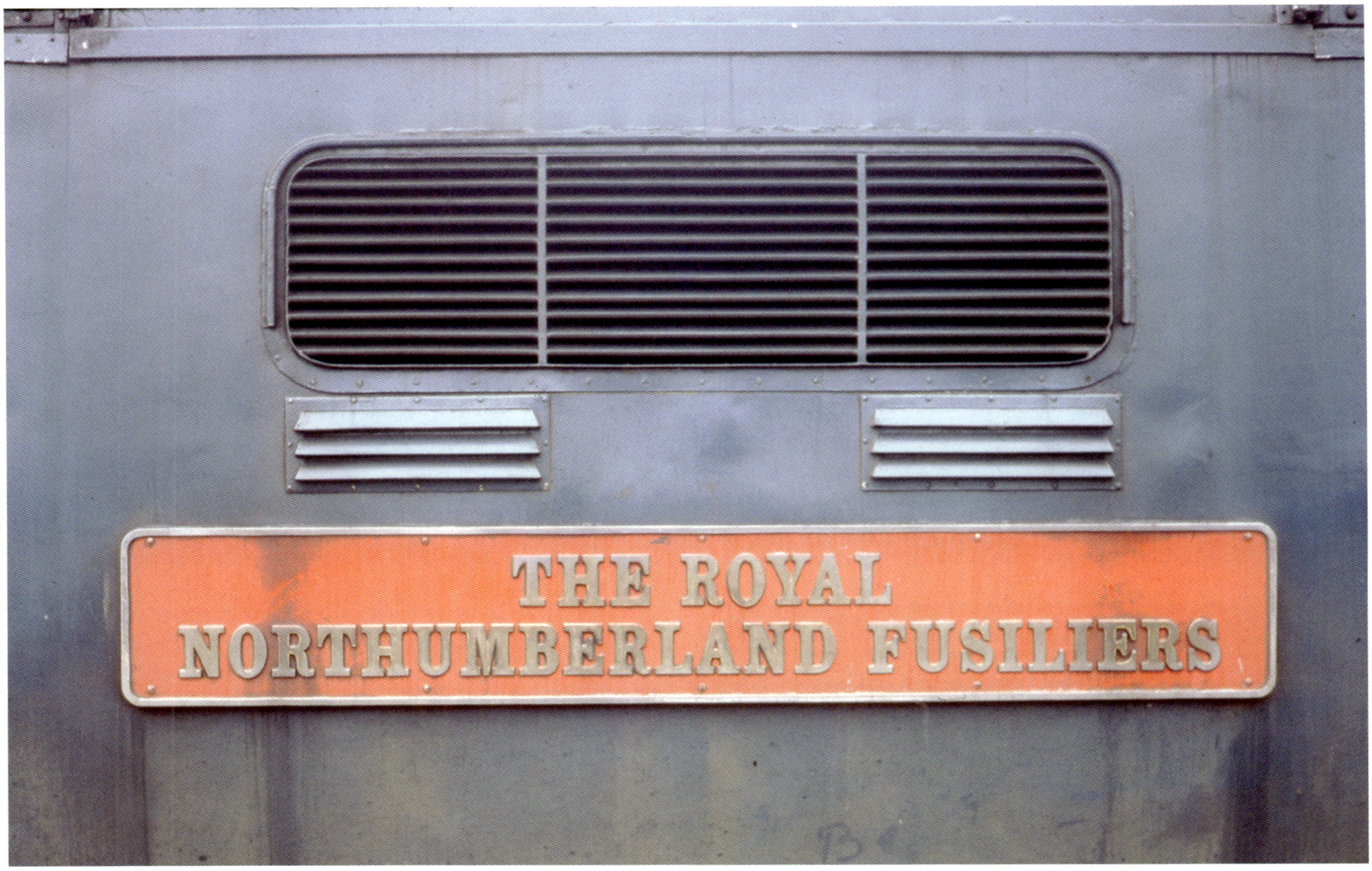

The naming ceremony was held at Newcastle Central on 28 May 1963, and the locomotive remained Gateshead based until May 1979 when the concentration of the class at York was made. ***Graham Courts***

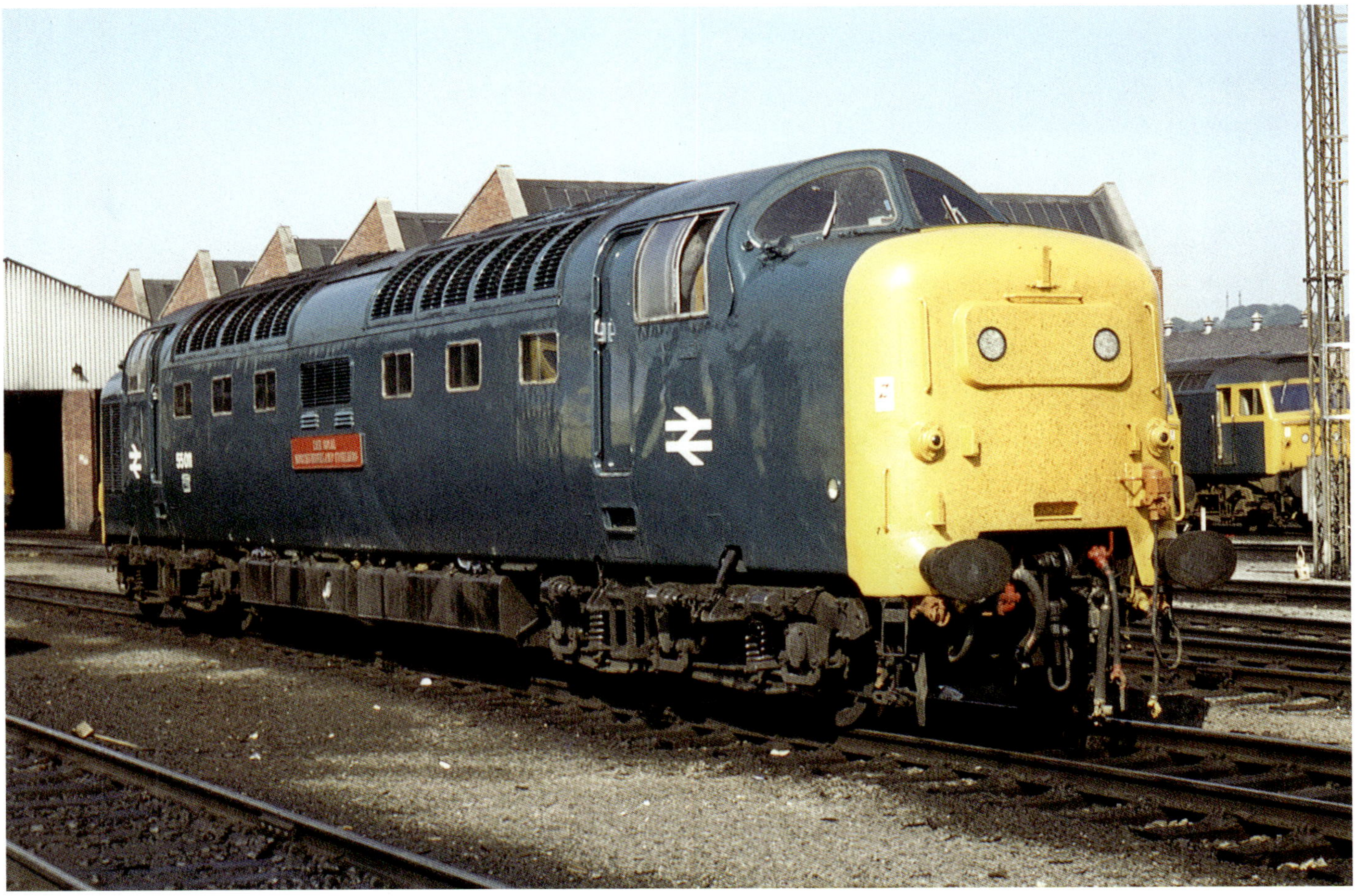

Standing in the sunshine at Edinburgh's Haymarket depot on 4 June 1978 the locomotive's career would conclude on withdrawal on 8 November 1981 in the dying weeks for the class, with cutting up taking place twelve months later. ***John Chalcraft/Rail Photoprints***

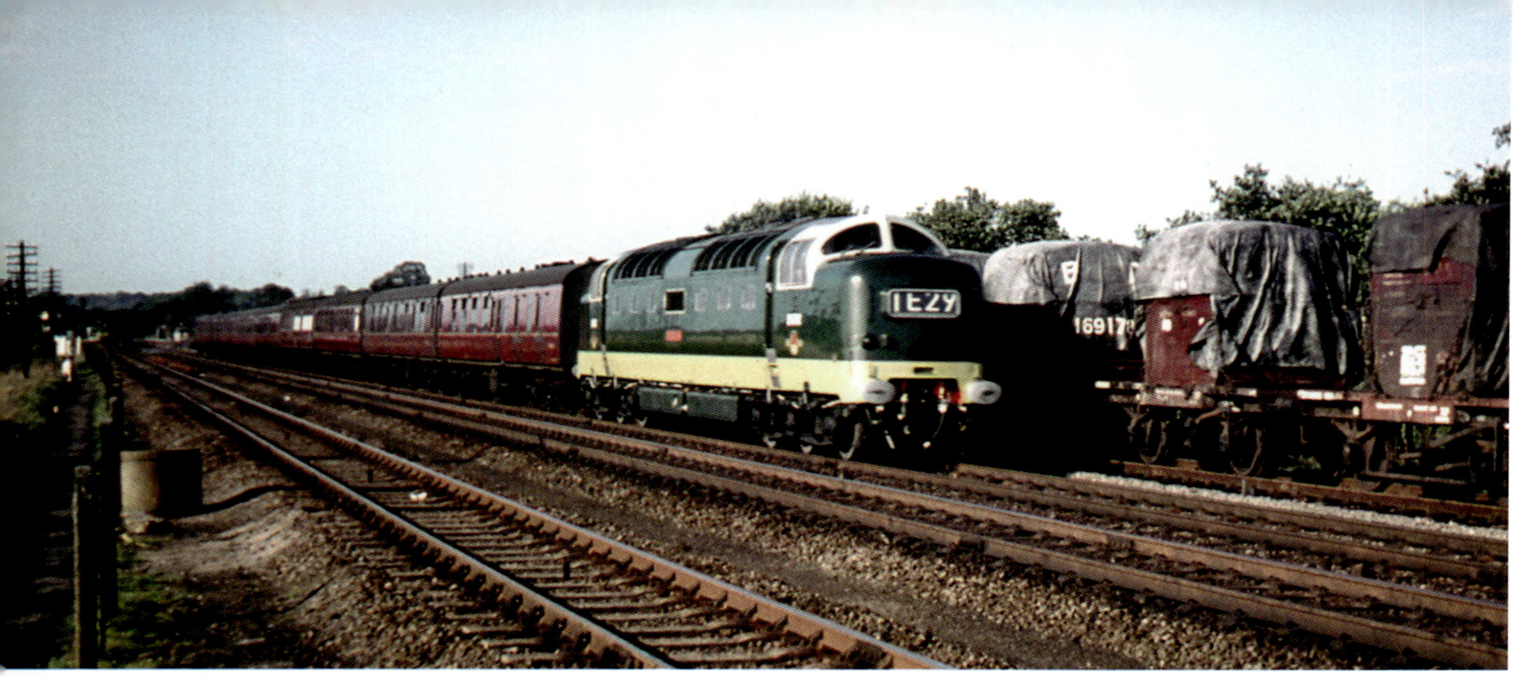

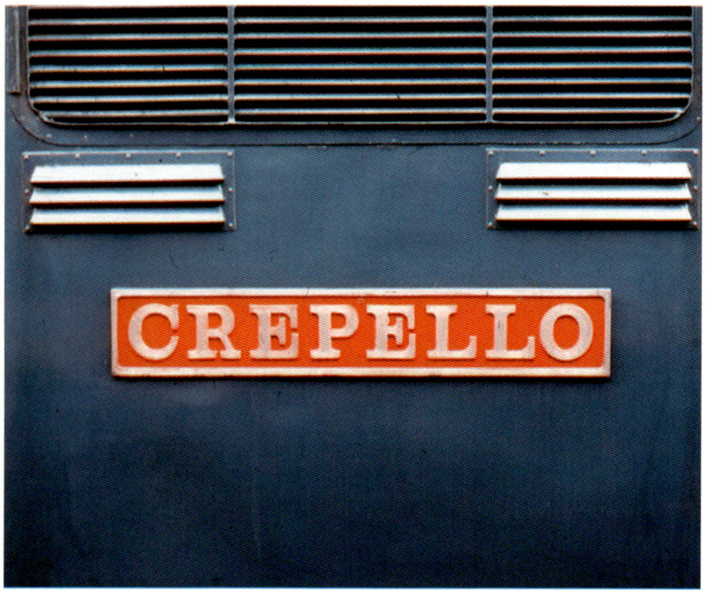

Contrast for D9012 Crepello seen on the 12.20 from Hull at Brookmans Park when new on 9 September 1961 against the locomotives condition when seen below at Doncaster on 29 December 1978. ***Photos: D Twibell/ Transport Treasury, Steve Burdett and Nev Sloper***

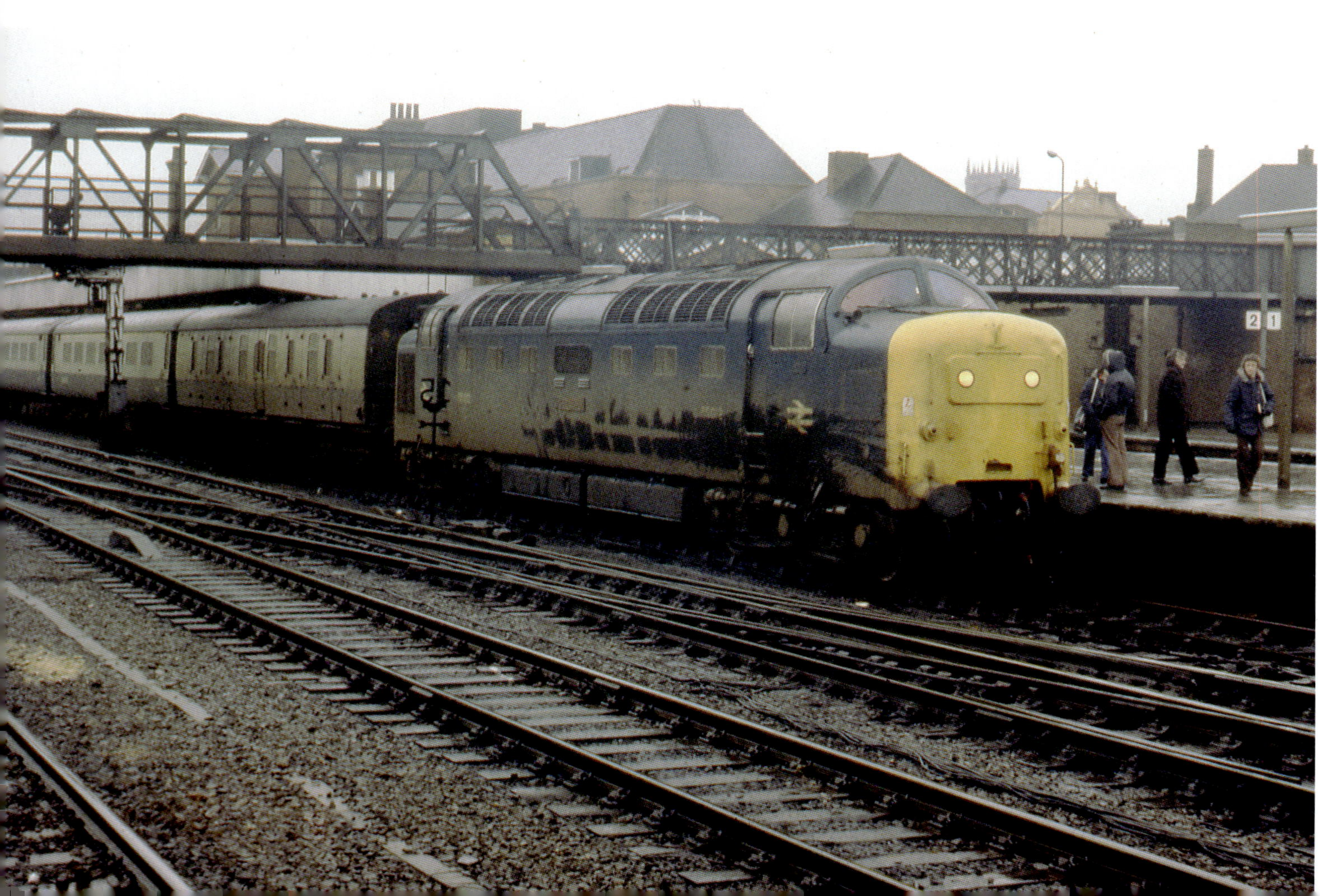

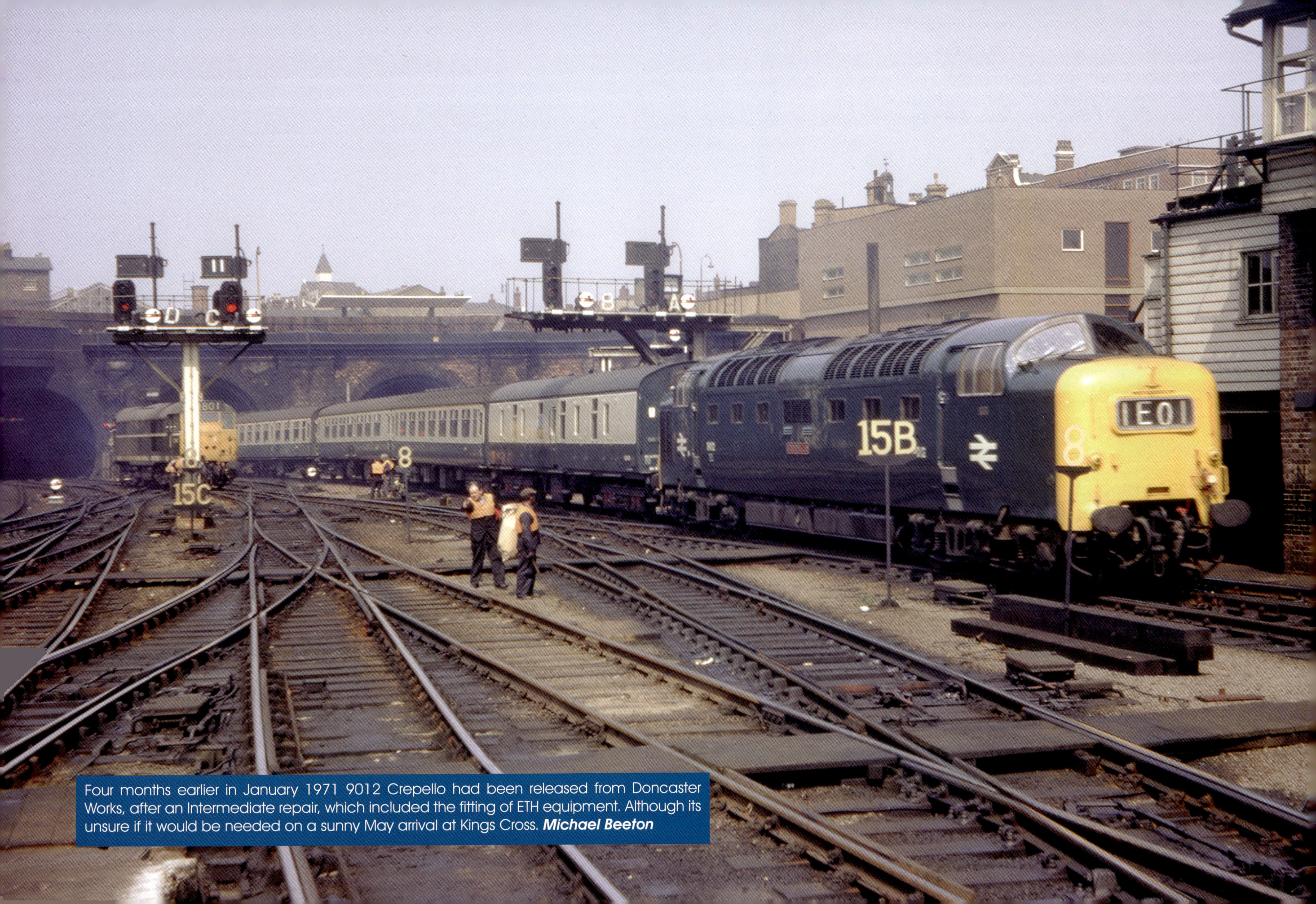

Four months earlier in January 1971 9012 Crepello had been released from Doncaster Works, after an Intermediate repair, which included the fitting of ETH equipment. Although its unsure if it would be needed on a sunny May arrival at Kings Cross. ***Michael Beeton***

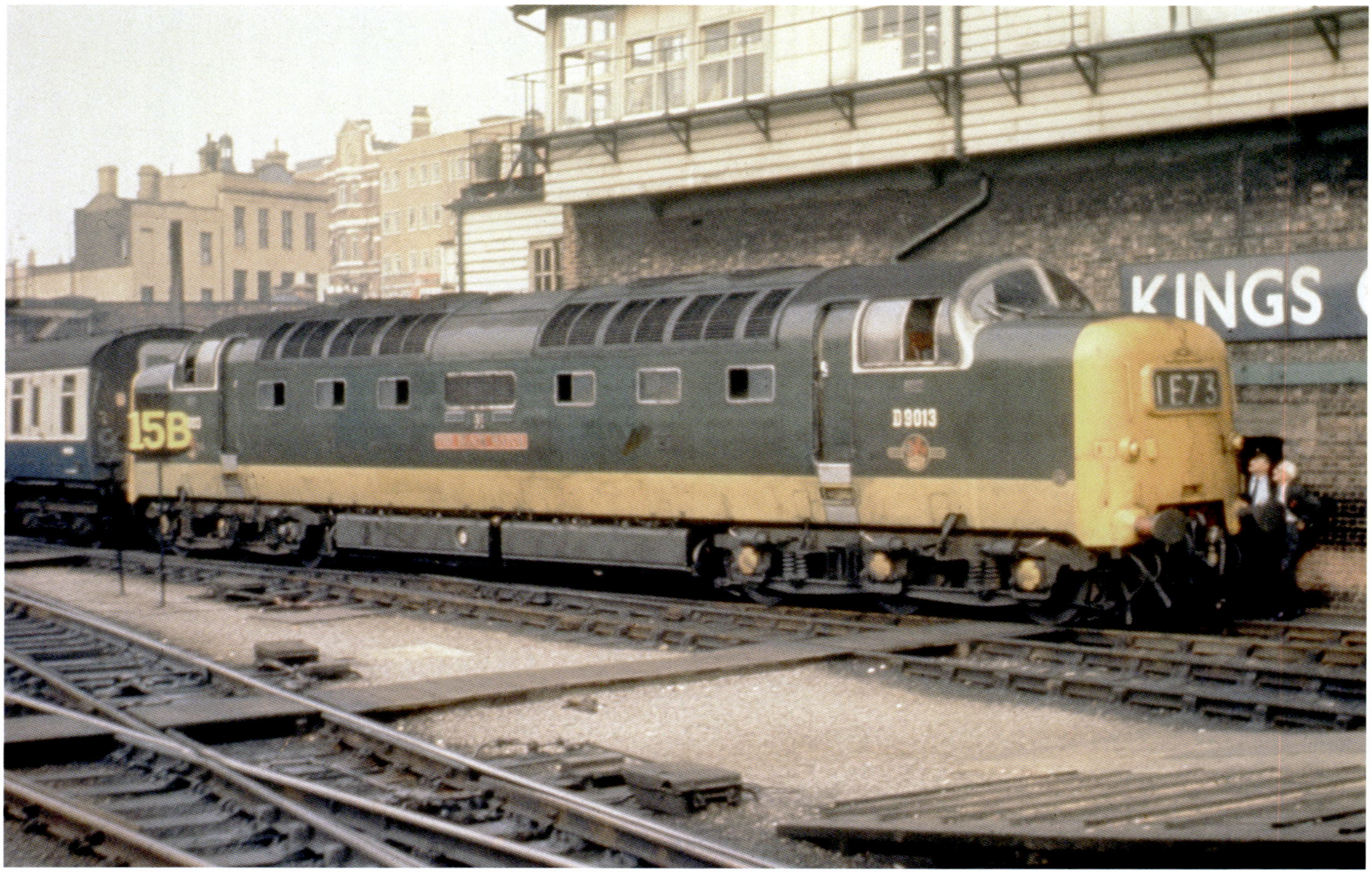

Taking up the name of The Black Watch at Dundee in a ceremony on 16 January 1963 D9013 also gained the regimental badge above its name plate as seen here in August 1967. ***Grahame Wareham***

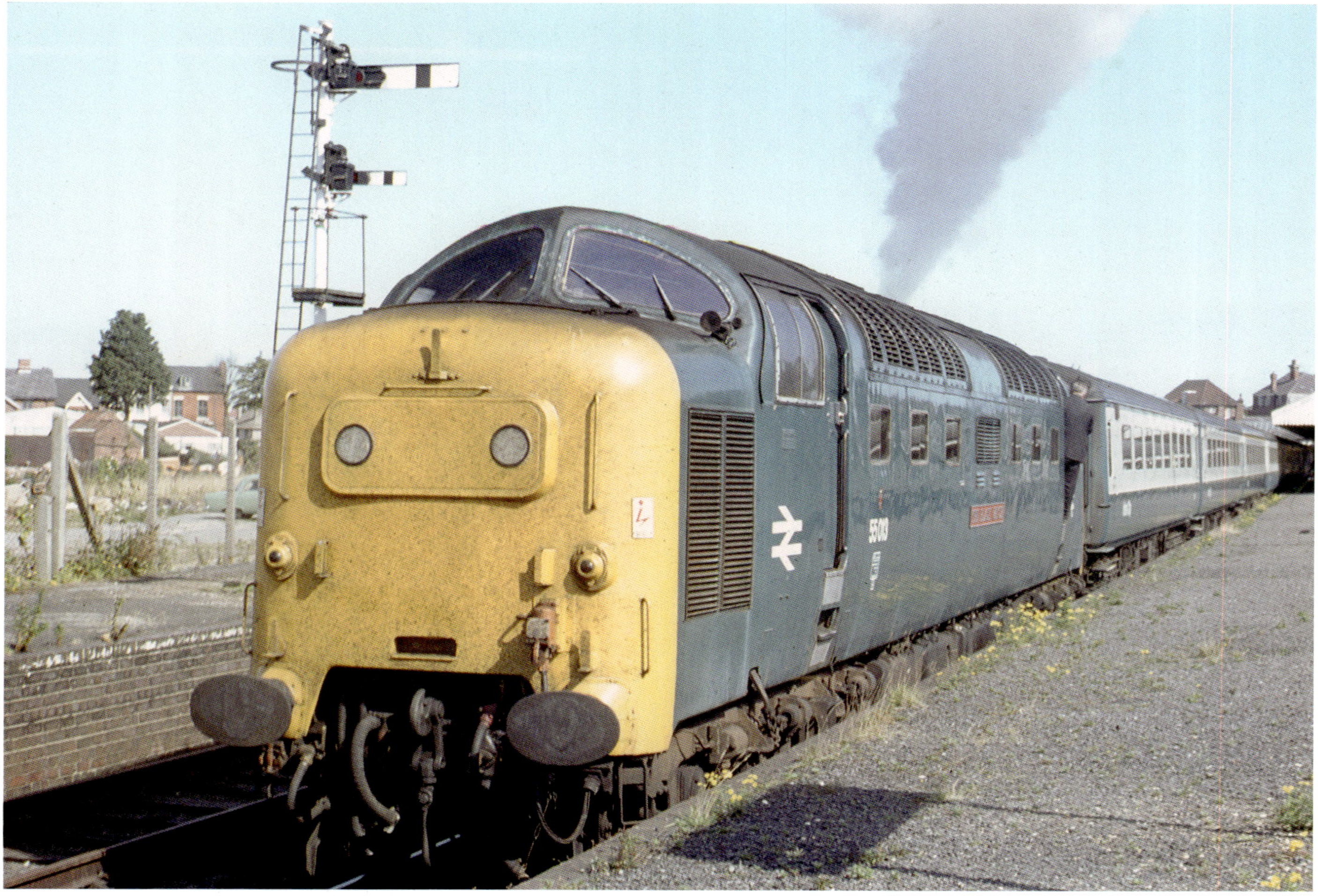

The locomotive took on blue livery on release from Doncaster Works a few months later in December 1967, so far we have not found any shots of it retaining the badge from this point. The ever so bracing Skegness air reverberates to the sound of Napier Deltic engines on 15 September 1979 as 55013 The Black Watch has a day out at the seaside. ***Strathwood Library Collection***

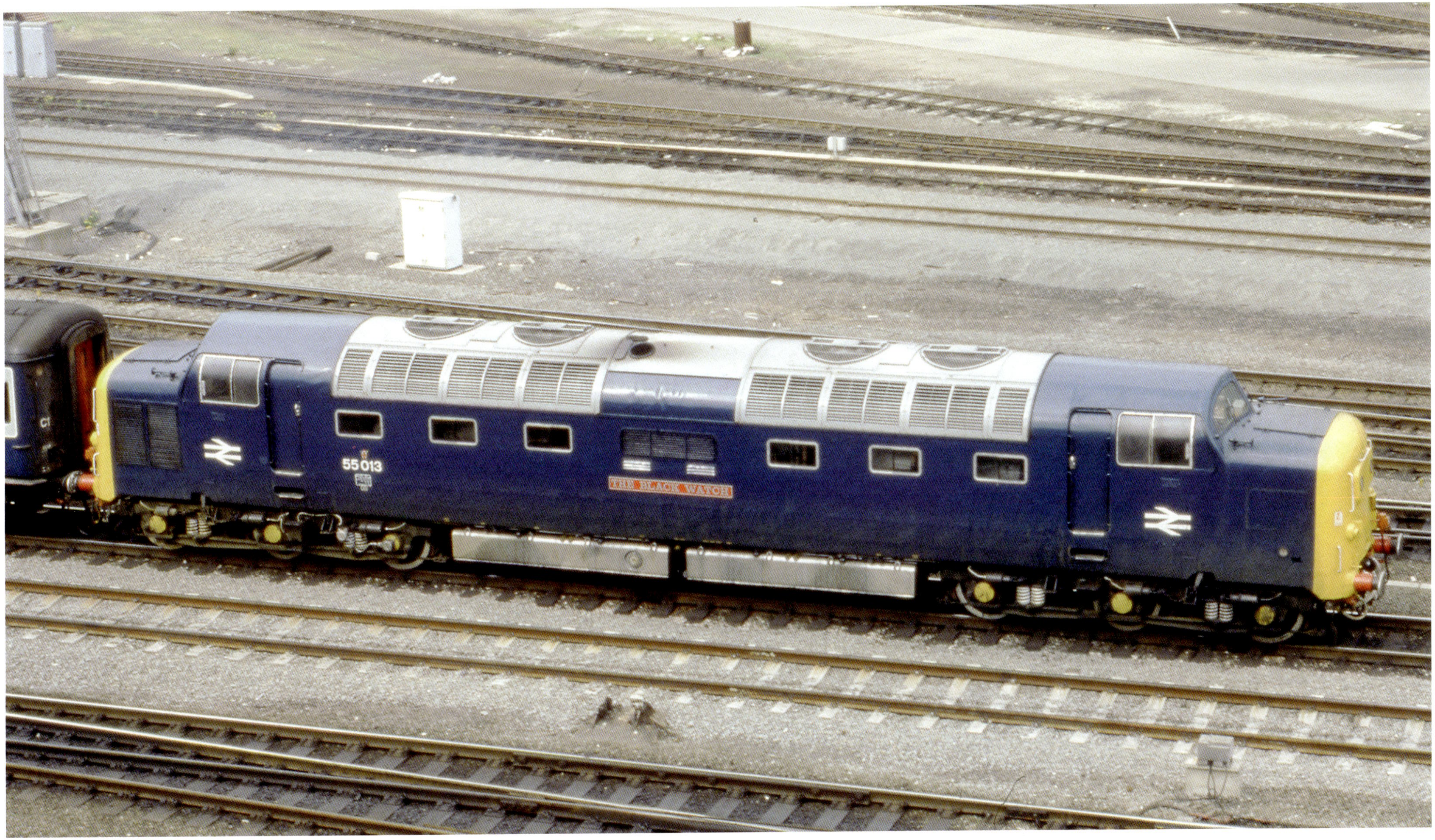

During May 1980 York depot carried out a full C exam and special preparation for the Rainhill celebrations for the locomotive. In the event it was 55015 Tulyar that was sent instead. On 25 May 1980 55013 The Black Watch adorned with extra paintwork took the 08.05 Kings Cross to Hull onwards from Doncaster. The Deltic's last service train would be on 16 December 1981 as the 07.23 Peterborough to Kings Cross, however engine failure at Wood Green required assistance to the terminus from 31292. Briefly stored at Finsbury Park and withdrawn four days later, the final movements would be to Doncaster Works on 23 January 1982 and final dismissal taking place within the works in December. ***Colin Whitbread***

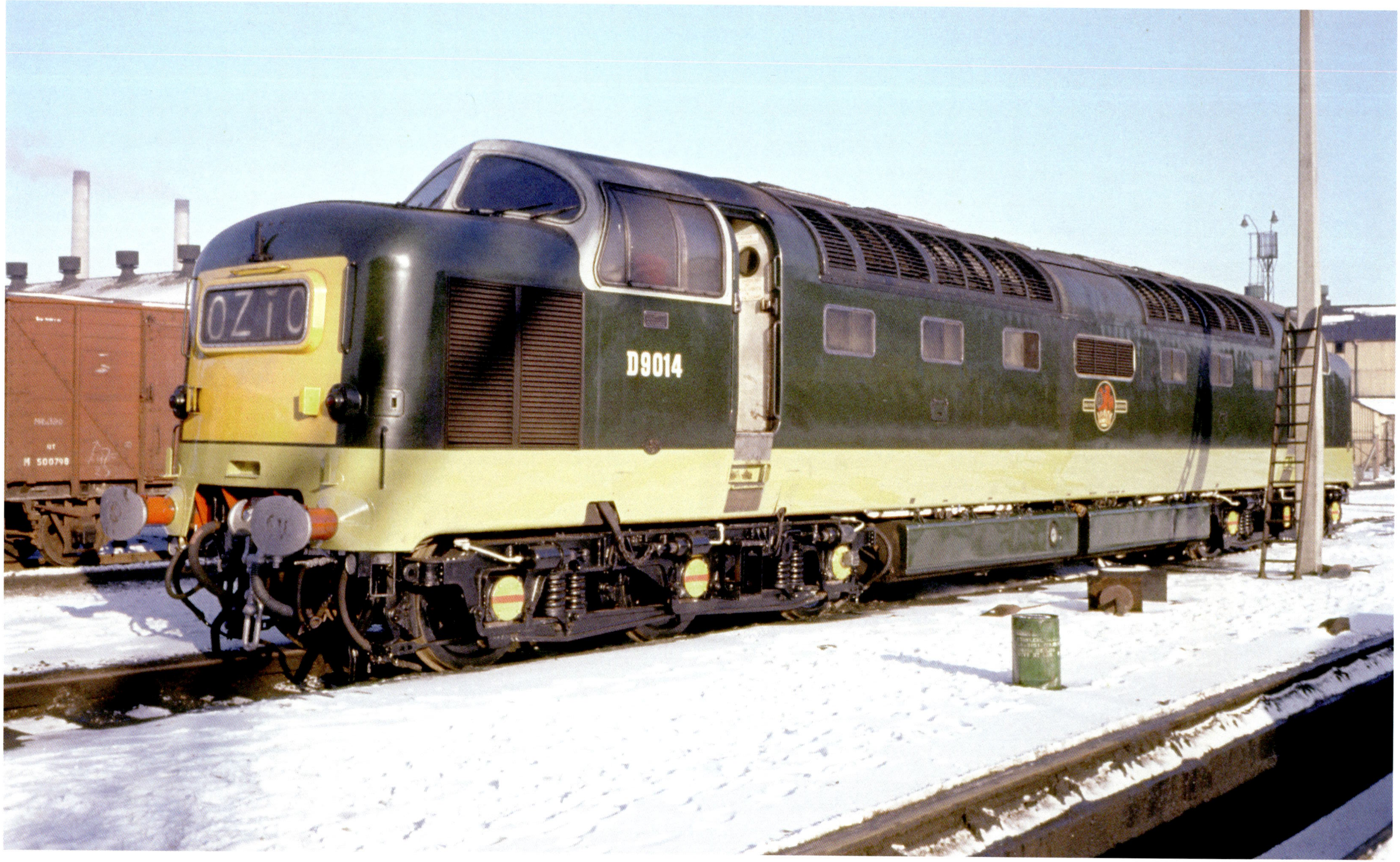

A return to Doncaster Works during the harsh winter of 1962-3 for D9014 still to be named as The Duke of Wellington's Regiment in a ceremony which will come on 22 October at Darlington with Major-General K.G. Exham Colonel of the regiment unveiling the nameplates. The officer also being presented with a nameplate taken from Royal Scot 46145 The Duke of Wellington's Regt. (West Riding) and a Hornby-Dublo model of the IDeltic. ***Strathwood Library Collection***

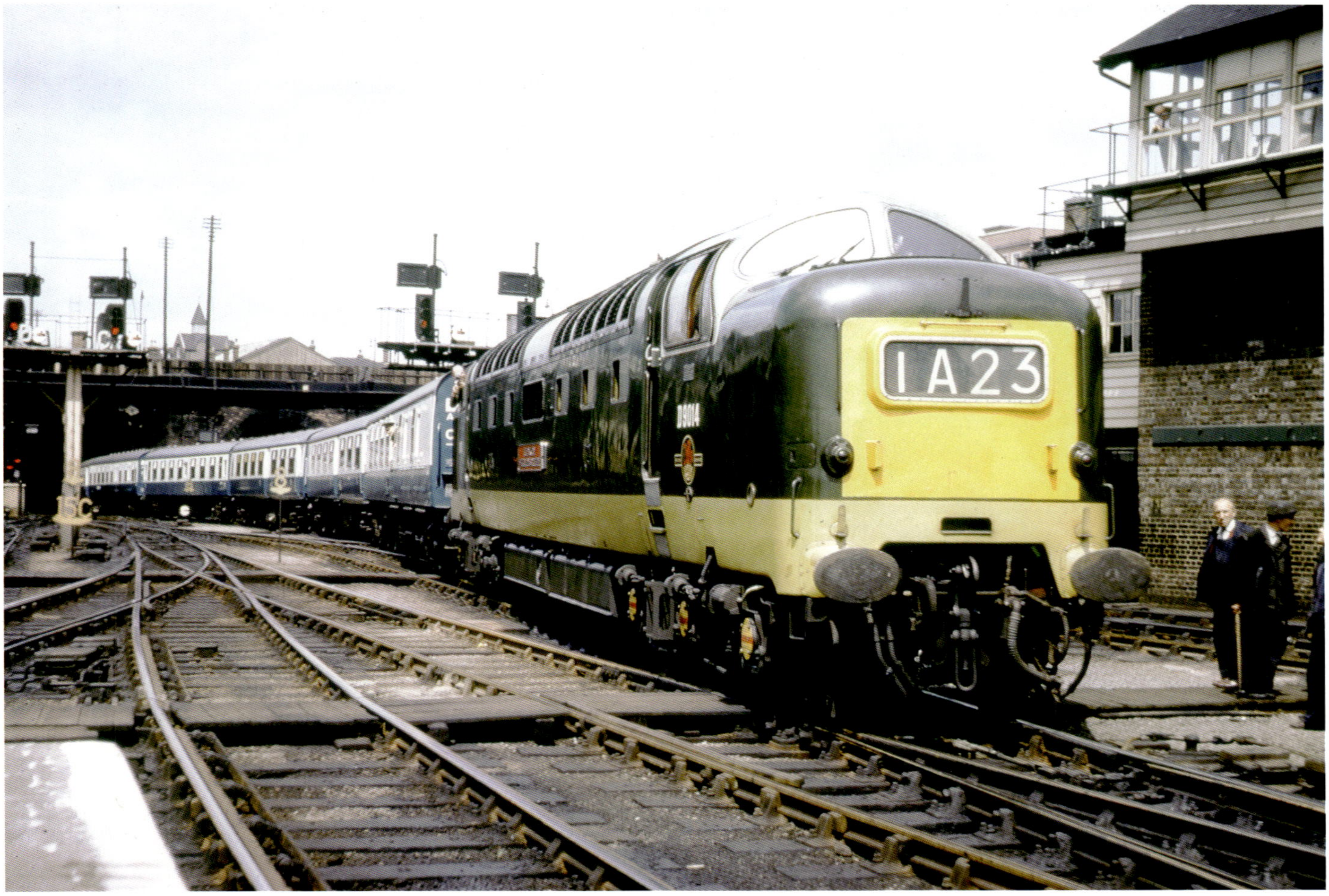

In June of 1964 D9014 The Duke of Wellington's Regiment had a number of experimental XP64 coaches within its rake for an up Talisman service on arrival at London's Kings Cross station. ***Strathwood Library Collection***

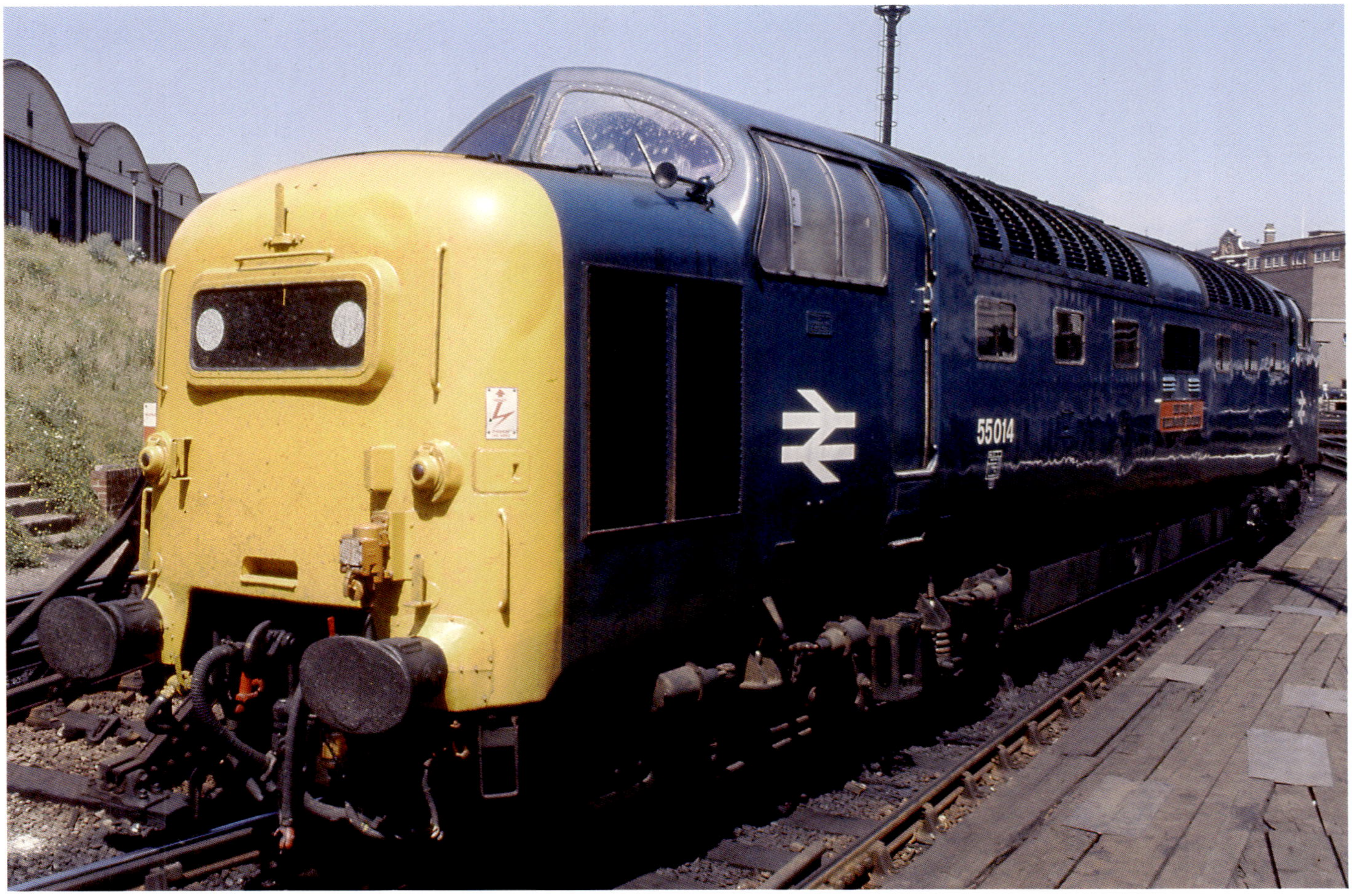

Not too many cameramen ventured around to the parcels platforms at Kings Cross to gain angles such as this one of 55014 The Duke of Wellington's Regiment in 1977. ***Strathwood Library Collection***

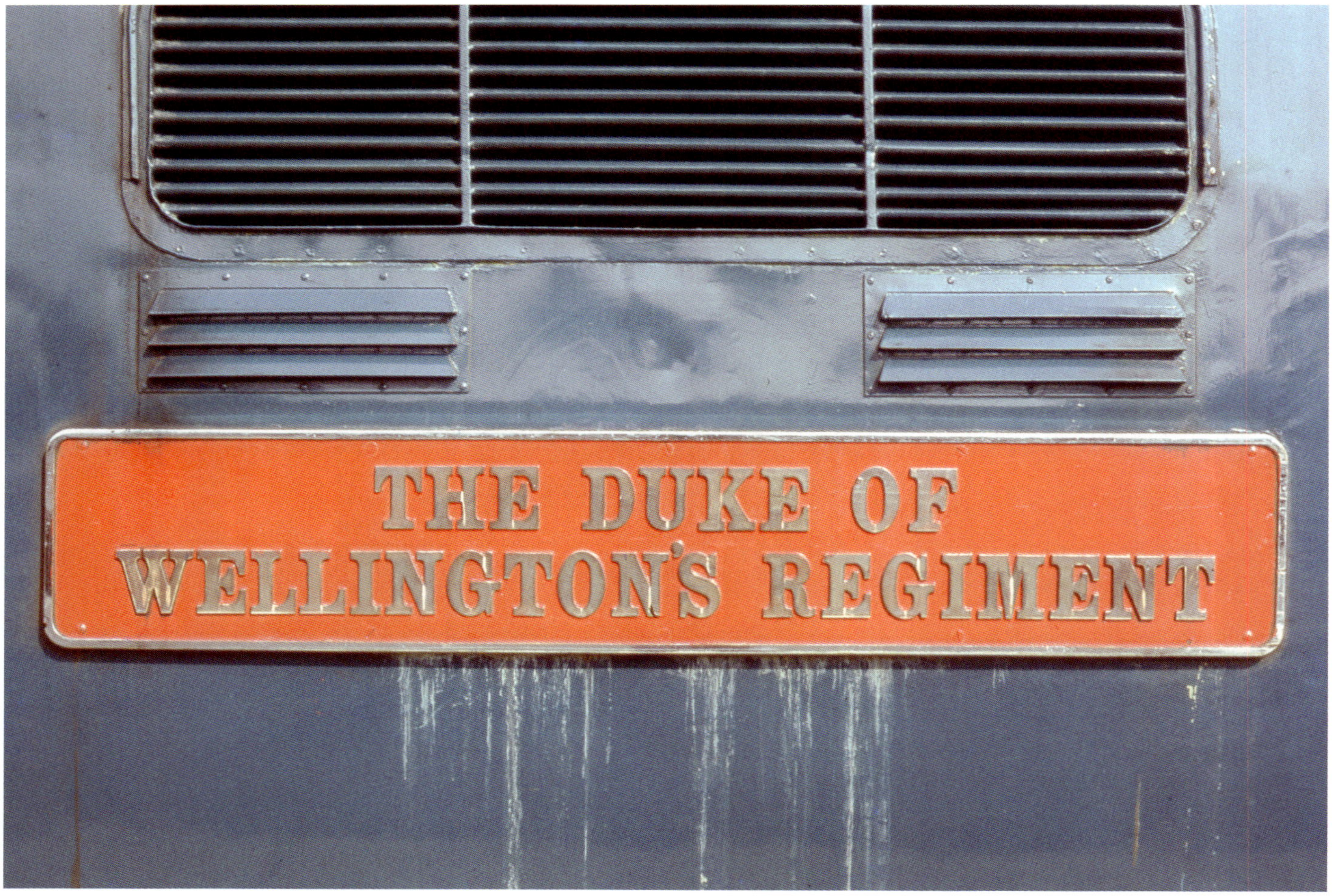

The chromium plating looks good on the nameplate although the chemical staining from the rear of the plate lets down the locomotive's appearance in this late 1970s view. ***Late Pete Walton/Sid Steadman***

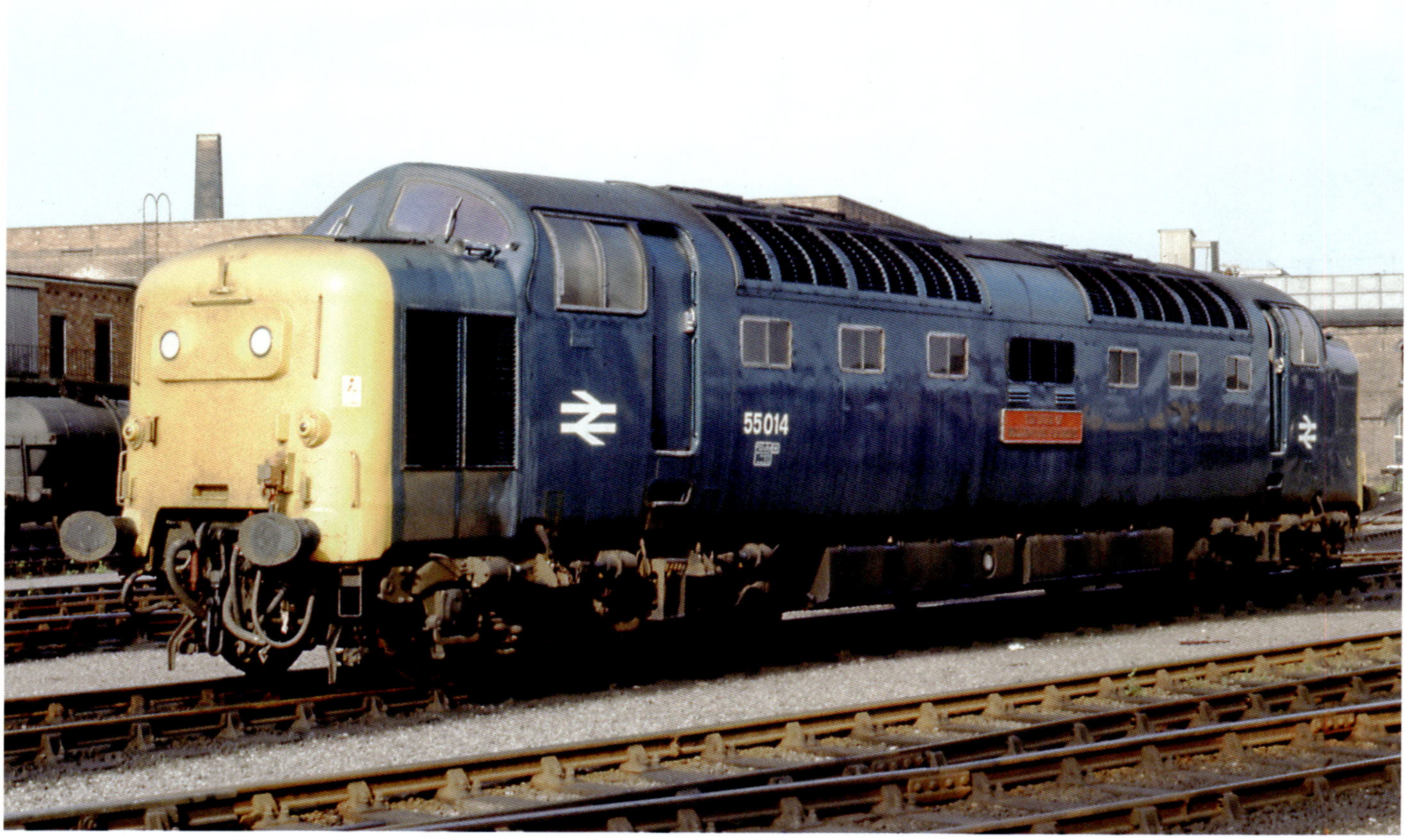

At Leed's Holbeck on 29 July 1978 Gateshead's 55014 The Duke of Wellington's Regiment graced the depot. It had been the last Deltic to be painted into blue livery which took place in November 1969. Then as 9014 taking up the TOPS number of 55014 for the start of February 1974. It would be engine failure whilst working the 08.10 Newcastle to Edinburgh at Cramlington that required assistance to its destination from 37082 another English Electric product on 10 November 1981 that put paid to the locomotive's career. ***Len Ball***

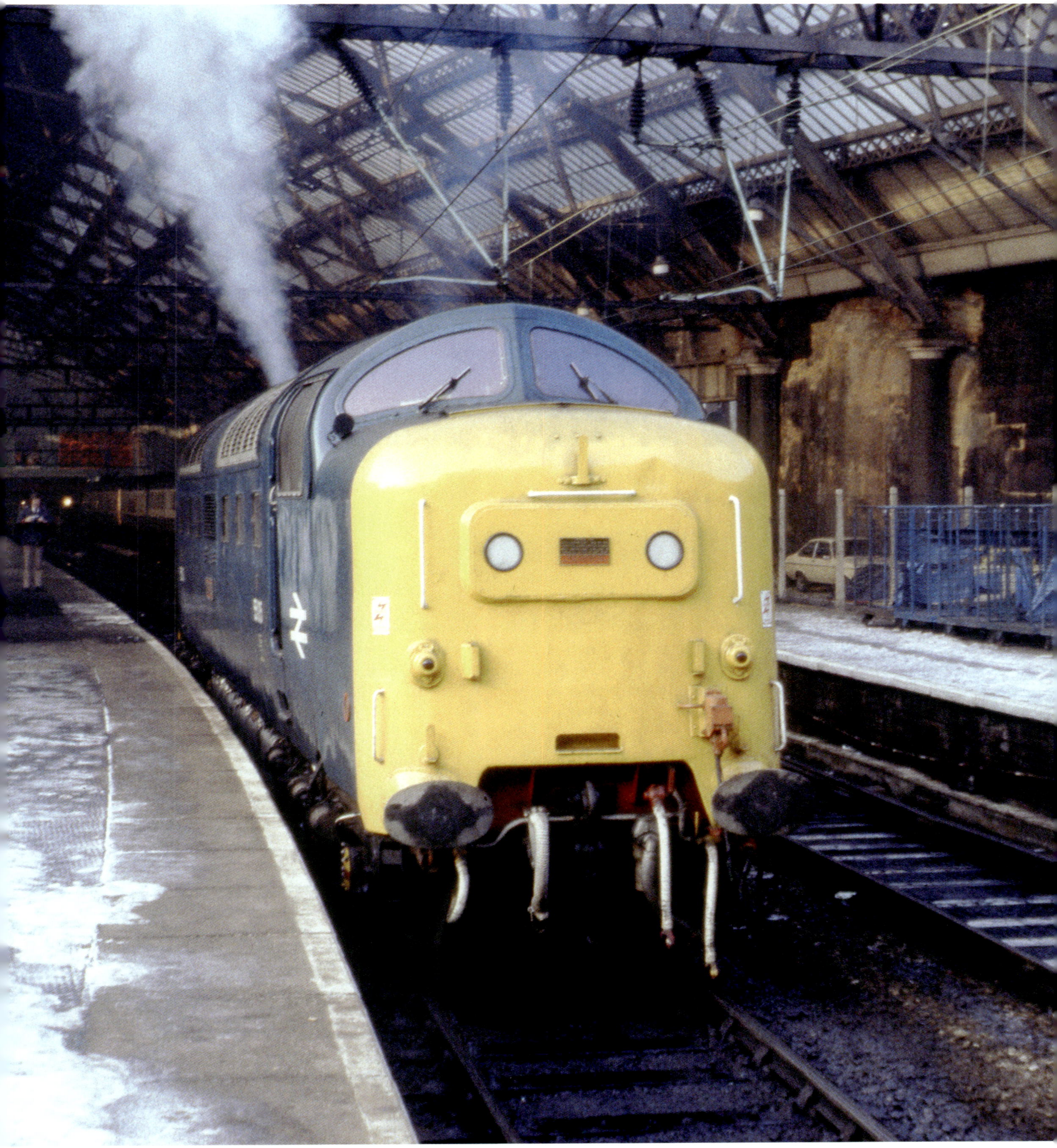

Both engines on 55015 Tulyar are throwing their exhausts into the overall roof at Liverpool Lime Street 23 December 1980 whilst working on the trans Pennine route from York. Here was another of the Deltic racehorses named from new, however this time an even more interesting and impressive pedigree. Owned by the Aga Khan and trained by Marcus Marsh. In 1952, ridden by Charlie Smirke, he won the Derby, St. Leger and Eclipse Stakes. Tulyar remained un-defeated as a three year old and won prize money totalling for the time an amazing £76,417. Such was this achievement Tulyar was honoured with the Tulyar Stakes a race run at Lingfield. Most notable among Tulyar's descendants was Shergar, winner of the 1981 Derby and King George VI & Queen Elizabeth Stakes, the horse allegedly taken for ransom by the IRA in the early 1980's and never to be seen again. ***Matthew Hall***

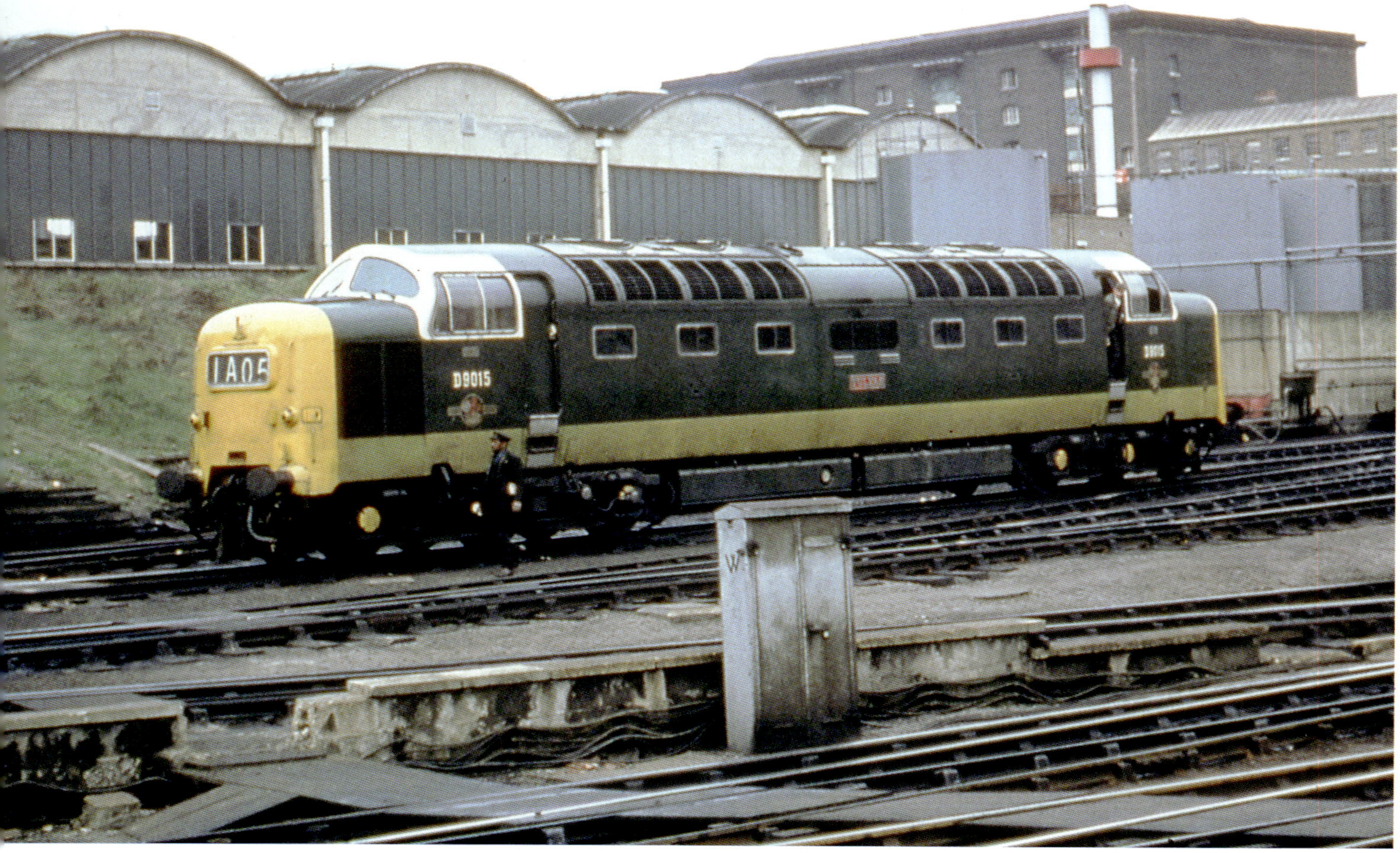

As a Finsbury Park Deltic D9015 Tulyar was a regular at Kings Cross as here on 6 April 1968. The full yellow ends had been applied in February 1967 and the next repainting would be into blue in May 1969. ***Strathwood Library Collection***

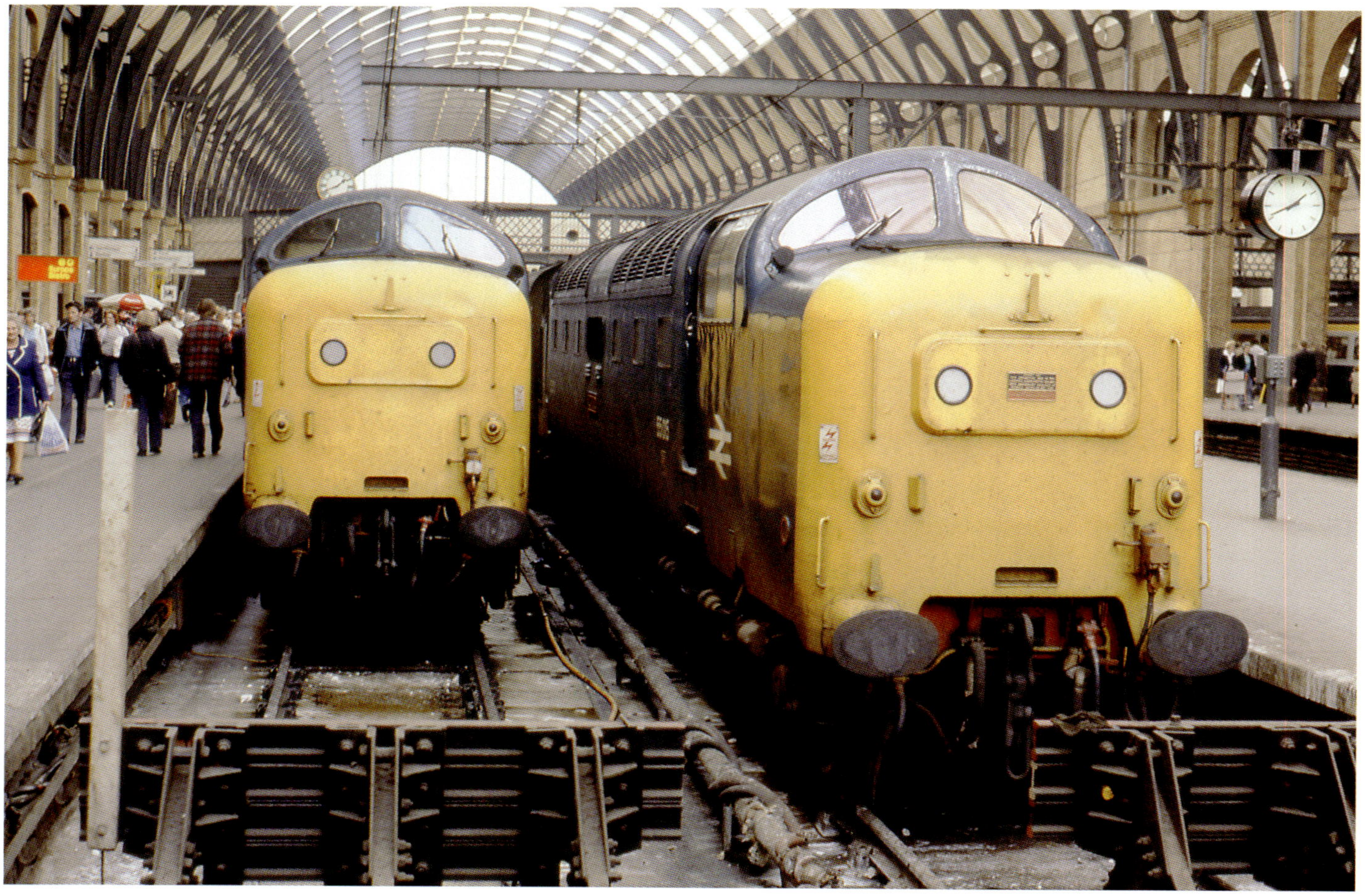

For just on twenty years passengers and enthusiasts would be often greeted by two or more Deltics at the concourse of Kings Cross as here with 55015 Tulyar alongside 55016 Gordon Highlander in 1980. ***Strathwood Library Collection***

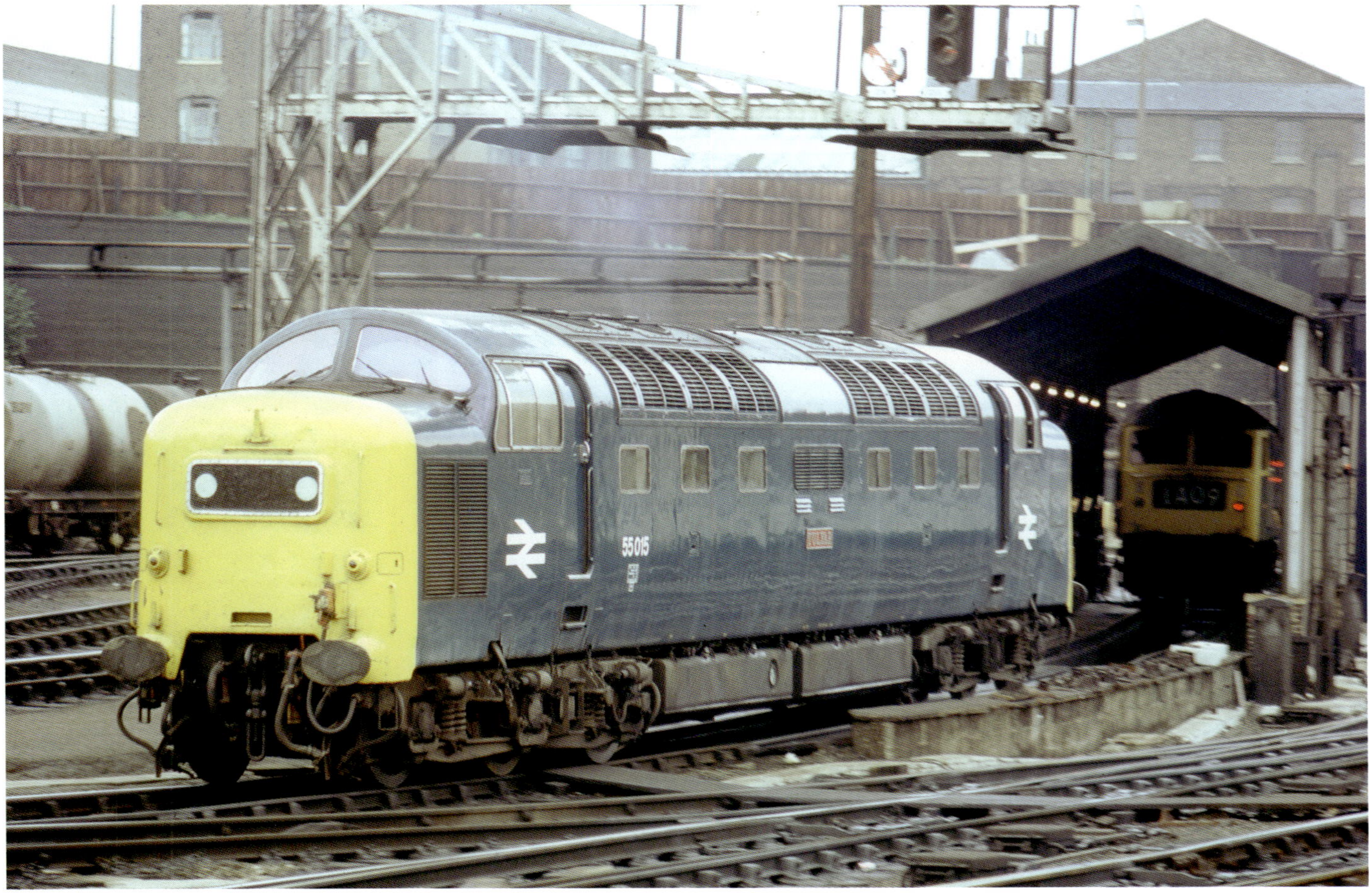

On 26 April 1975 55015 Tulyar was making its way off the servicing point at Kings Cross to take up a postion at the head of another departure from London. ***Aldo Delicata***

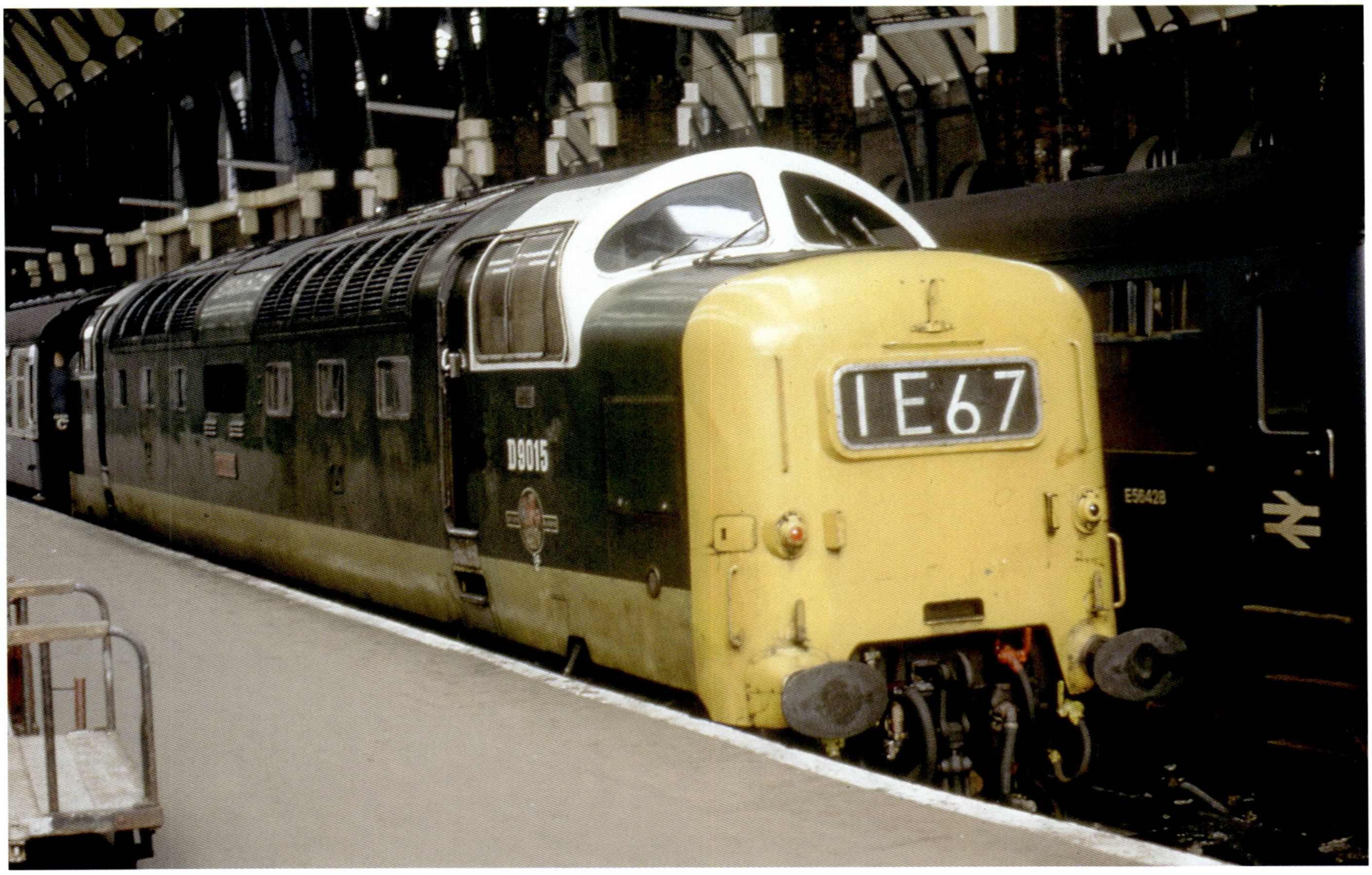

Very often the Deltics would be shut down whilst at the buffer stops to keep the exhaust fumes at a minimum, the sound of them being started up again at the point of being readied for moving out once more being a very evocative sight and sound. Here is D9015 Tulyar once again awaiting release from the station in April 1969 just before that repaint into blue livery. ***Strathwood Library Collection***

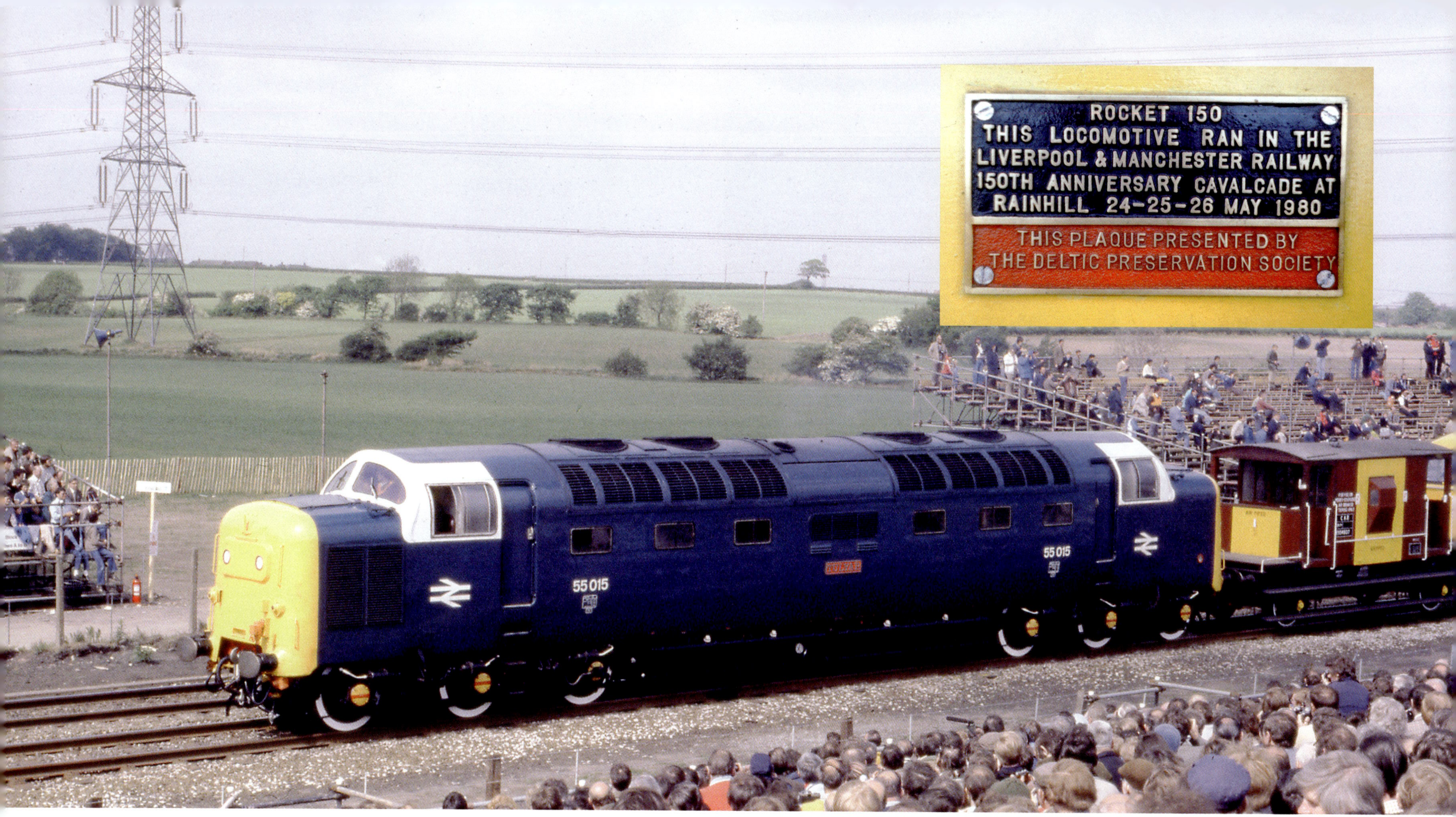

The treatment given to 55013 The Black Watch by York depot as seen on page 51 is visually different to 55015 Tulyar for preparation for possible exhibition here at the Rainhill 150 celebrations. Finsbury Park had Tulyar in for a B exam, and power unit repairs at the start of May and carried out this repaint to present the locomotive in its best condition and was seen here on 24 May 1980. The following year on 17 March, Tulyar was affixed with commemorative plaques denoting its part in these Rocket 150 cavalcades. Two plaques were fitted and unveiled at Finsbury Park by Neville G. Davies (Divisional Maintenance Engineer, Kings Cross) in the presence of Alan Baker (Manager, Finsbury Park) and David Carter (Chairman of the Deltic Preservation Society). It is likely these plaques actually saved 55015 from withdrawal in May 1981 when the locomotive was more overdue for a classified overhaul at Doncaster than its sister 55012 Crepello, which was withdrawn instead. ***Photos; Ian James & Matthew Hall***

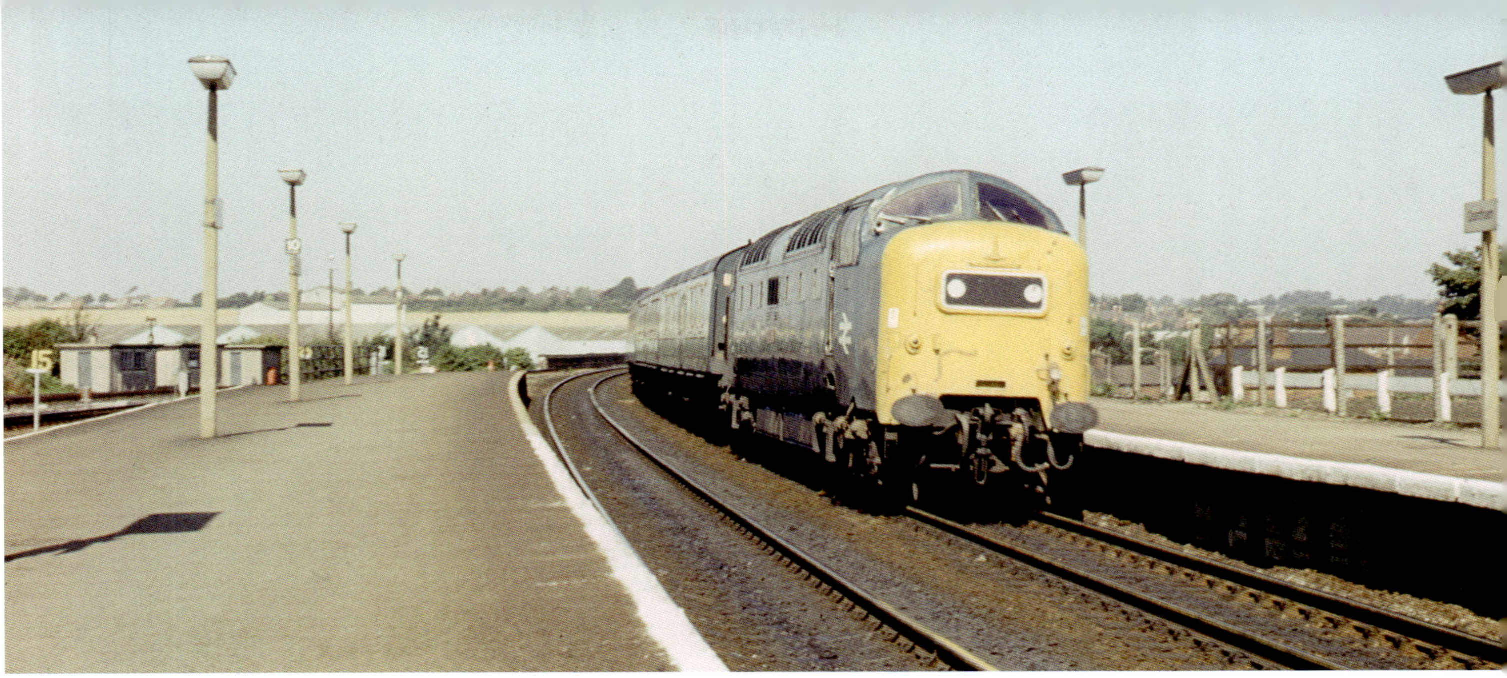

Here is Tulyar leaning into Grantham on 29 August 1977 and early morning at Hull Paragon on 25 July 1981 having brought in the 03.55 from Doncaster having reverted to blue window surrounds once again. ***Photos: Nev Sloper, Aldo Delicata & Colin Whitbread***

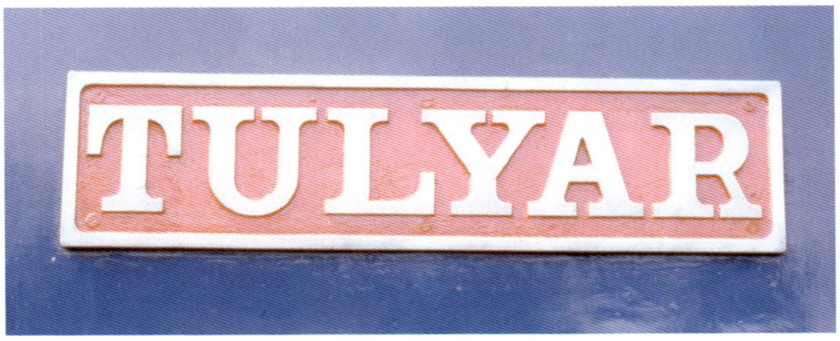

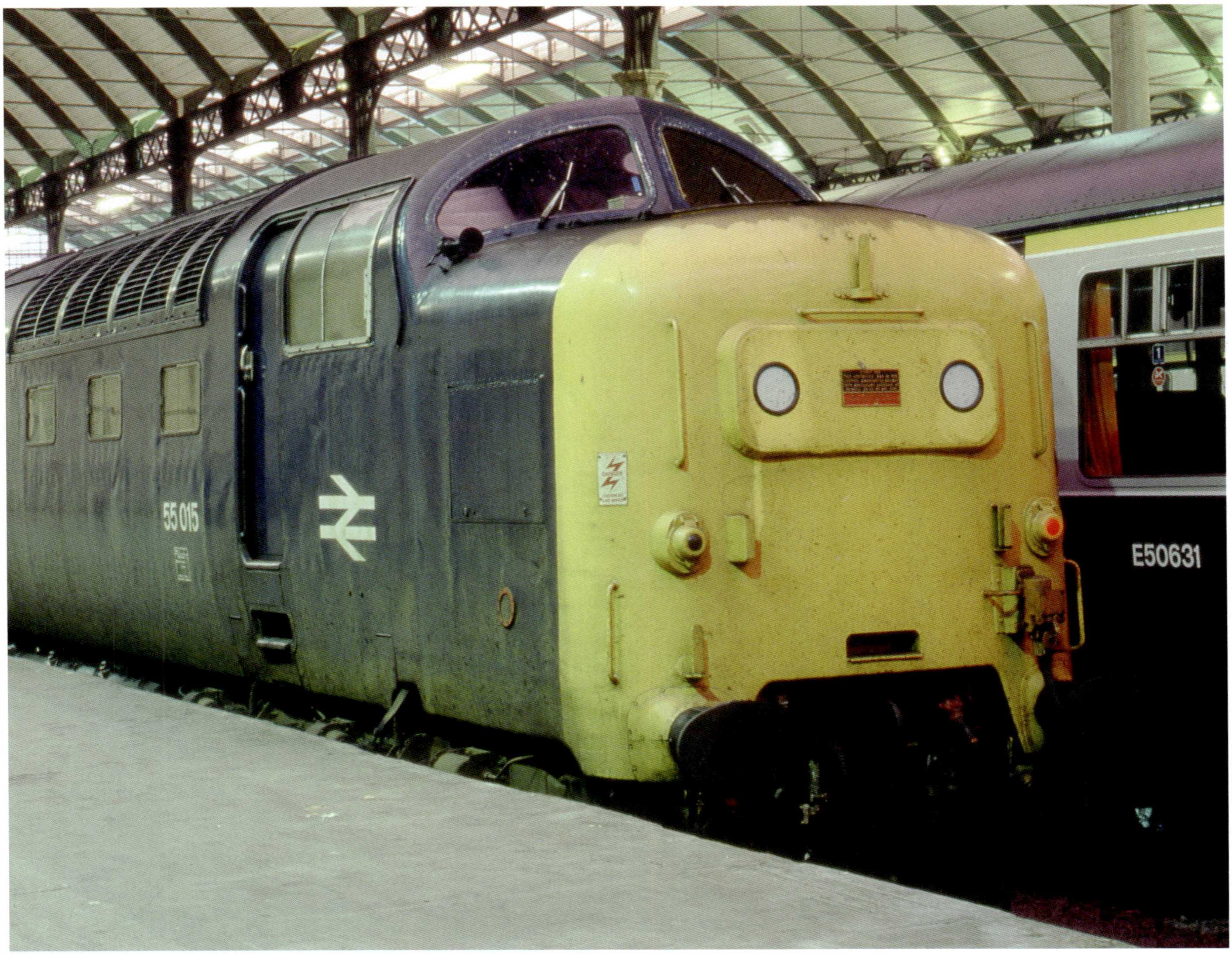

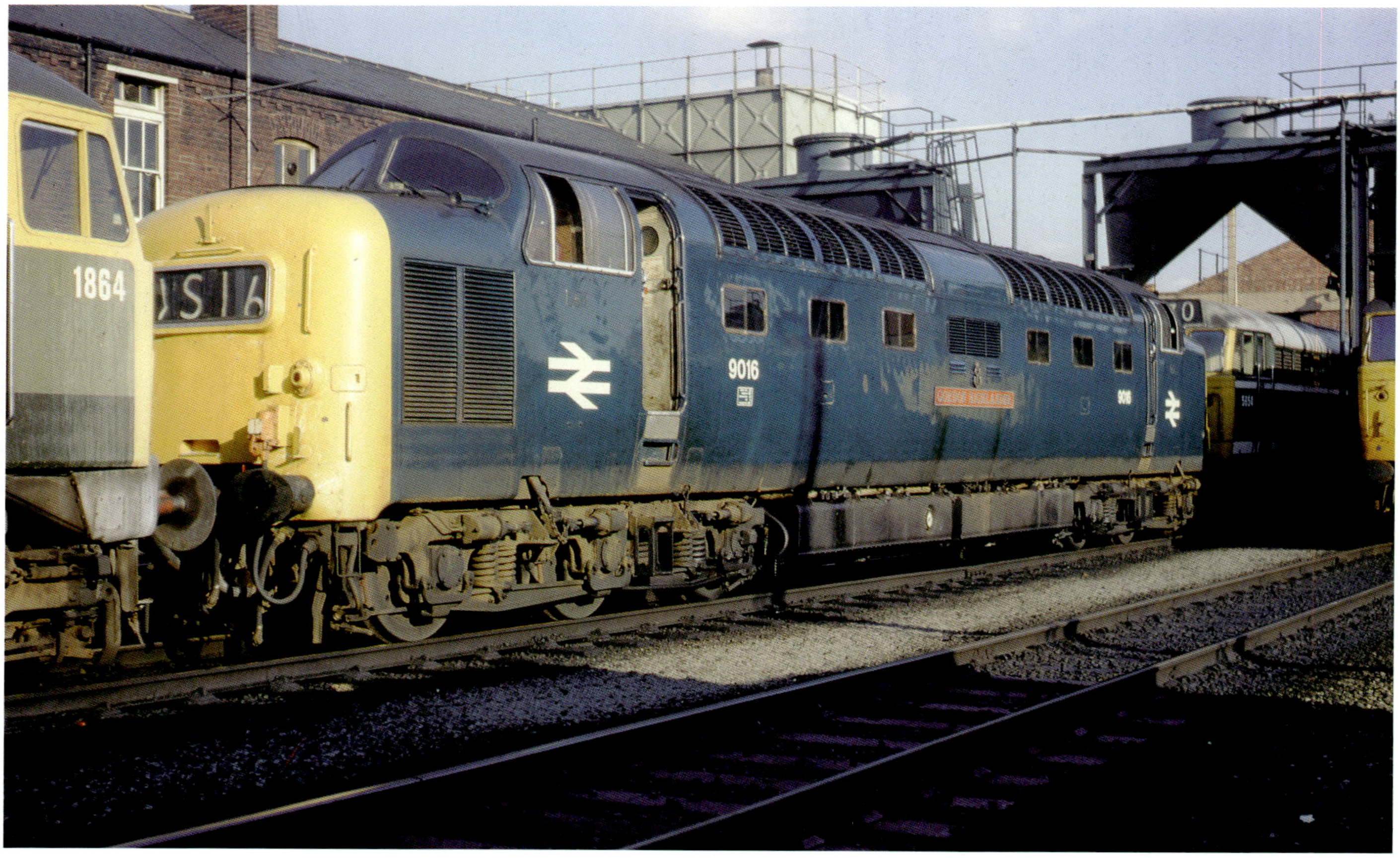

Another one of the earlier repaints into blue was undertaken on 9016 Gordon Highlander in October 1967 after being the first to be fitted with dual braking. In September 1972 it was parked up surrounded by green examples of Brush Types 2 and 4. ***Strathwood Library Collection***

Another view taken at Grantham on 29 August 1977 rewards us with 55016 Gordon Highlander using its braking capacity to bring its train to a stand in the station. ***Nev Sloper***

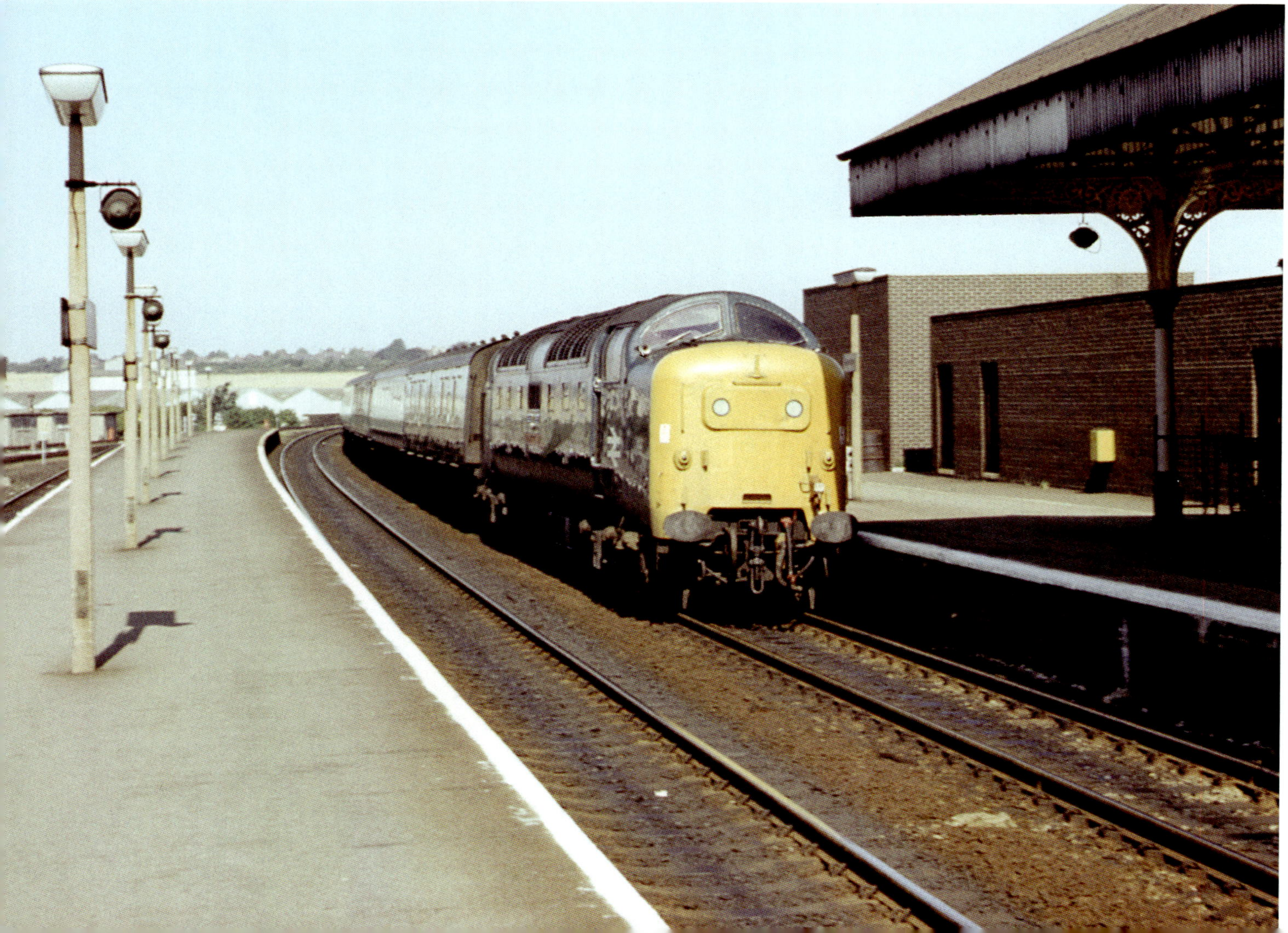

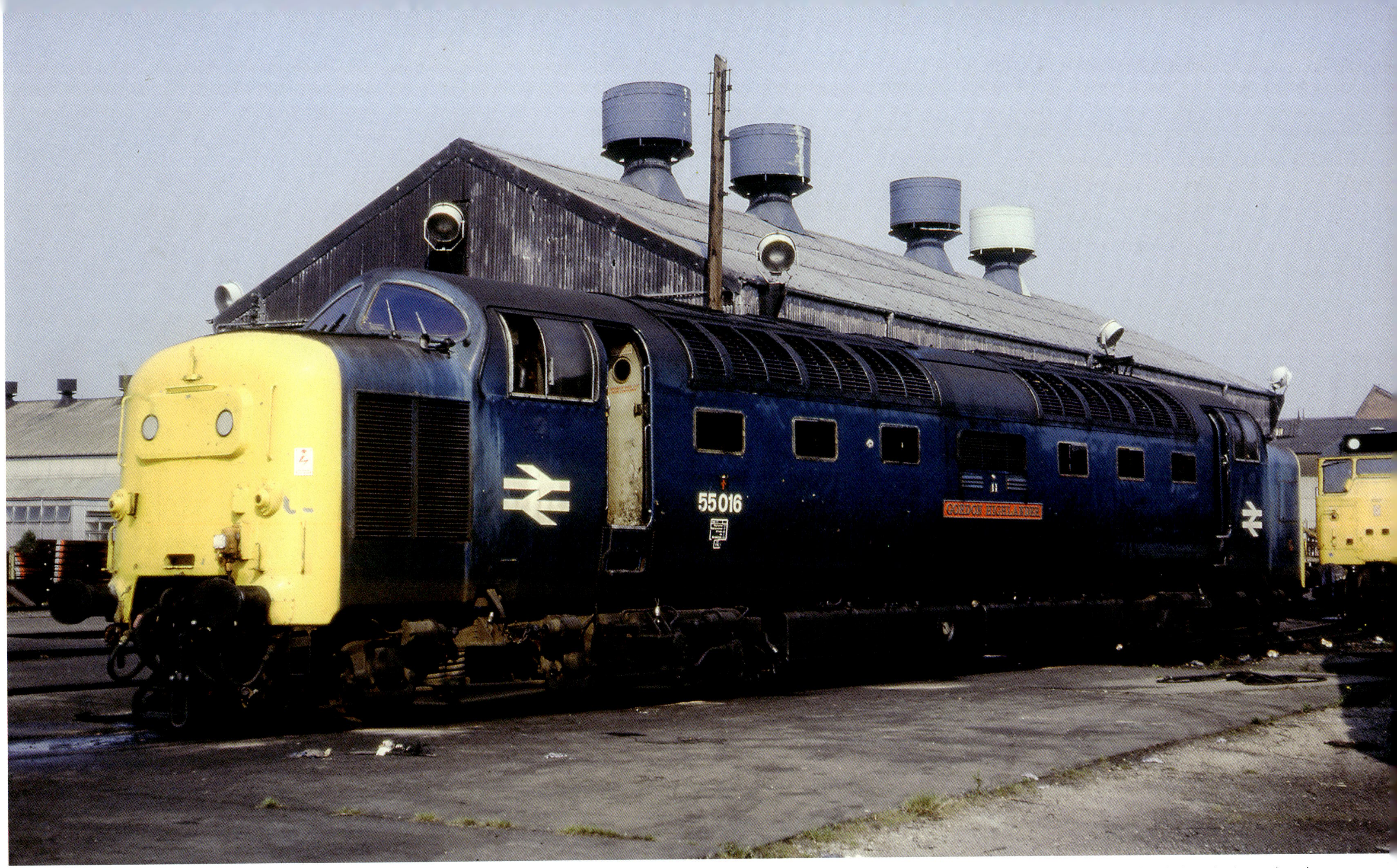

Back again to Doncaster on 6 September 1981 where we find 55016 Gordon Highlander within the works complex. With just a shortwhile still to go in service the locomotive would find work on The Deltic Devonian deputising for the failed 55002 The King's Own Yorkshire Light Infantry on 28 November. Then on 21 December whilst working the 08.07 York to Kings Cross it was stopped at Peterborough for the fire brigade to put out an exhaust fire. Un-deterred it was sent out again on 23 December for one last turn on the 19.40 Kings Cross to Hull working the ecs back to York. Official withdrawal came on 30 December 1981. ***Strathwood Library Collection***

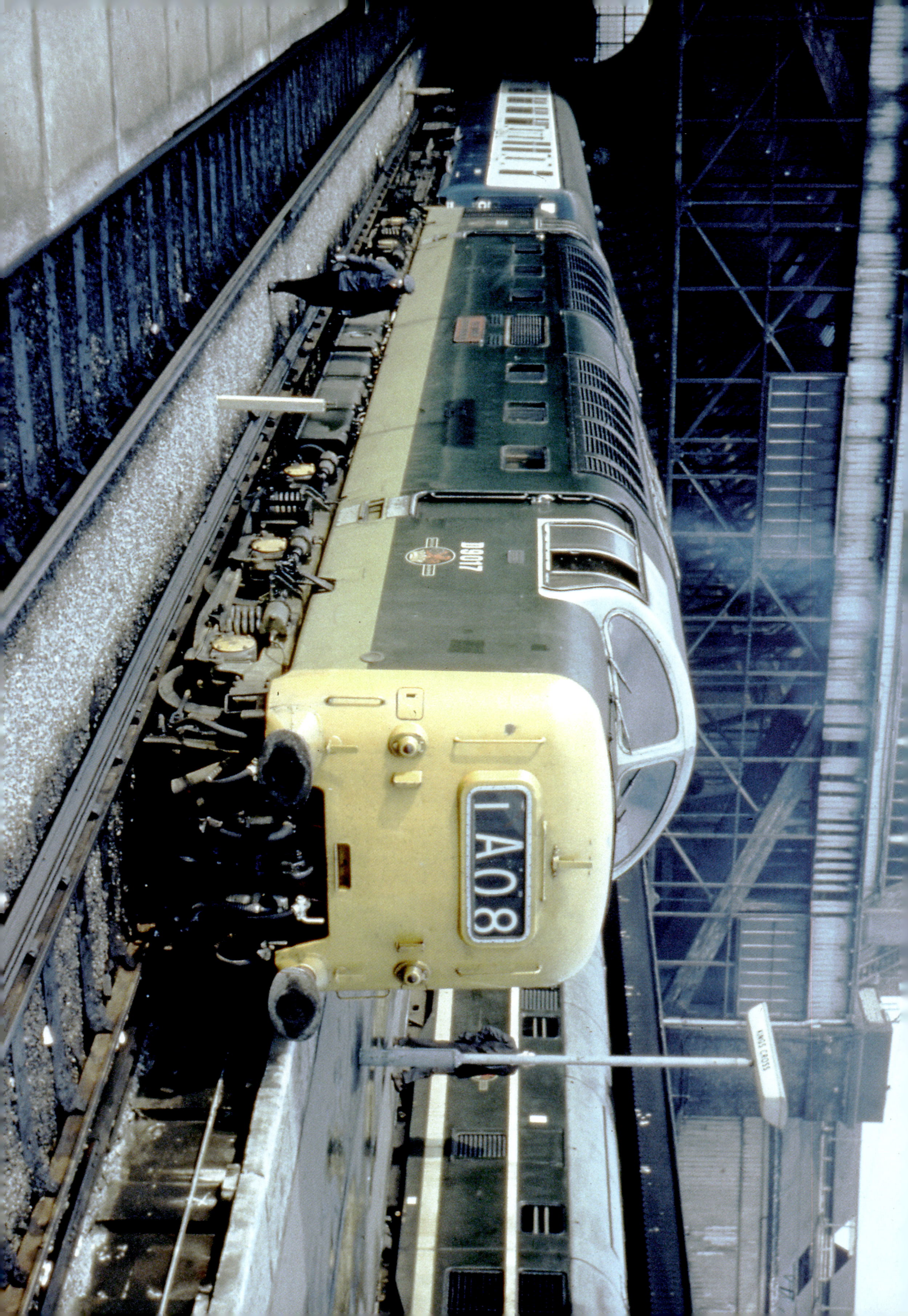
D9017
1A08

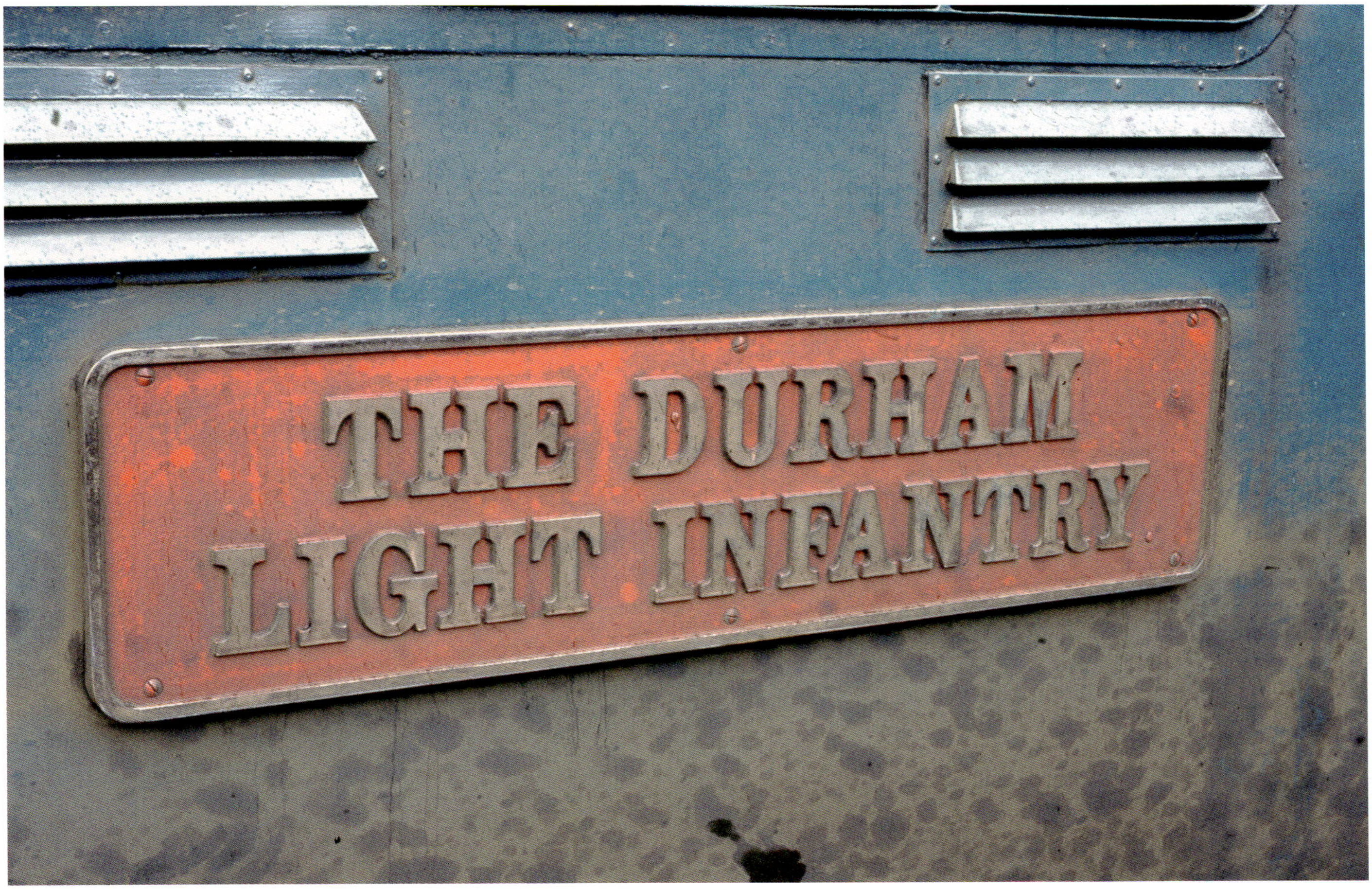

Standards of cleanliness were poor on 14 March 1978 when this nameplate shot was taken, no doubt all was shining for the naming ceremony at Durham station on 29 October 1963. ***Colin Whitbread***

Below: A conversation about releasing locomotives from the somewhat cramped stabling point at Kings Cross in 1975 with 55017 The Durham Light Infantry involved. ***Les Byatt***

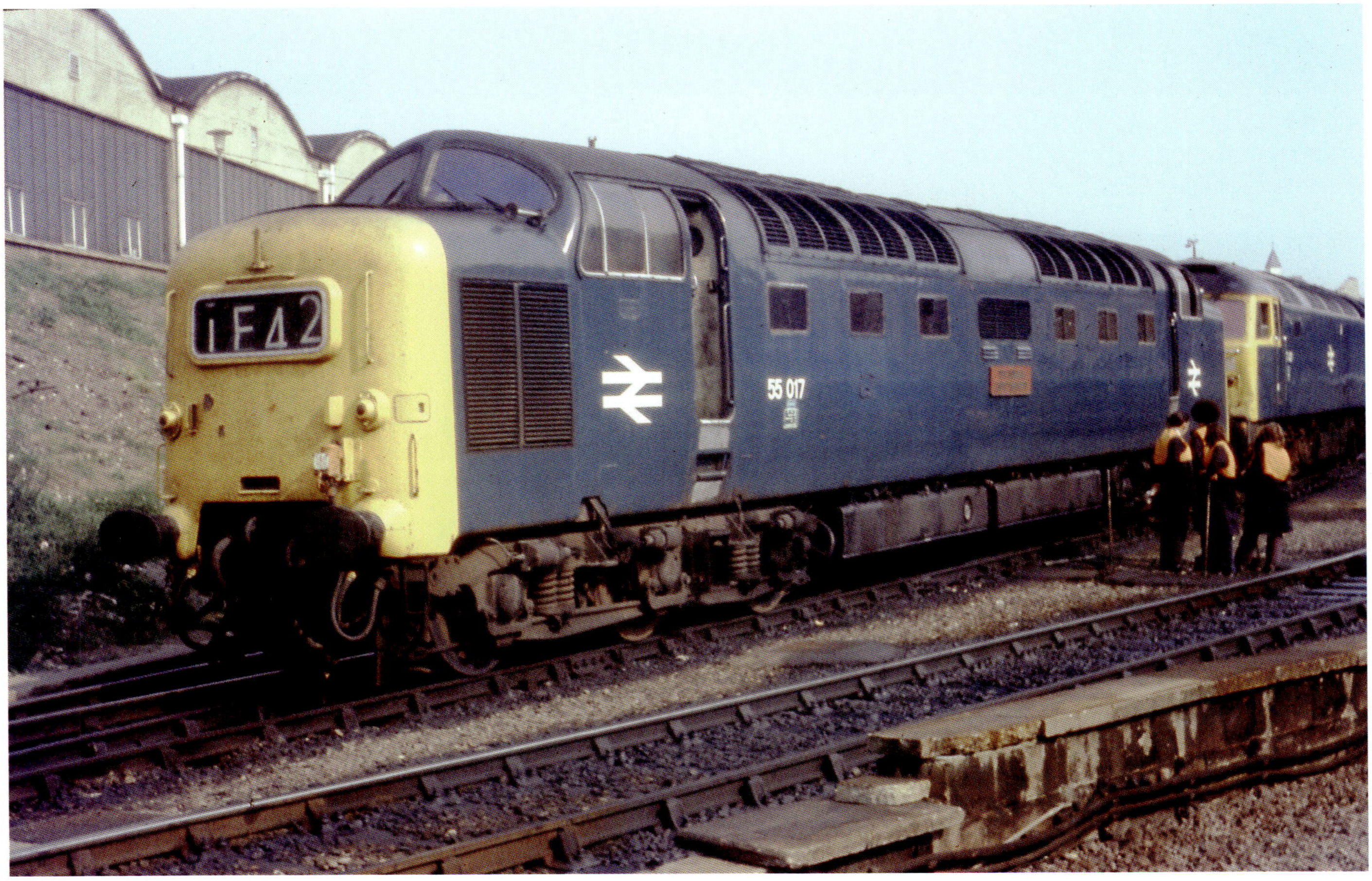

Page opposite: Having acquired full yellow ends in April 1967, D9017 The Durham Light Infantry is ready for another run northwards at Kings Cross away from the capital. ***Strathwood Library Collection***

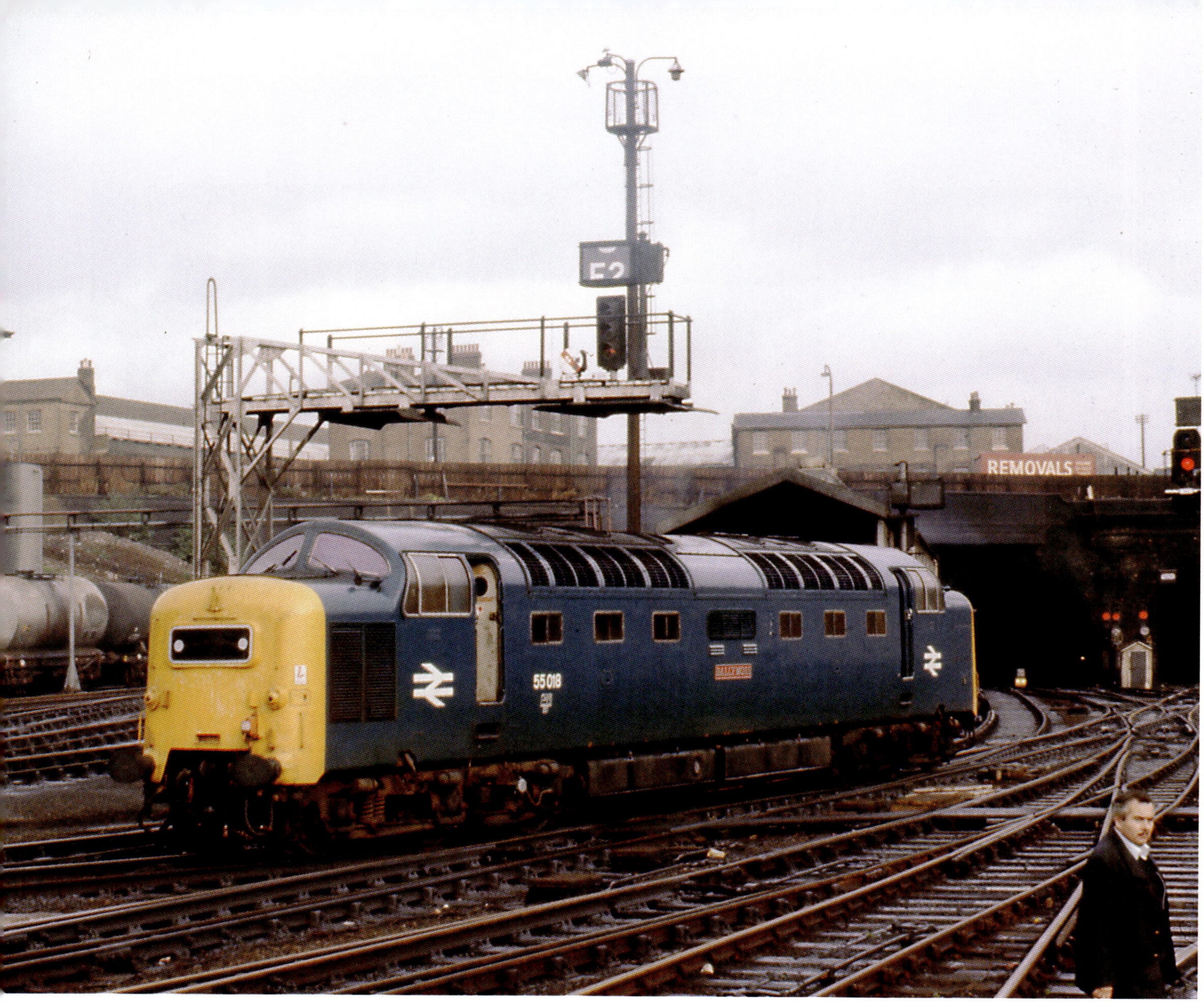

The marker dots applied to 55018 Ballymoss at first were smaller than those used on other class members when seen here at Kings Cross in 1976. ***Roger Griffiths***

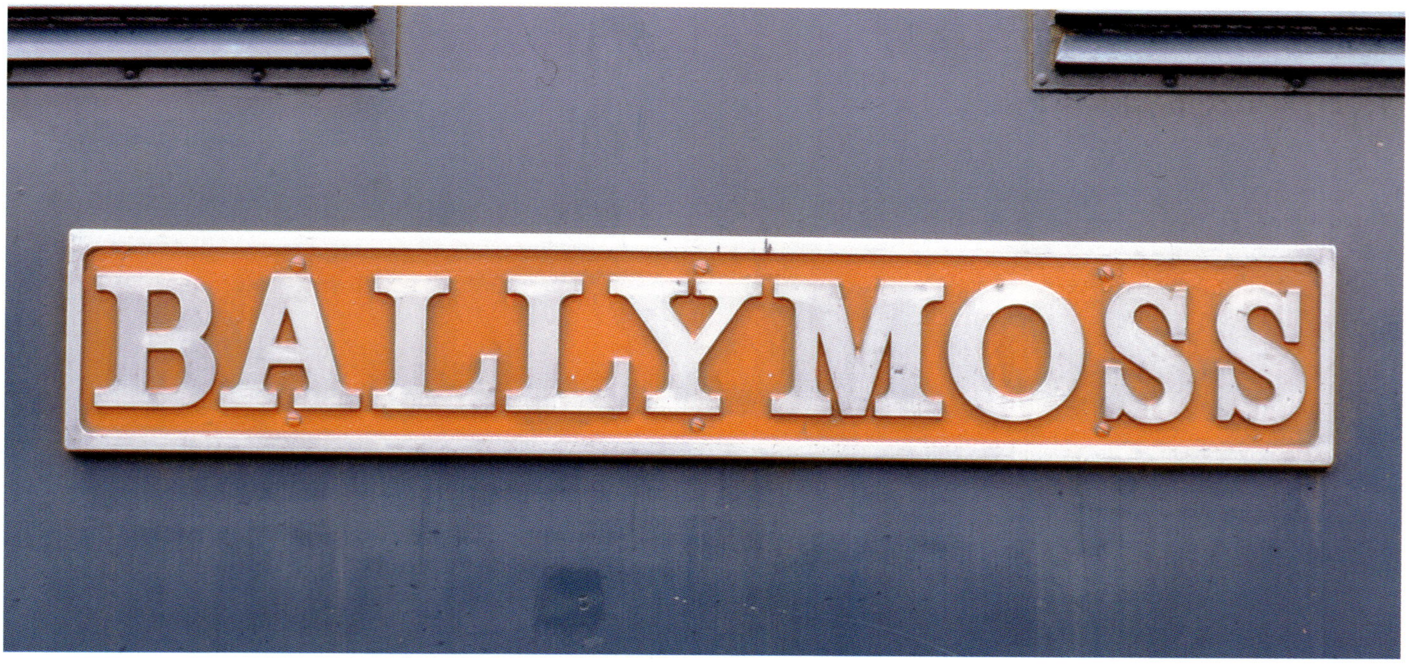

Ballymoss was foaled in 1954 and would become one of the greatest Irish racehorses of the era. In 1957 he won the St. Leger and the Irish Derby and was beaten into second place that year by Crepello in the English Derby. Arriving at Doncaster Works new from Vulcan Foundry on 24 November 1961 the nameplates were fitted without ceremony within the The Plant before being sent to take up service from Finsbury Park. ***Strathwood Library Collection***

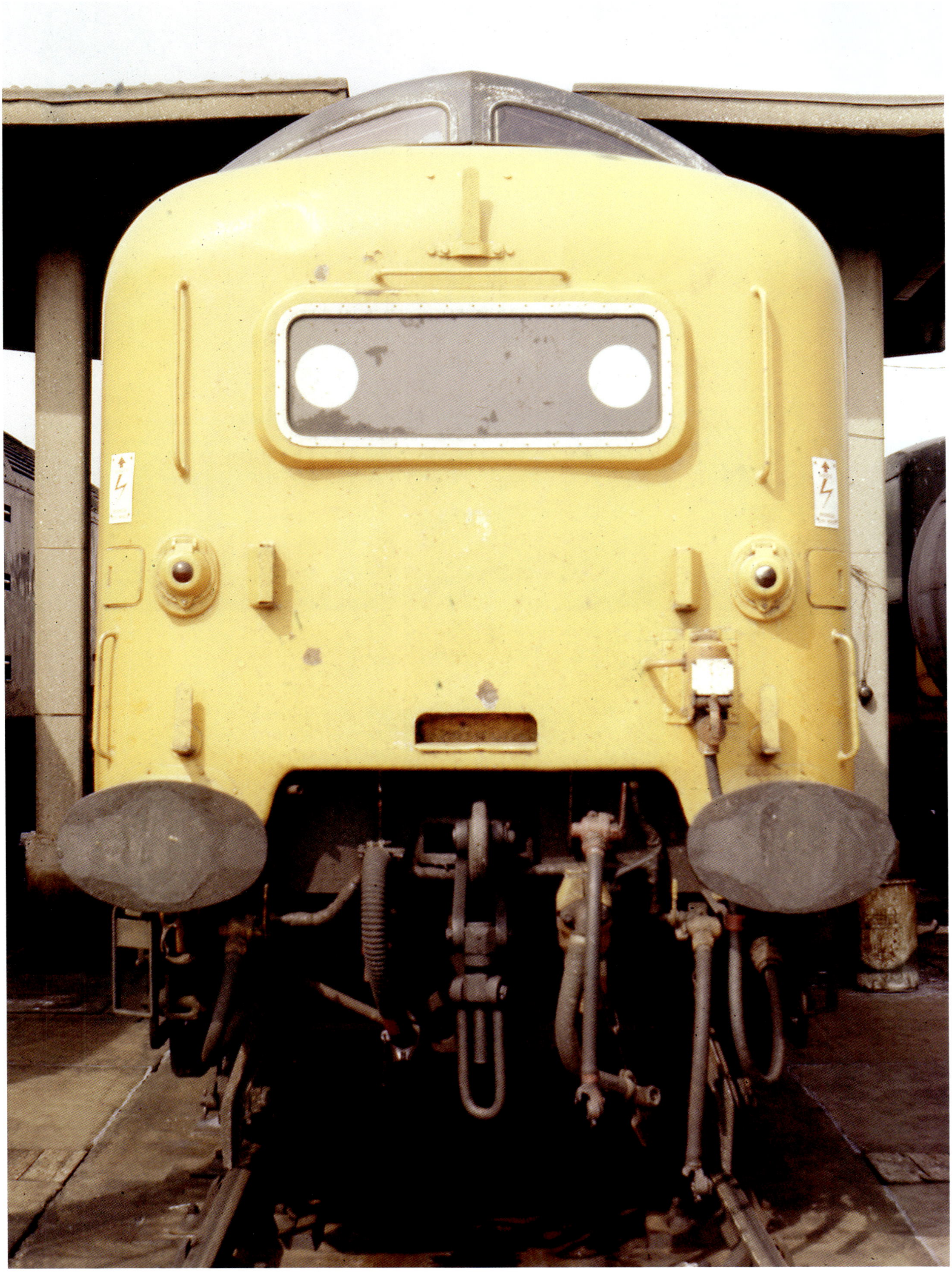

Finsbury Park would be the long term base for 55018 Ballymoss where we see the locomotive on 5 June 1976 now fitted with larger marker dots. York would take over responsibilty for Ballymoss in May 1981 briefly before the locomotive was withdrawn on 12 October when it was then sent to Stratford for stripping of any usefull componants. A return to Doncaster Works one day short of its twentieth anniversary of entering service on 23 November 1981. By the end of January it was no more, the cutters having made sure it would not appear at the famous Deltic Open Day weeks later. ***Derek Everson***

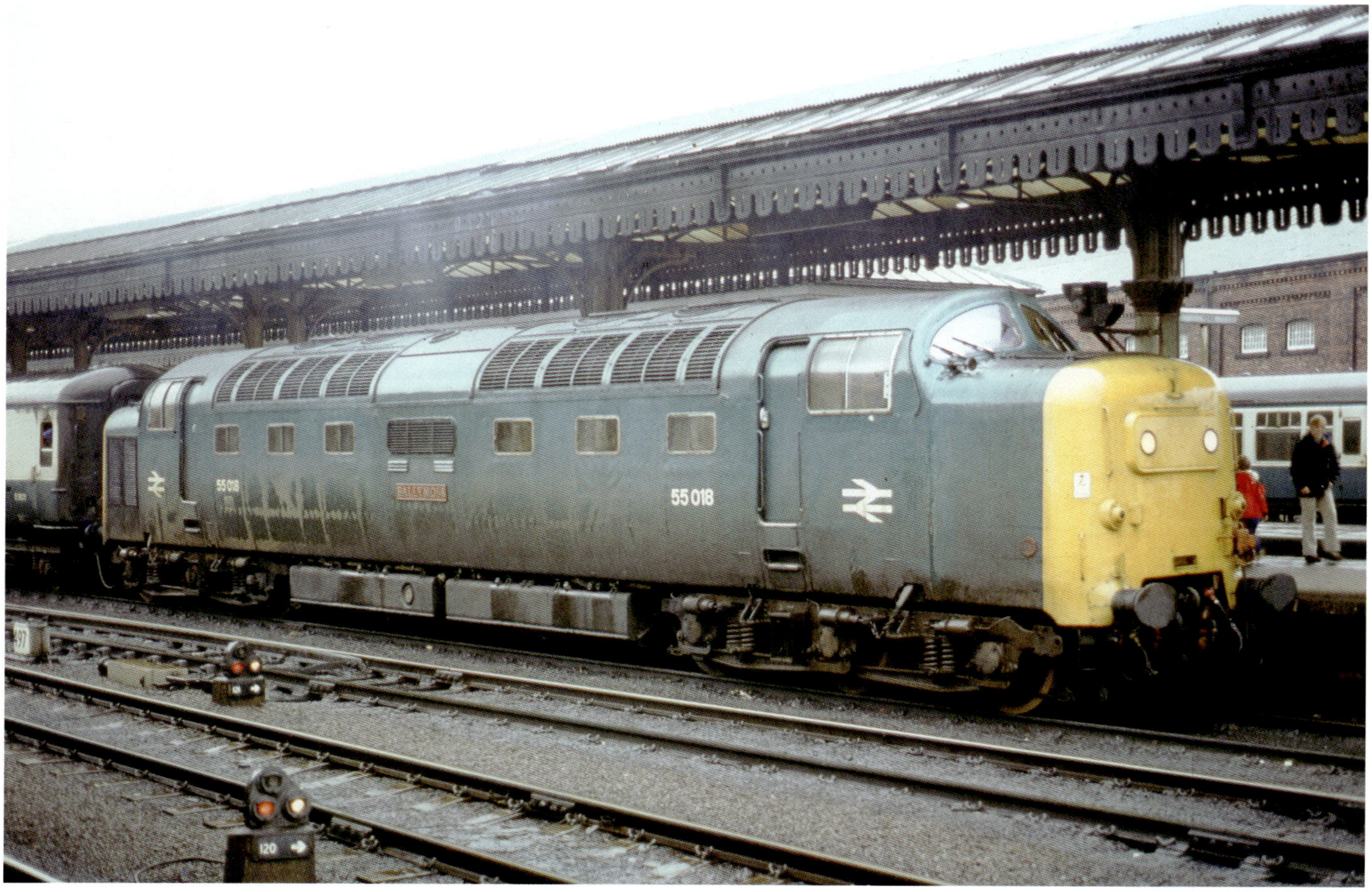

In happier times Ballymoss is seen around 1978 at York with two sets of 55018 numbers along its flanks.
Bruce Smetham

However this side shows Ballymoss to have just one set of numbers when seen near Ferryhill on 29 May 1978.
Sid Steadman

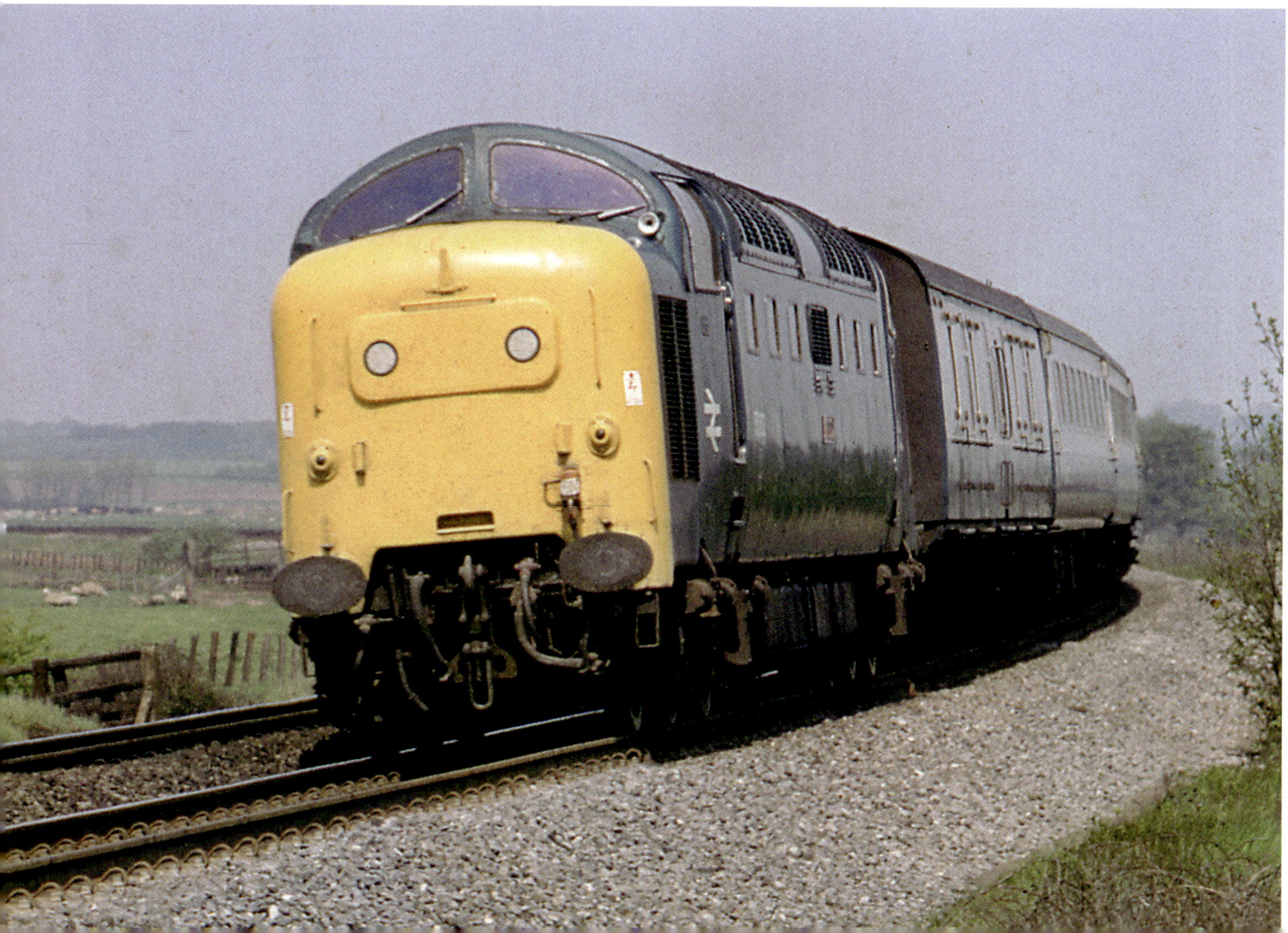

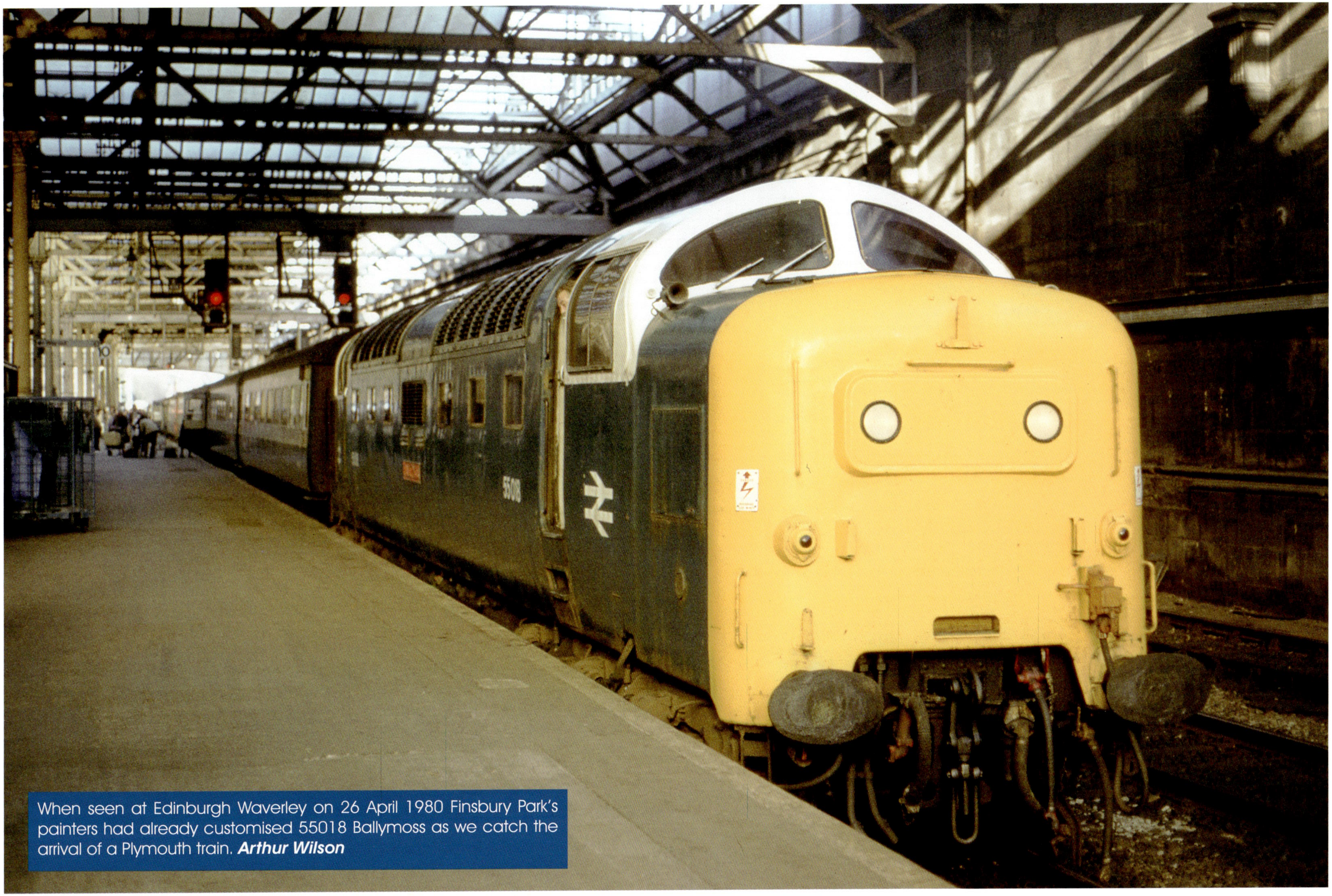

When seen at Edinburgh Waverley on 26 April 1980 Finsbury Park's painters had already customised 55018 Ballymoss as we catch the arrival of a Plymouth train. ***Arthur Wilson***

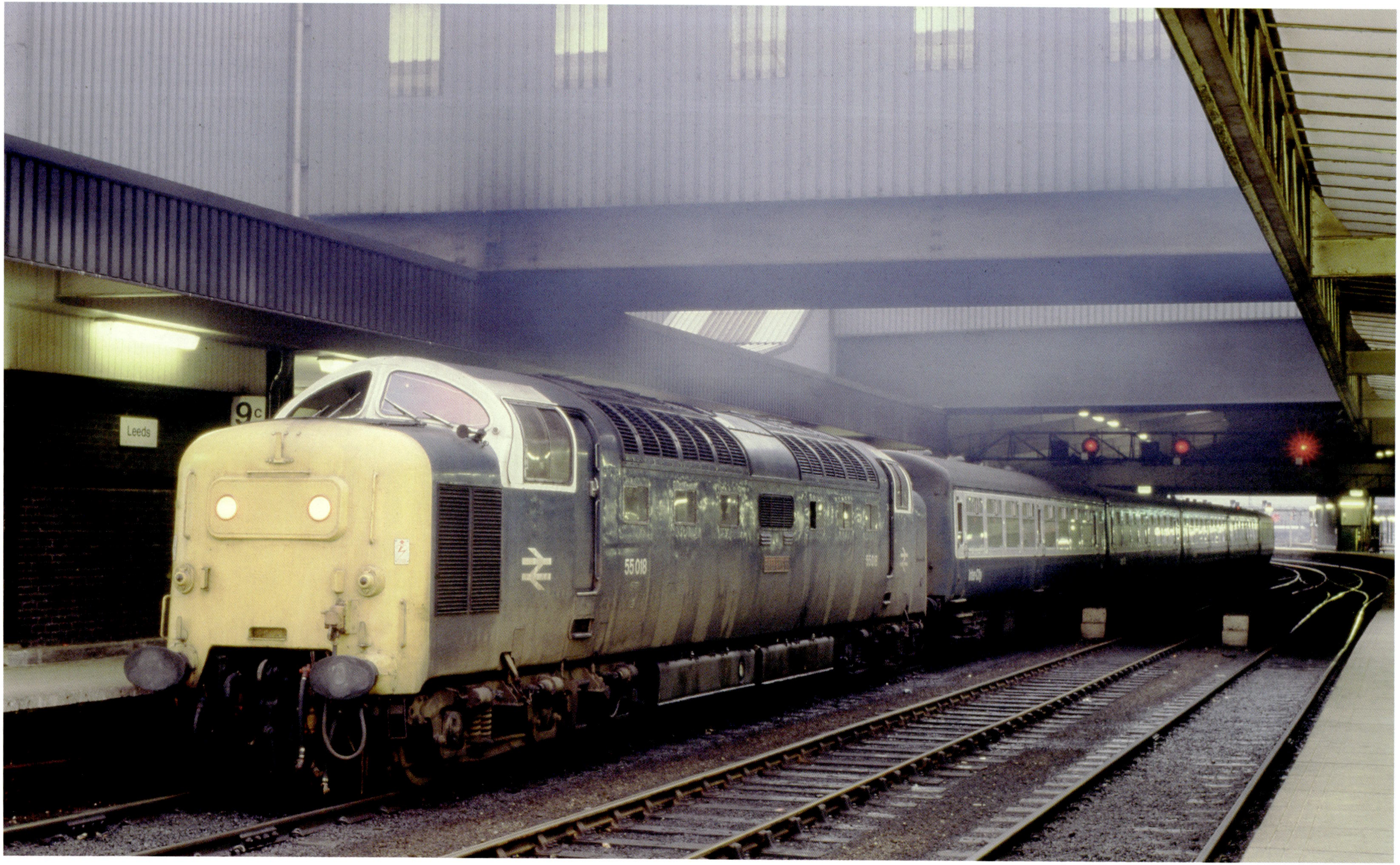

Captured in the fading light of a cold and damp Wednesday evening of 11 March 1981 in Leeds, 55018 Ballymoss makes a stop with the 16.05 Liverpool to Newcastle service. ***Colin Whitbread***

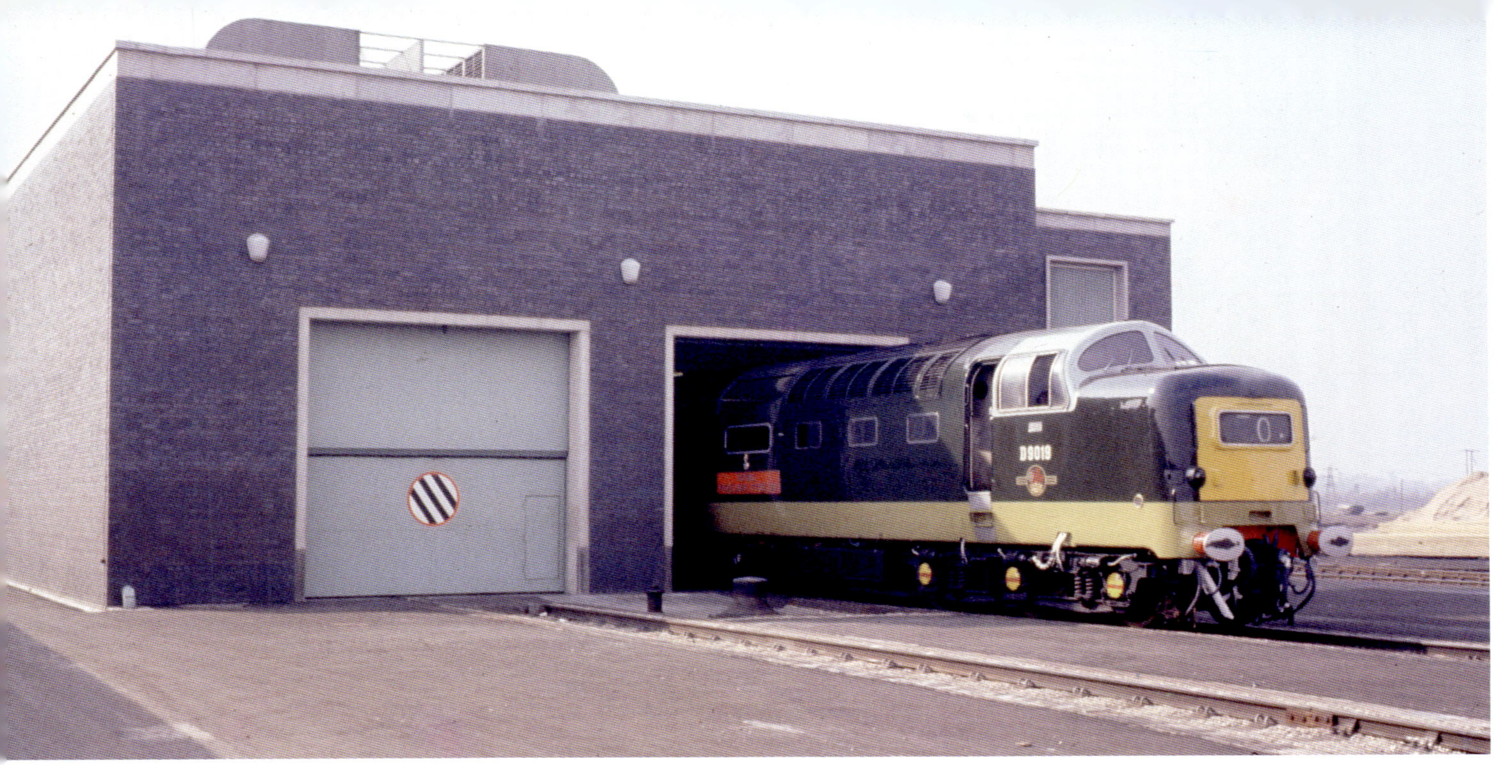

The Test House at Doncaster Works would see Deltics run up to full power before release to traffic, in this scene from September 1965 D9019 Royal Highland Fusilier has become the last of the Deltics to be named adopting nameplates and badges of the regiment at Glasgow Central on the eleventh of the month in front of dignitories. ***Both Photos: Strathwood Library Collection***

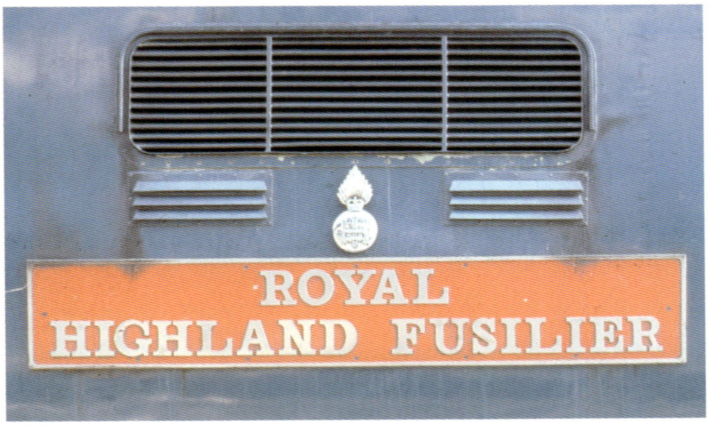

Seen at the head of D1874 arriving at Doncaster on 19 September 1969 was 9019 Royal Highland Fuslier thought to be assisting a stricken Class 47. ***Exe Rail***

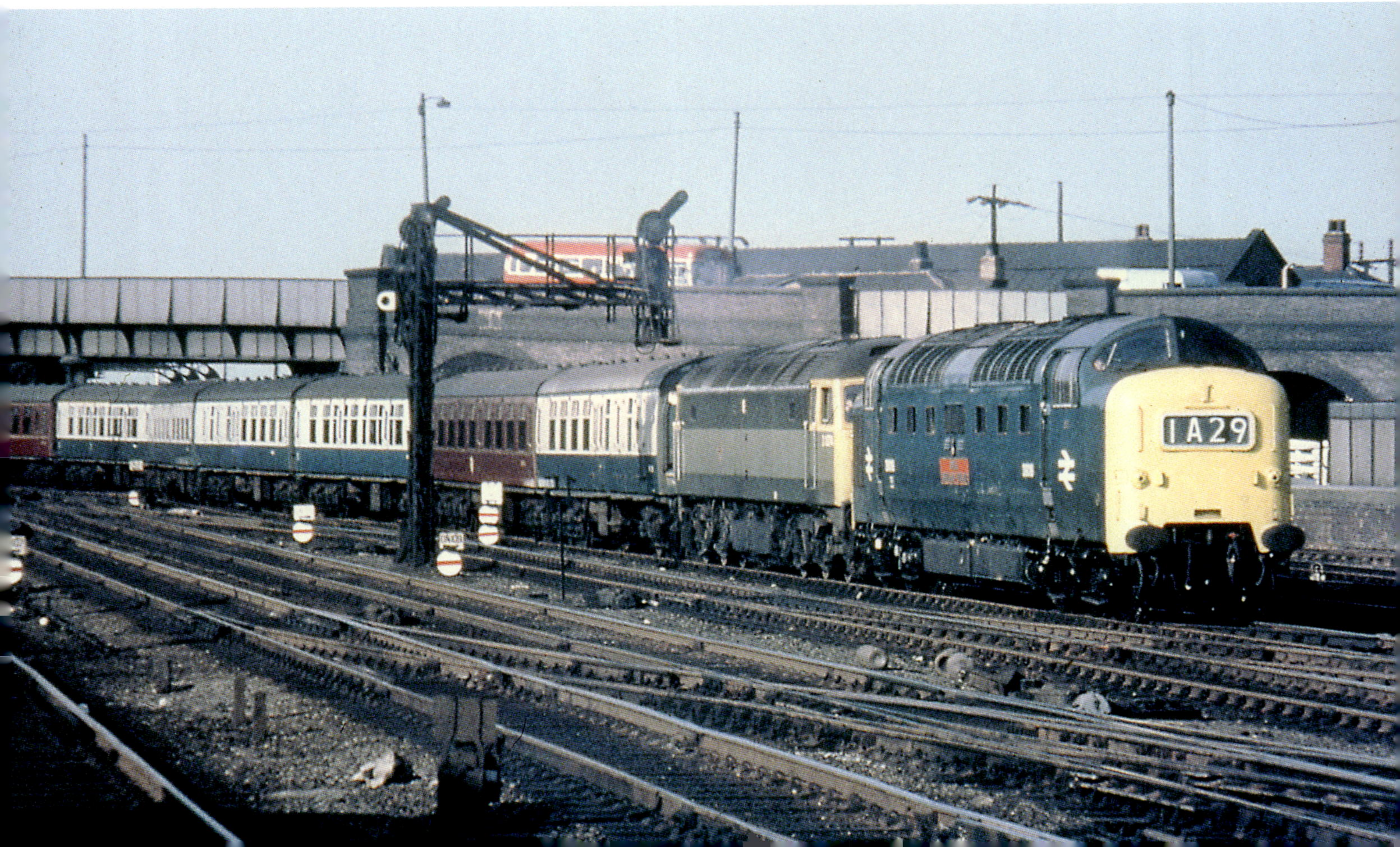

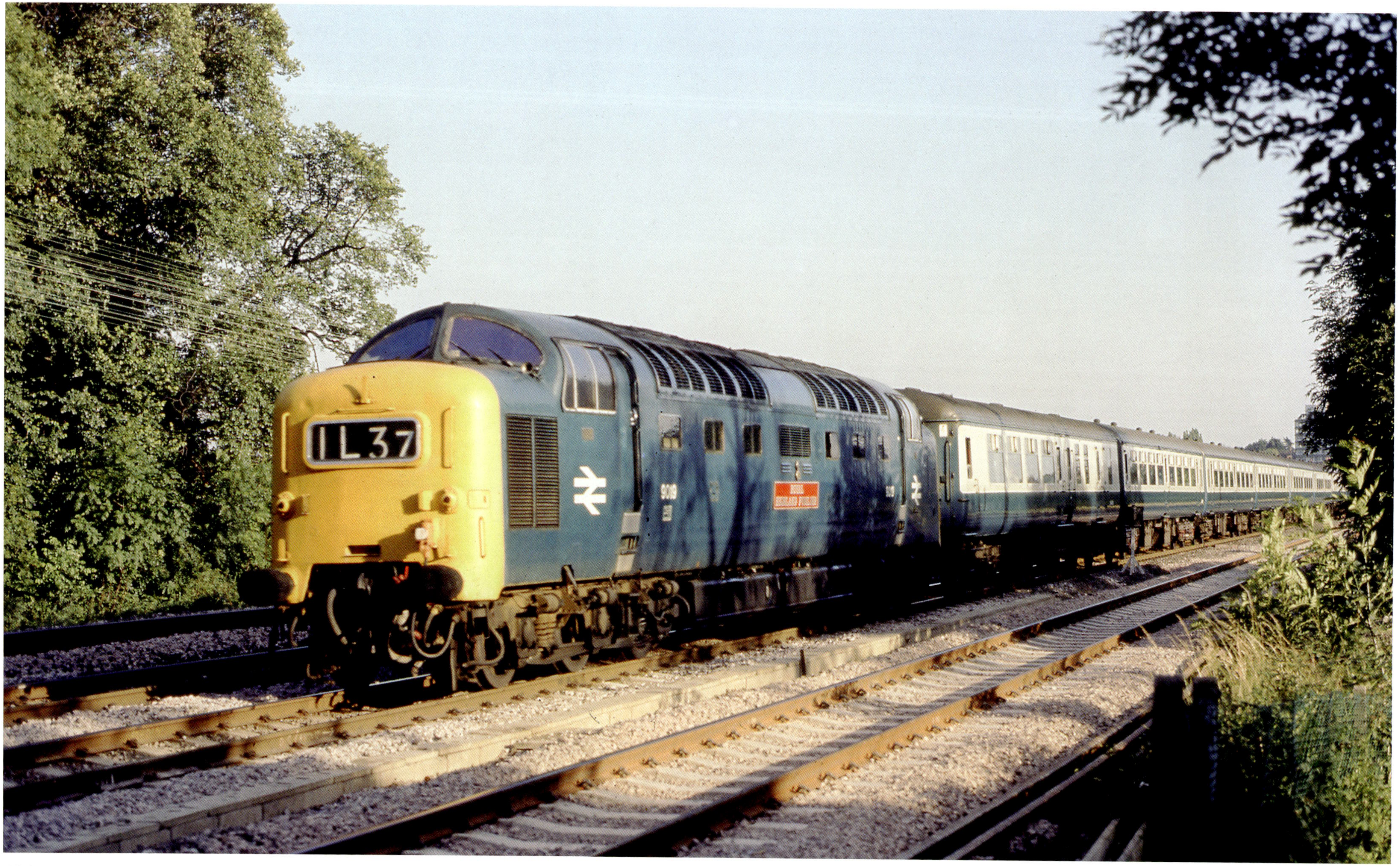

All is well again on 15 July 1971 at Hadley Wood as 9019 Royal Highland Fuslier flashes past with a Leeds service. By December 1973 the locomotive had clocked up 2,000,000 miles which in spite of the Deltic's reputation for being unreliable has to be taken into context with the high mileages the class averaged throughout their lives on the East Coast Main Line. ***Strathwood Library Collection***

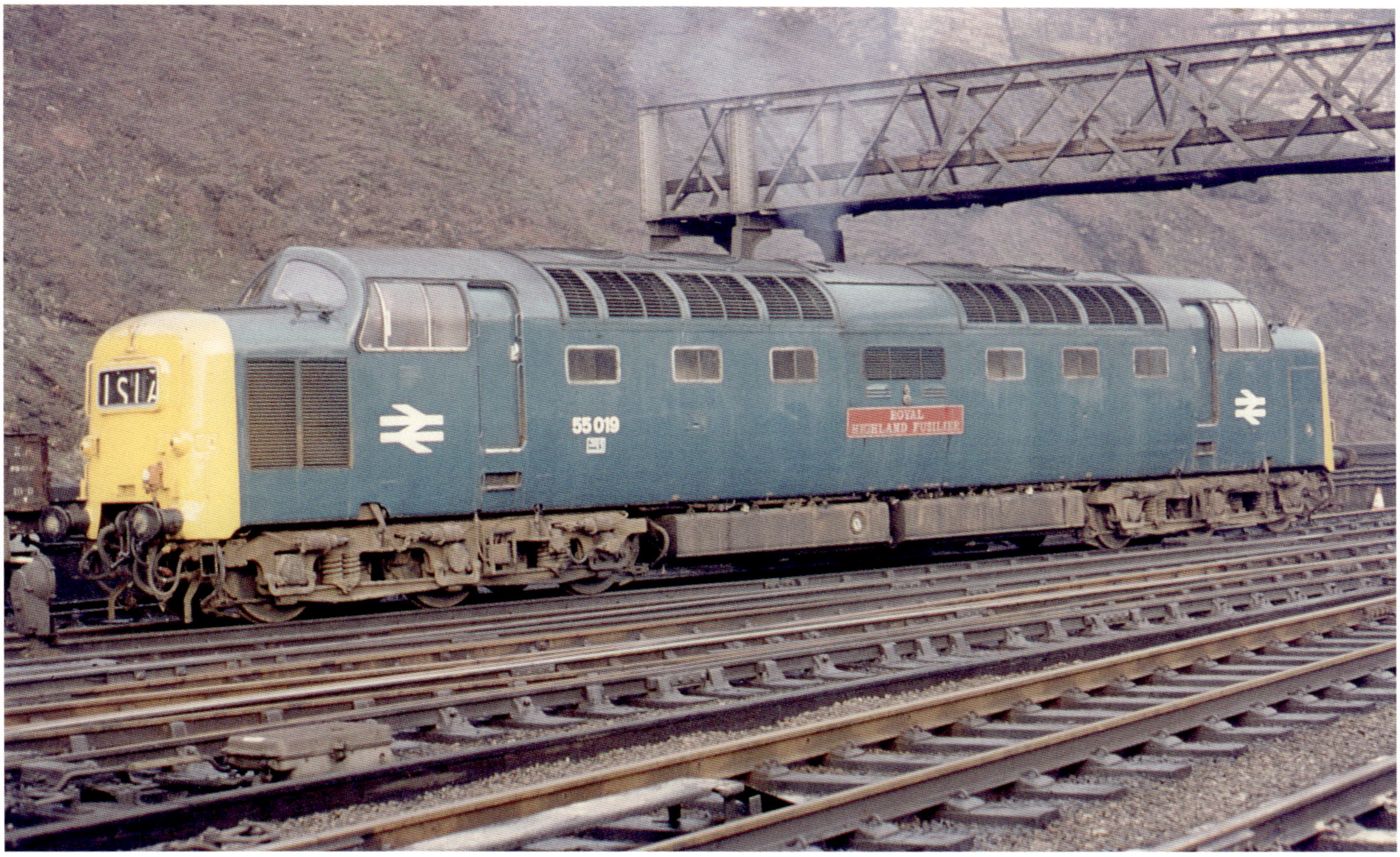

The change into the TOPS style of numbering occured for 55019 Royal Highland Fusilier on 23 November 1973 we see it at one of the more popular locations for cameramen namely the platform ends at Edinburgh's Waverley station on a festive Christmas Eve of 1973. ***Tom Bigley/Strathwood Library Collection***

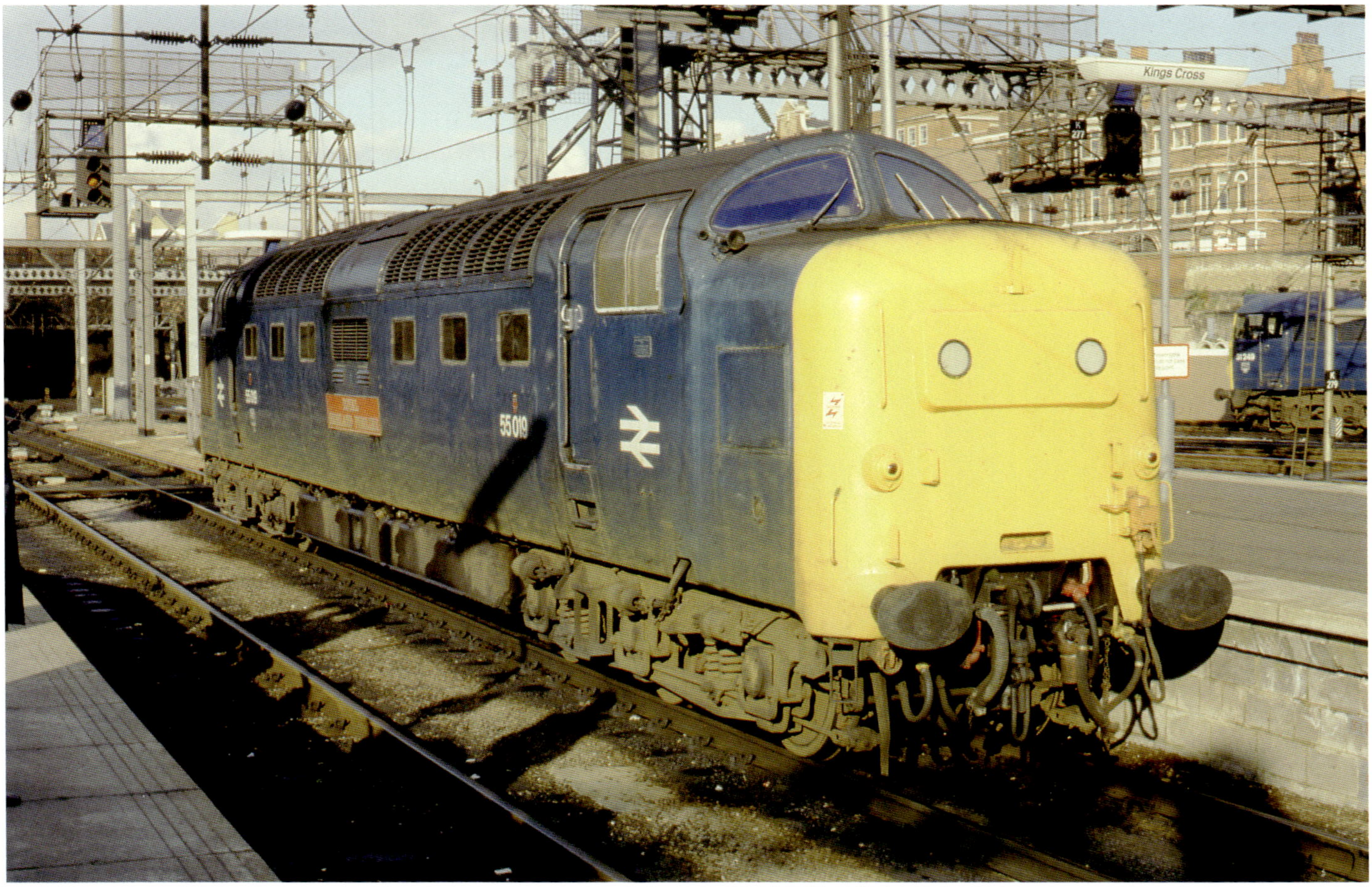

Along with Doncaster and York the other favourite for Deltic photography was at Kings Cross. However by 29 October 1979 a sea of gantries and wiring was in place along the southern most stretches of the East Coast Main Line as 55019 Royal Highland Fusilier awaited clearance from the station. Soon even more powerful and faster electric locomotives would in turn oust many of the HSTs on the route as well. ***Colin Whitbread***

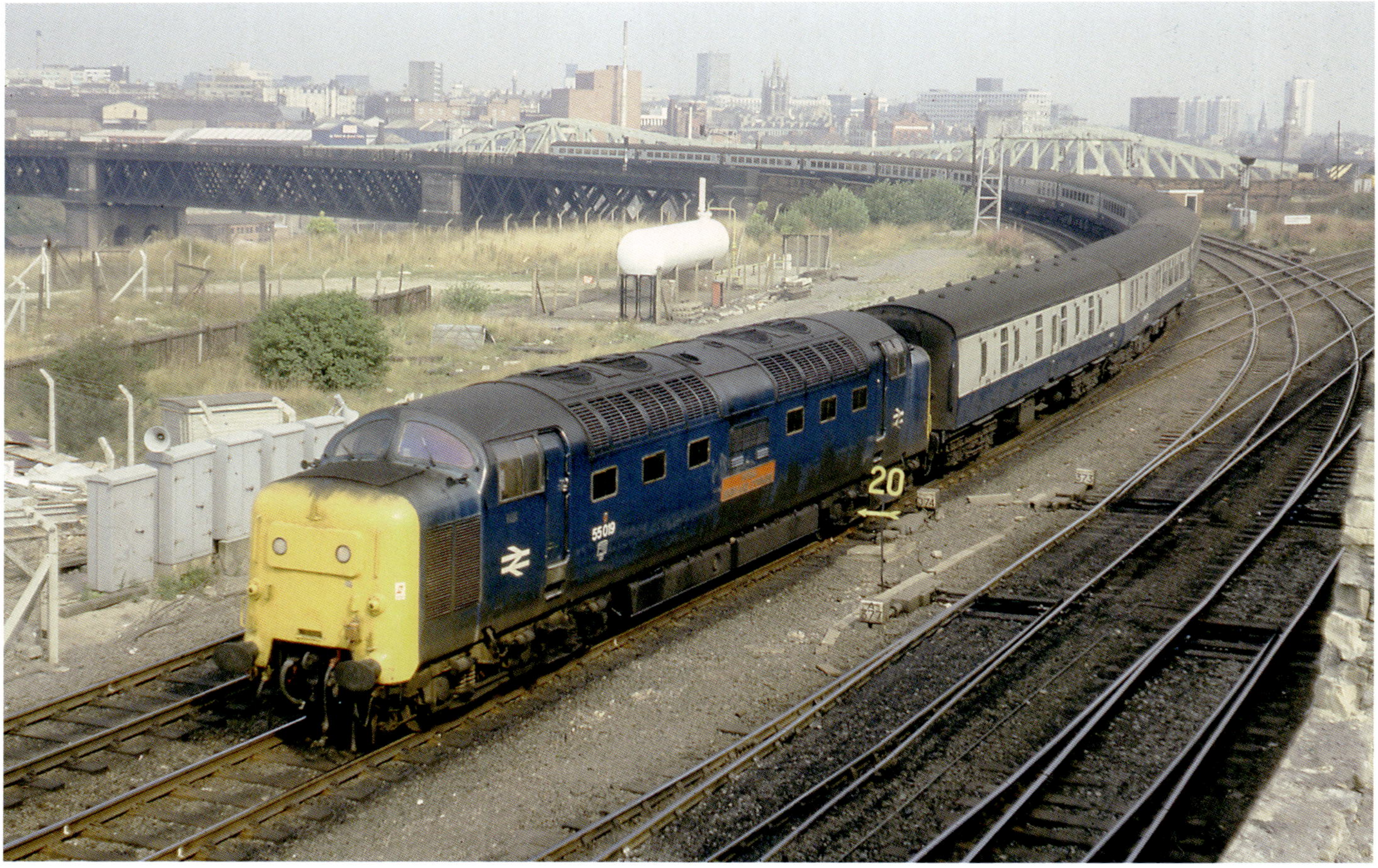

The electrification masts were yet to reach Newcastle on 4 September 1981 as 55019 Royal Highland Fusilier swept over the River Tyne with the 09.50 Edinburgh to Plymouth. ***Strathwood Library Collection***

A great deal of thought and expense would be exercised to take the electrification masts across the River Tweed on The Royal Border Bridge. This was the impressive view of the 05.50 Kings Cross to Aberdeen on 27 November 1981, as the last weeks of Deltic haulage counted down with 55019 Royal Highland Fusilier in charge today. ***Colin Whitbread***

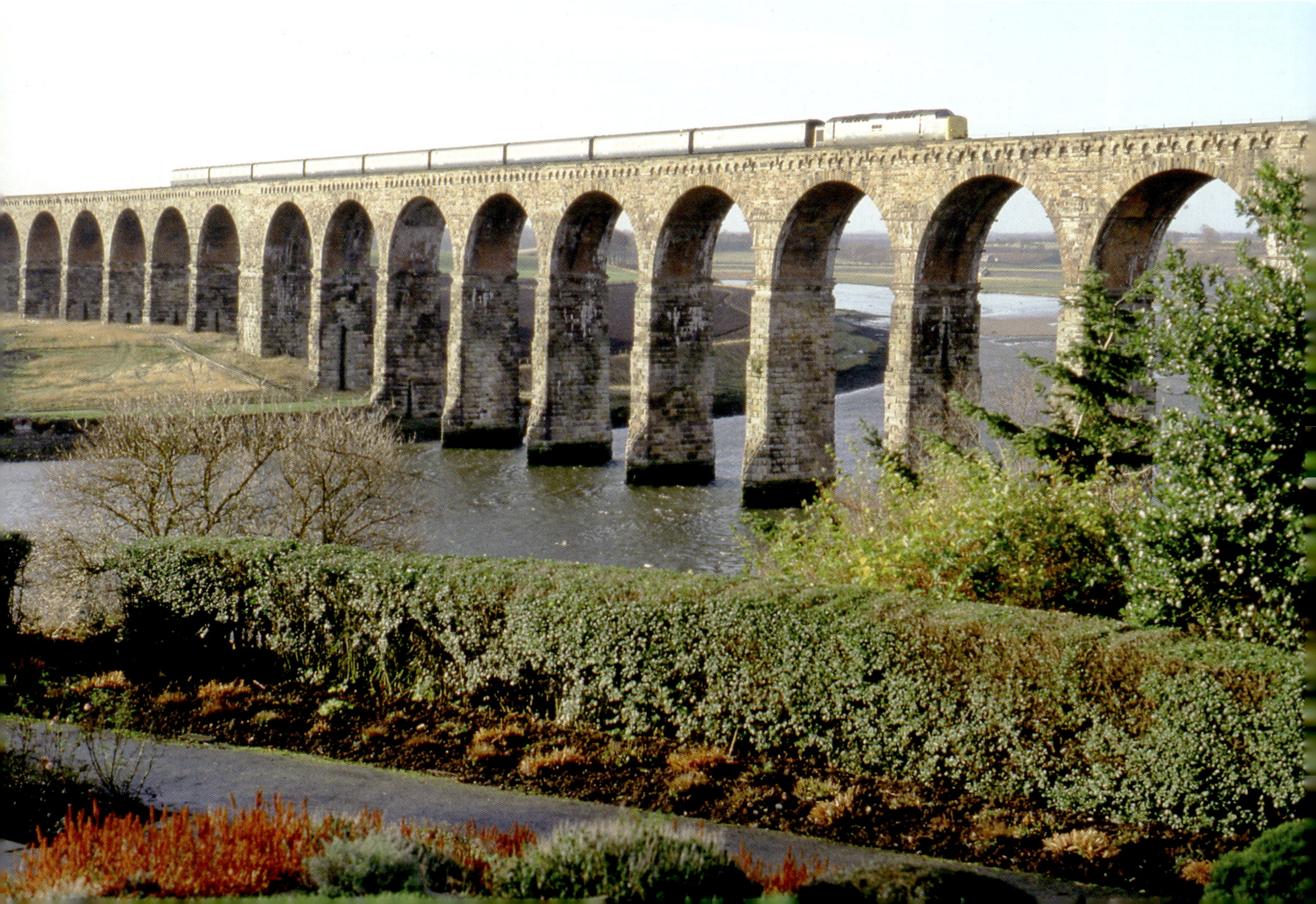

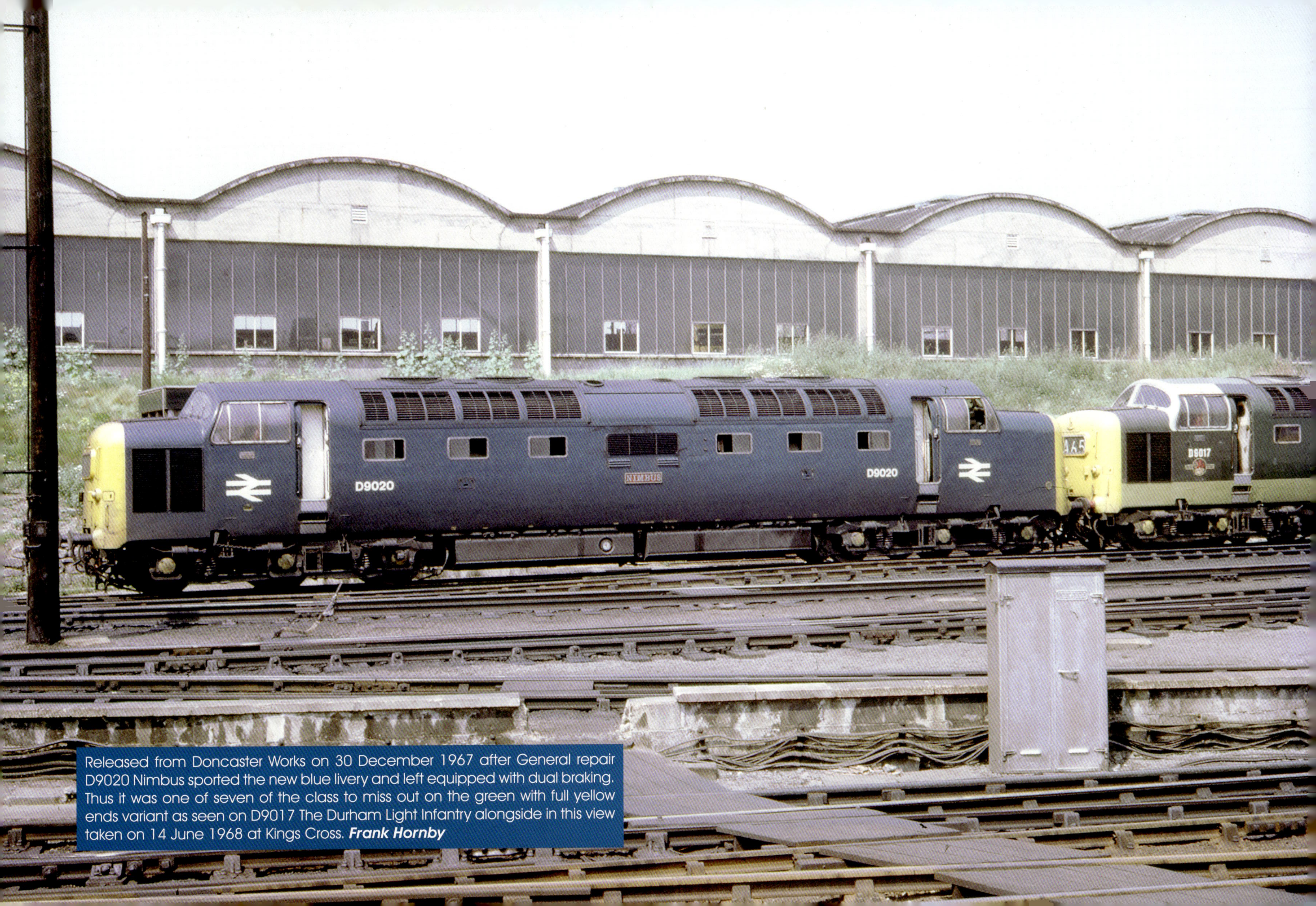

Released from Doncaster Works on 30 December 1967 after General repair D9020 Nimbus sported the new blue livery and left equipped with dual braking. Thus it was one of seven of the class to miss out on the green with full yellow ends variant as seen on D9017 The Durham Light Infantry alongside in this view taken on 14 June 1968 at Kings Cross. ***Frank Hornby***

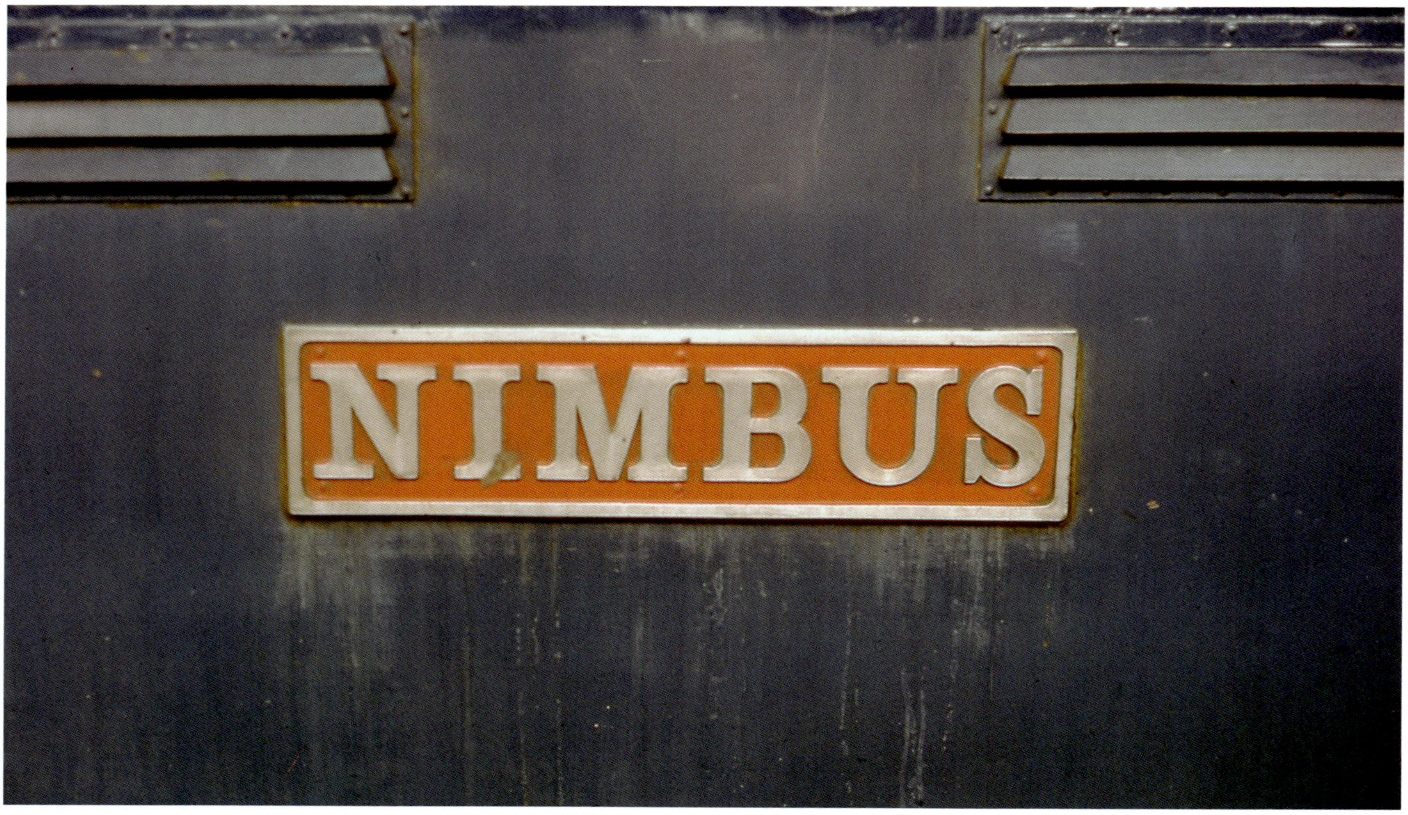

Nimbus was foaled in 1946, and was originally owned by William Hill who went on to sell the racehorse for £5,000 as a yearling to Mr H. A. Glenister who gifted it to his wife as a present. Nimbus would win the Derby, in the races first ever photo finish, and the 2000 Guineas in 1949. Nimbus retired to Japan as part of a stud program in 1963 and died there in 1972. ***David T Williams***

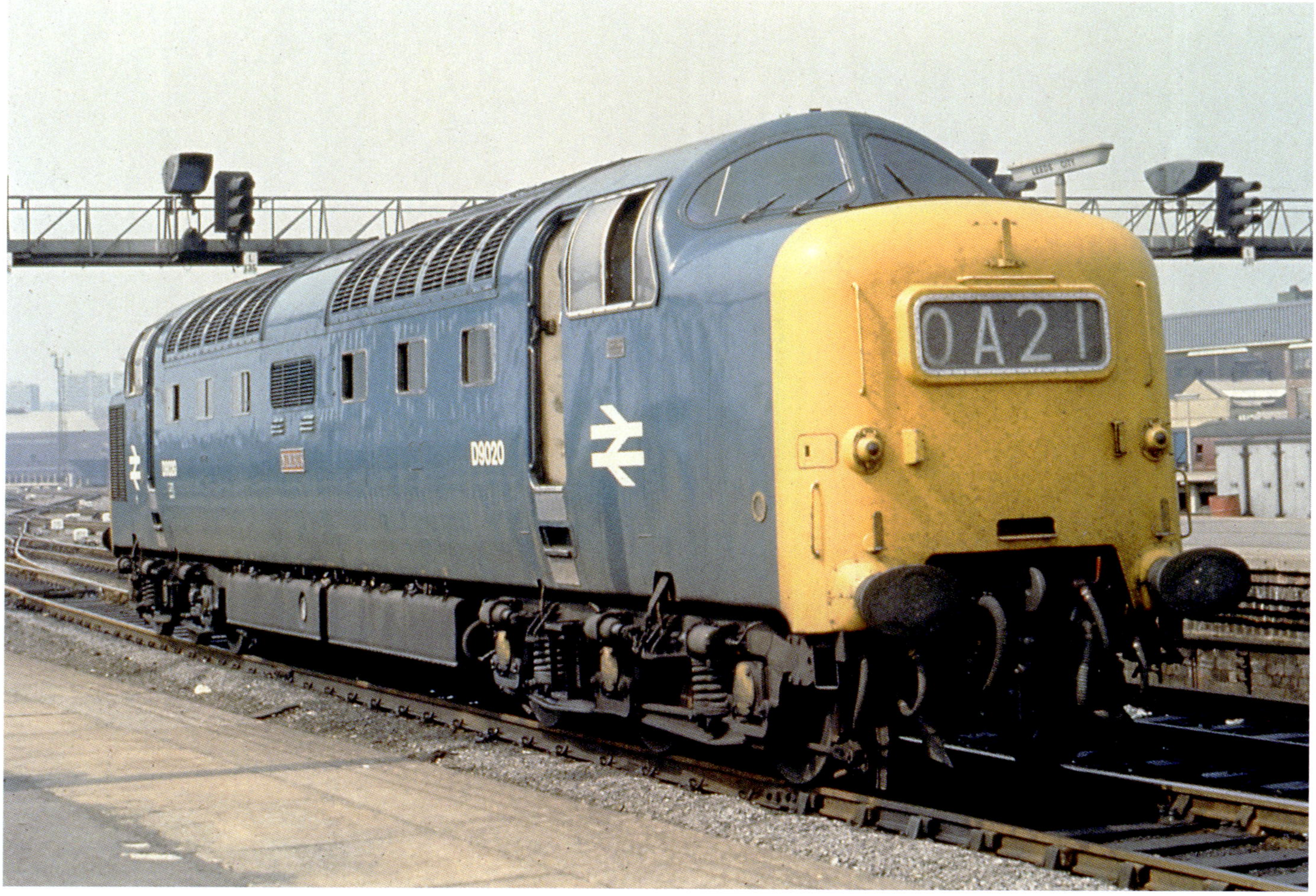

In fact D9020 Nimbus and D9021 Argyll & Sutherland Highlander were the only two class members to go into service from new with half yellow panels applied at Vulcan Foundry. In this view at Leeds from 1968 shows the D prefix still in place, this would be painted over by May the following year. Nimbus would be the first of her class to be renumbered on 10 November 1973 into TOPS as 55020. ***Strathwood Library Collection***

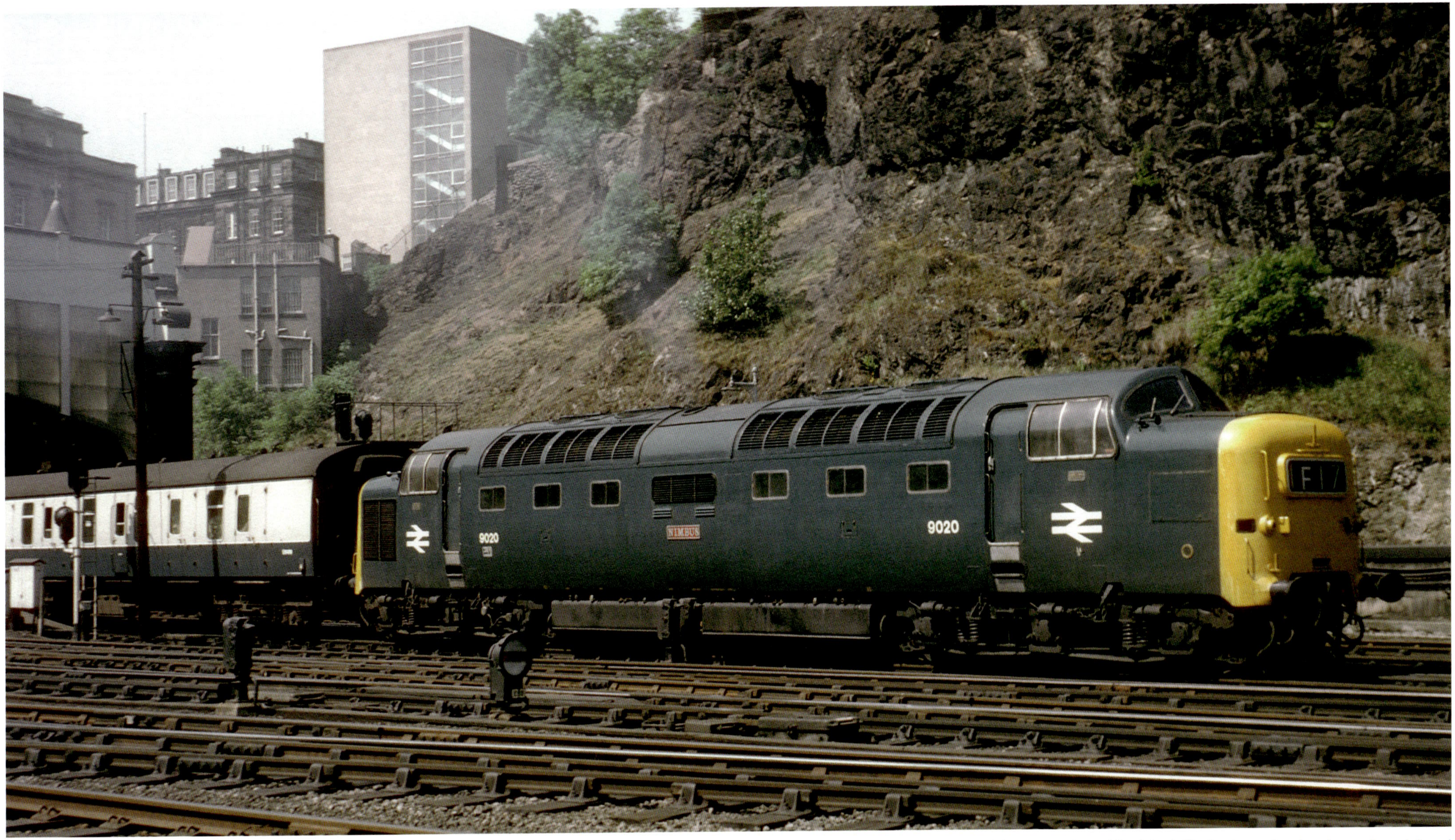

Departing south from Edinburgh Waverley with the 14.00 service for Kings Cross was 9020 Nimbus on 20 May 1969. All of the class aside from Nimbus would have their cab quarterlight windows plated over from the mid seventies. On 30 March 1978 the locomotive would make its last working on an Oxford to Newcastle parcels which it took over at York, this duty was undertaken on just one engine. Nimbus was to have a visit to Doncaster Works for power unit exchange, however, due to industrial action by Doncaster employees 55020 was instead held at Gateshead, who heavily robbed it of spares for the rest of their fleet. When Nimbus finally made it to Doncaster at the end of April it was parked up and those repairs were never to be approved, with the locomotive being the first of the Deltics now to be scrapped in January 1980. ***Jim Binnie***

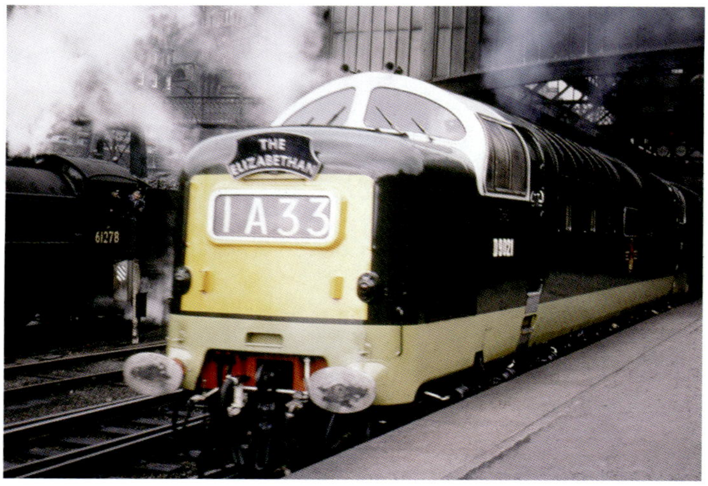

The last three Deltics entered service with their horns placed above the cabs as here on D9021 at Edinburgh Waverley in May 1962. Within a very short time the horns would be first repositioned under the bufferbeams in line with the rest of the fleet. Trials with D9007 Pinza having its horns mounted within grills on the nose, in the style of Class 40s were not satisfactory either. Further trials showed the best position for audibility and to stop the constant damage problems was mounting the horns on the nose by the windscreens with all of the class thus fitted by 1970. ***Strathwood Library Collection***

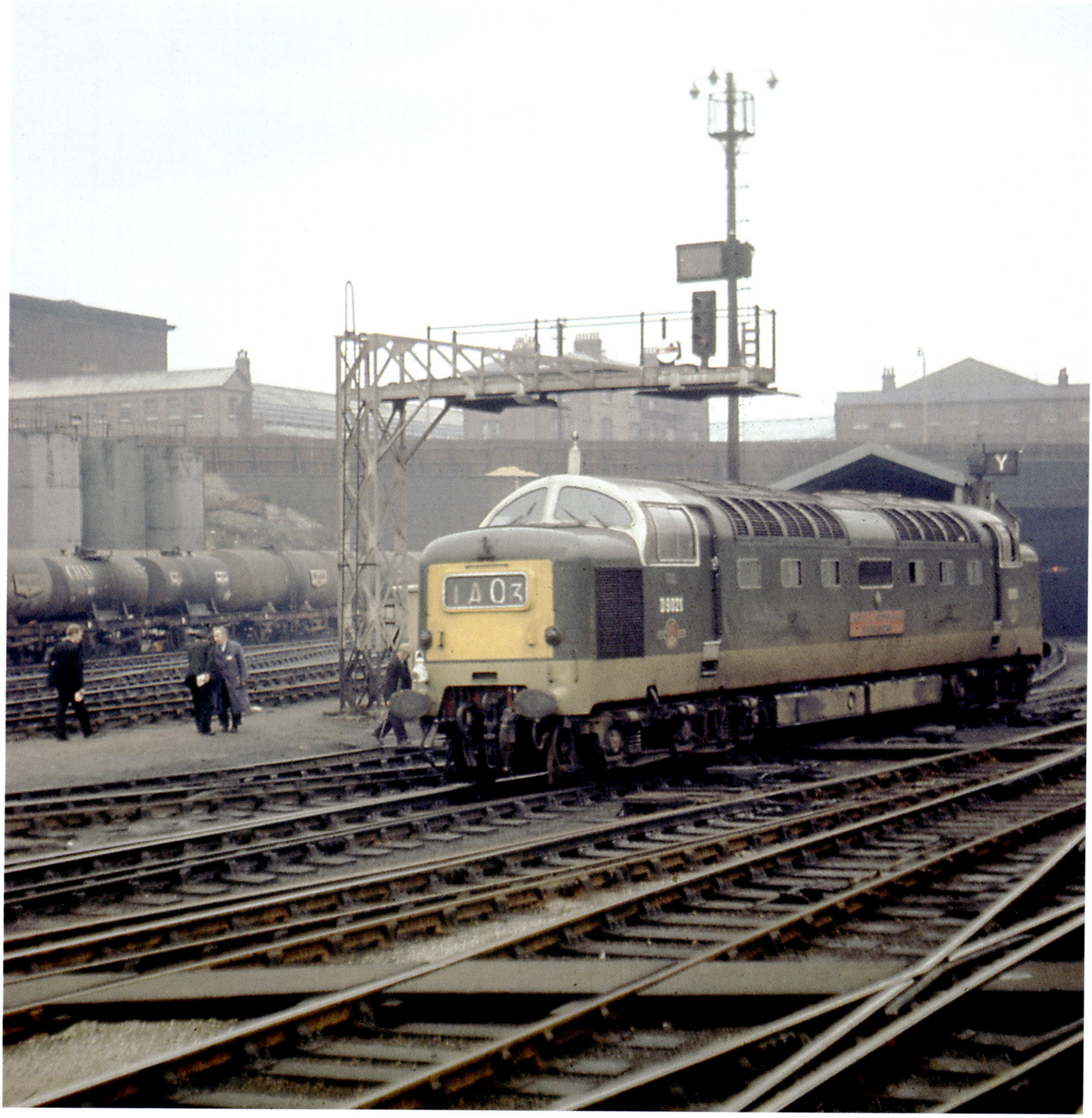

When seen at Kings Cross on 26 March 1965 the single larger British Railways emblem had given way to the fitting of a fine set of large nameplates to accomodate Argyll & Sutherland Highlander as a name along with the regimental badge. Two smaller British Railways emblems were now affixed on each side under the numbers. ***Gilroy A Kerr***

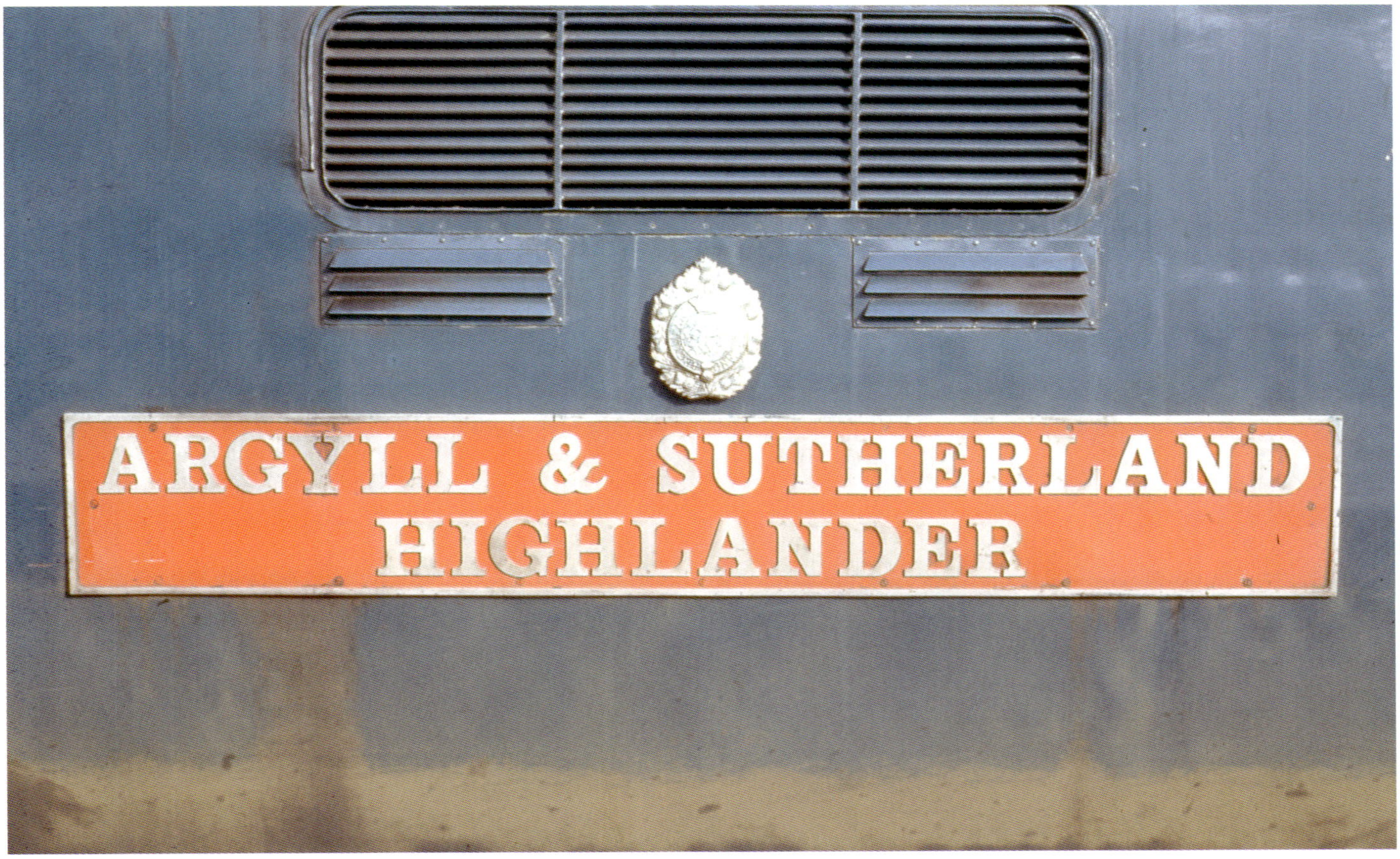

During the mid 1960s all of the class recieved this modification above their nameplates with the fitting of two additional ventilation grills below the existing side grills to attempt to cool the engine rooms. Even so it was common practice to run the locomotives most of the time with their engine room side windows open to cool the beasts. ***Colin Whitbread***

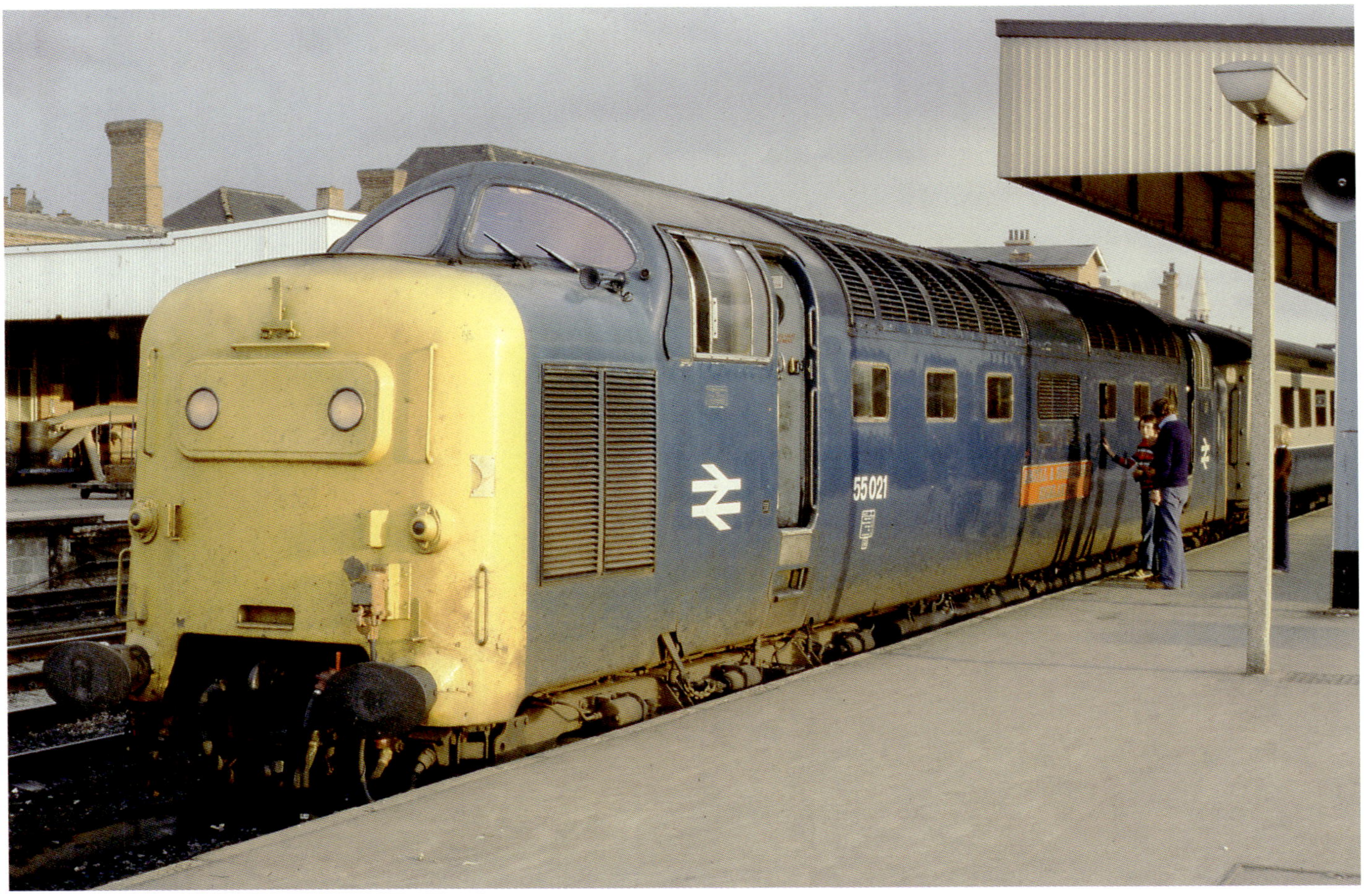

Two years after the nameplate view above and 55021 Argyll & Sutherland Highlander has lost its badges when we see it being admired by two spotters at Doncaster on 22 September 1979 whilst working the 17.05 Kings Cross to Hull. ***Len Ball***

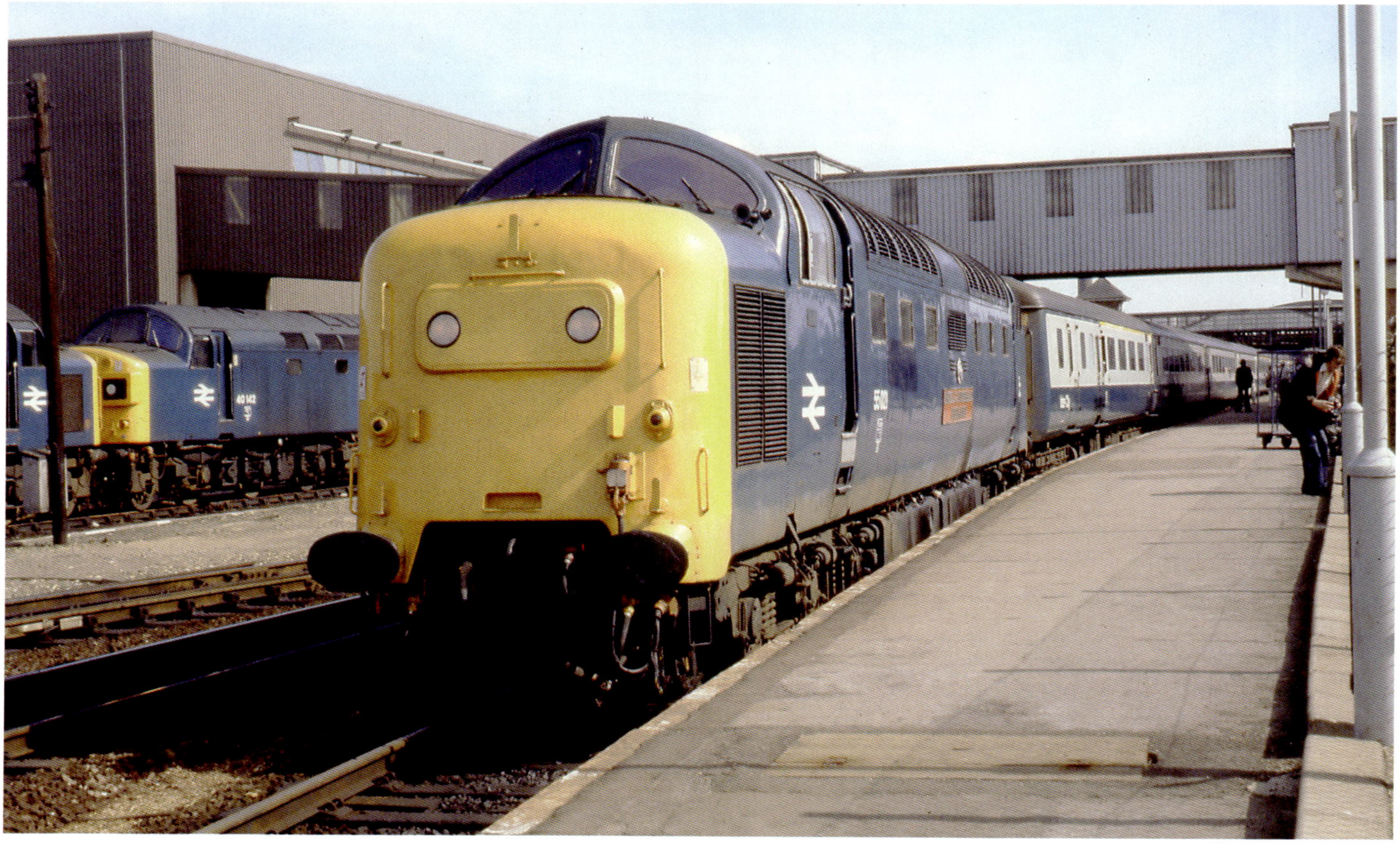

The locomotive had become 55021 in the TOPS scheme on 2 January 1974, when seen at Peterborough in the early summer of 1976 it had only been the fourth member of the class to have been given a Heavy General Repair at Doncaster Works. With the high costs involved in the renewal of inner and outer skins and re-wiring a decision was made to suspend the programme when 55013 The Black Watch followed Argyll & Sutherland Hinghlander out of the Plant a few weeks later. As the projected future use in light of HST deliveries meant the writing was now on the wall for the Deltics. ***Nev Sloper***

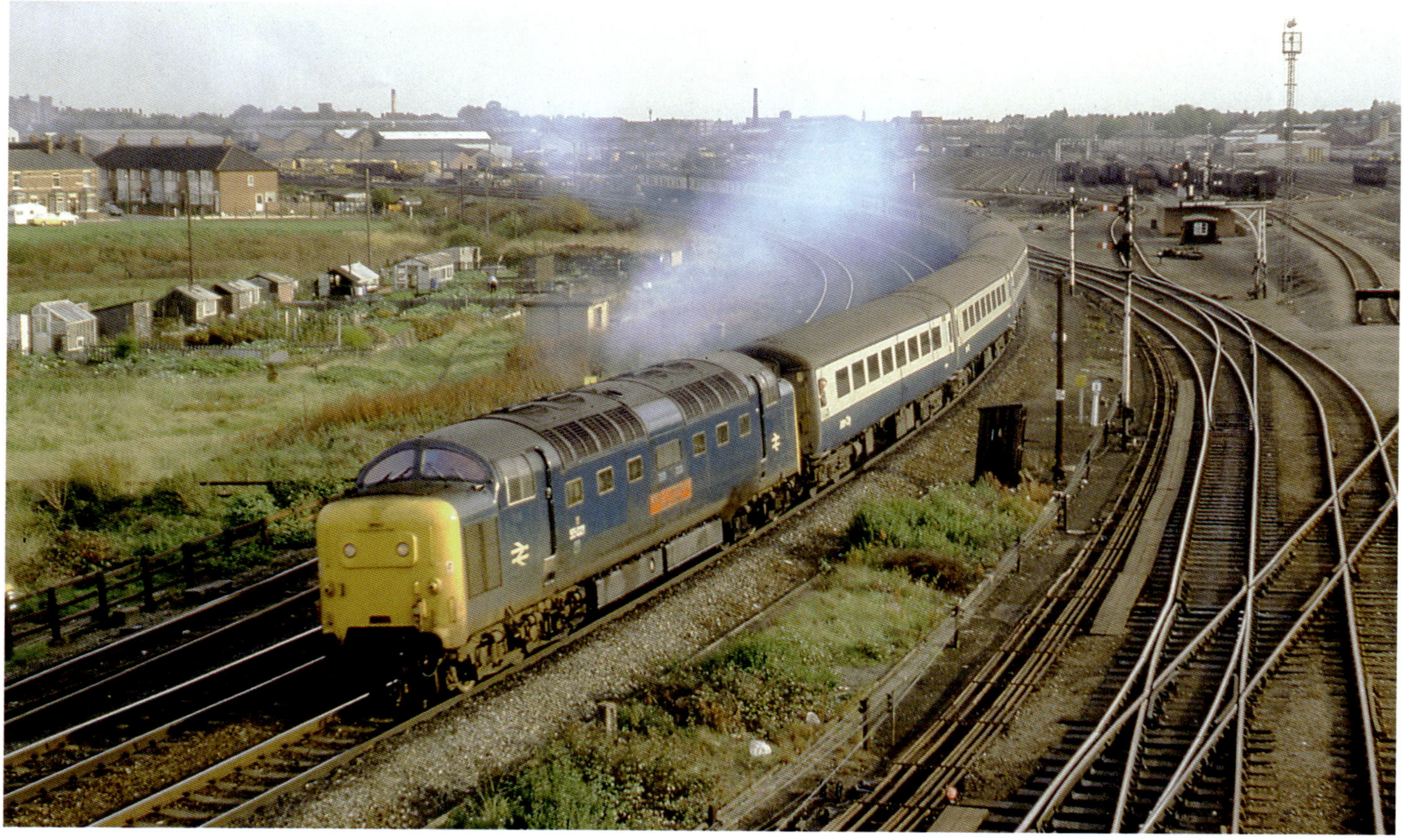

Another visit to Doncaster Works in 1978 for an exchange of power units in the summer of that year would last the locomotive through to withdrawal. Although by November 1981 at least one power unit looks sickly as 55021 Argyll & Sutherland Highlander takes Clifton Curve at York with a Plymouth to Edinburgh service. That last run would be a few weeks later on New Years Eve with a trip from Kings Cross to York, where the locomotive was taken onto the depot and switched off and withdrawn. ***Strathwood Library Collection***

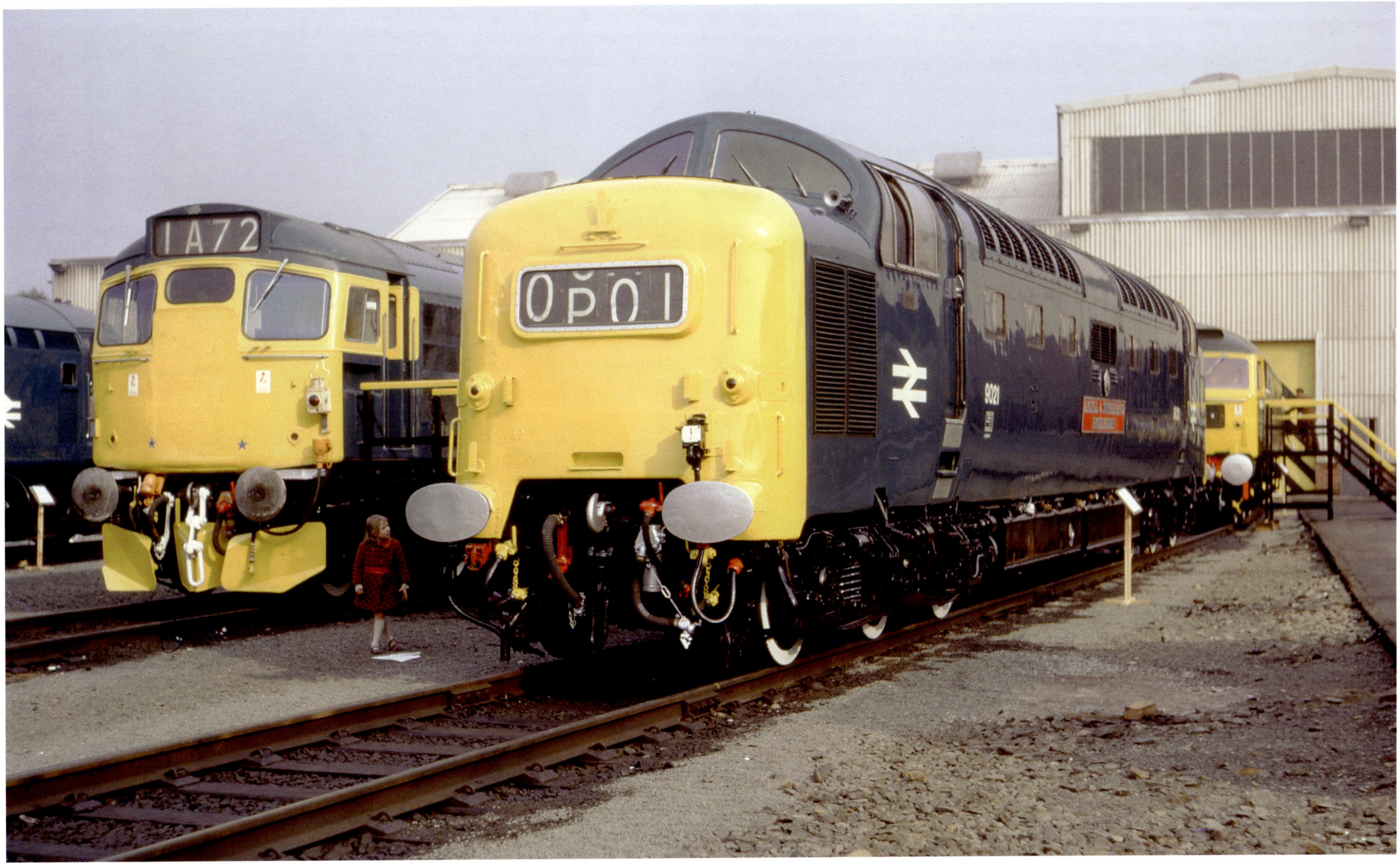

To conclude this review of the Deltic fleet we have chosen this view of a spotless 9021 Argyll & Sutherland Highlander as exhibited over the weekend of 16-17 September 1972 at Eastfield as the star attraction of the open days for Railfair 72. ***Arthur Wilson***

Nocturnal Napiers

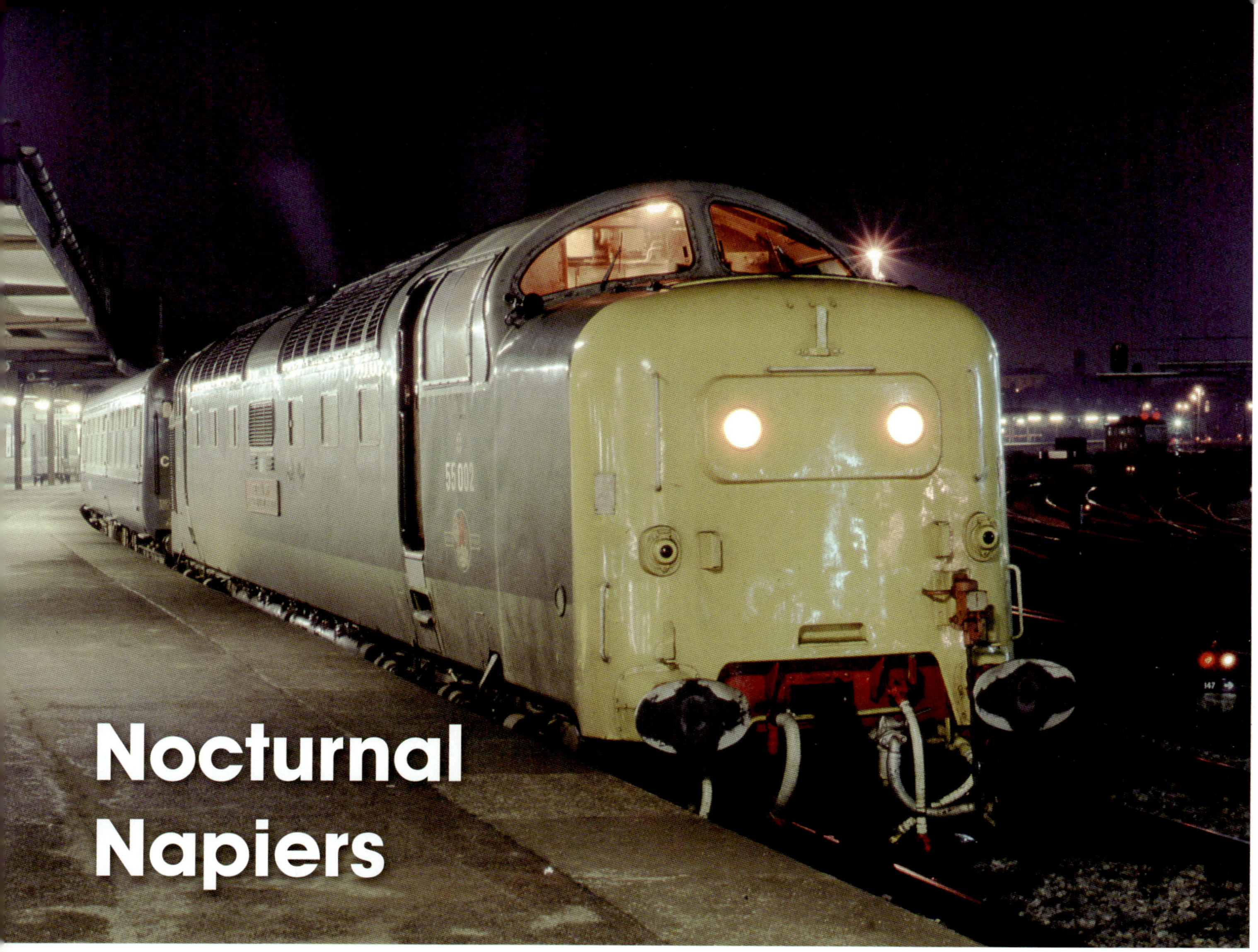

With just weeks to go before the cessation of Deltic workings 55002 The King's Own Yorkshire Light Infantry had just arrived at York on Thursday 19 November 1981 with the 20.40 from Liverpool Lime Street. ***Colin Whitbread***

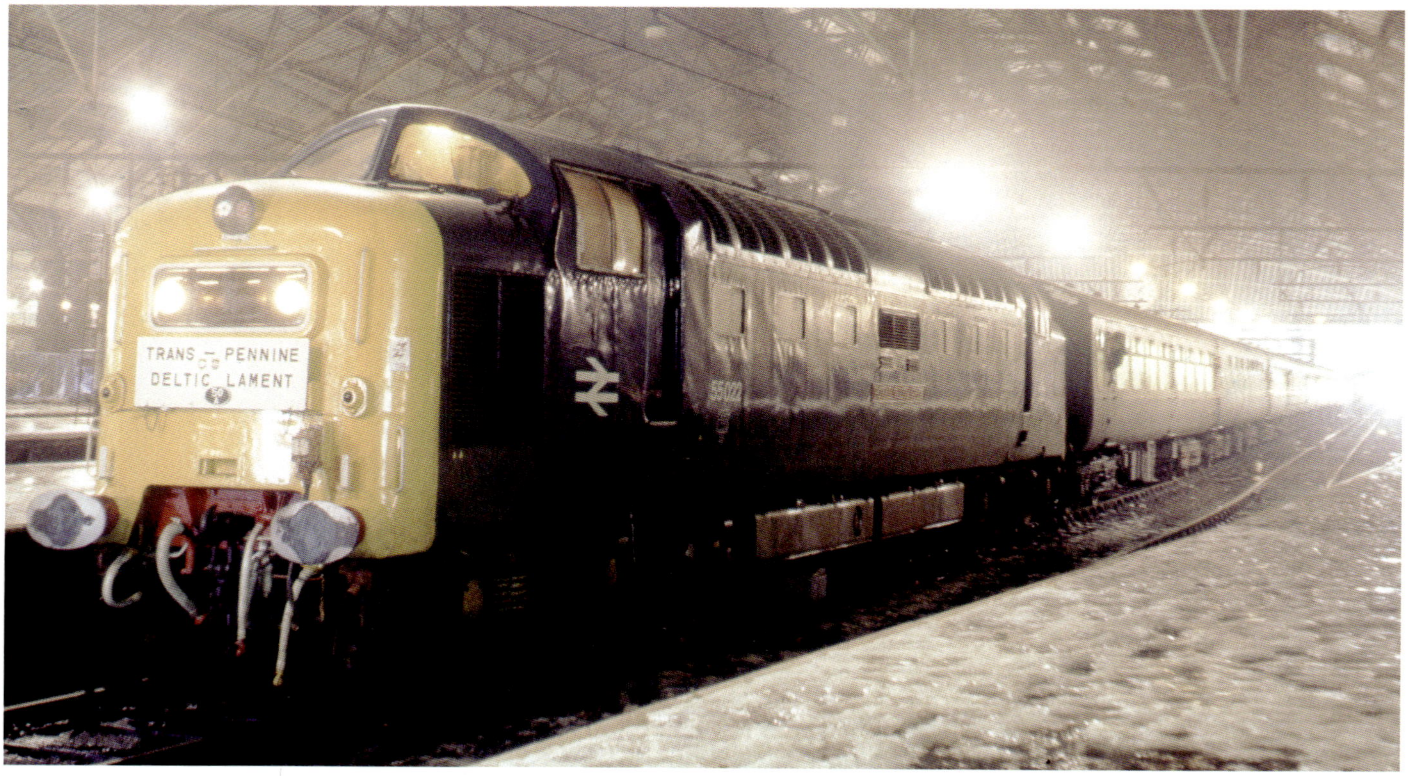

Next to a snowy Liverpool Lime Street itself to capture 55022 Royal Scots Grey on 20 December a month later at the head of the Trans Pennine Deltic Lament. ***Matthew Hall***

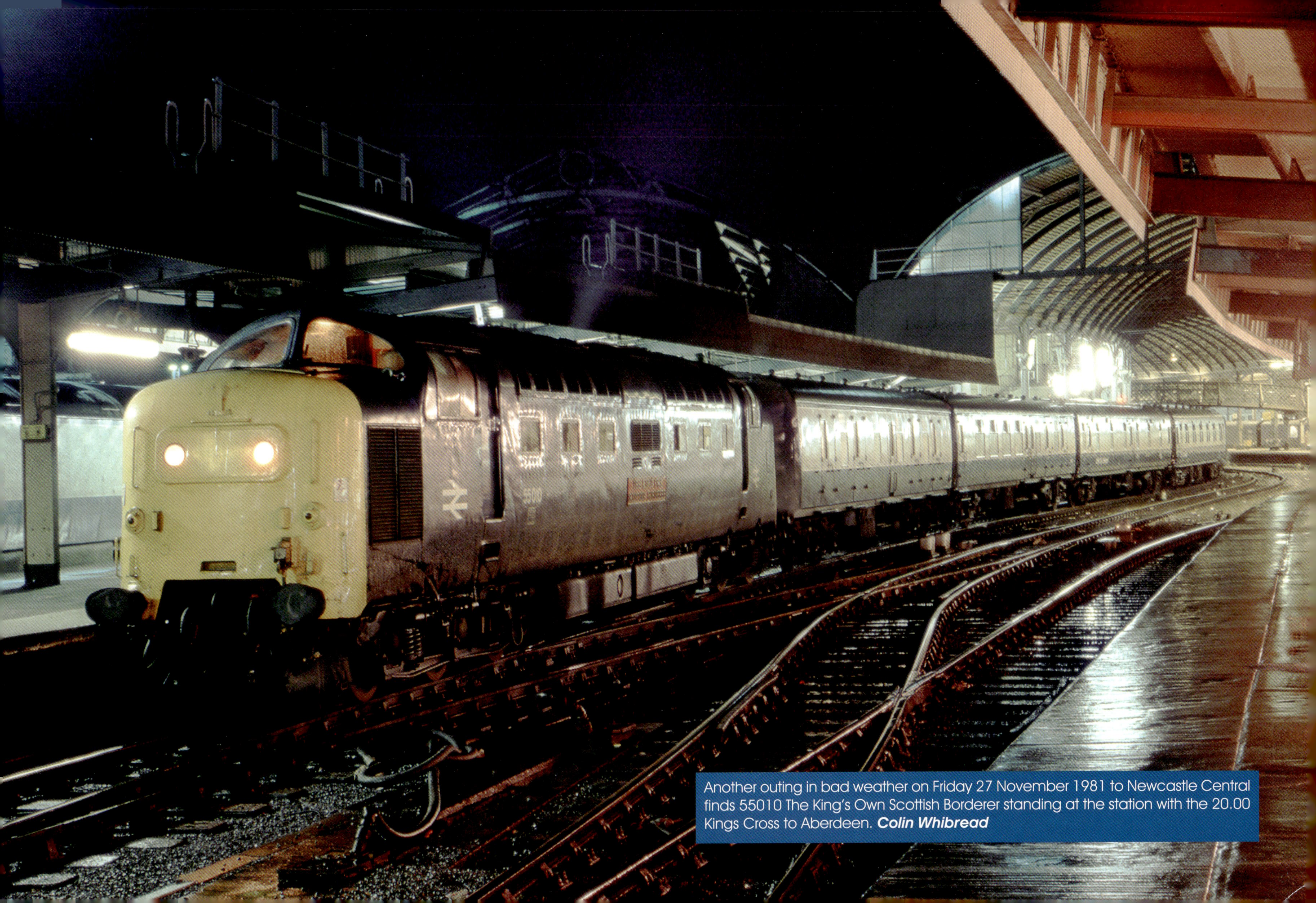

Another outing in bad weather on Friday 27 November 1981 to Newcastle Central finds 55010 The King's Own Scottish Borderer standing at the station with the 20.00 Kings Cross to Aberdeen. ***Colin Whibread***

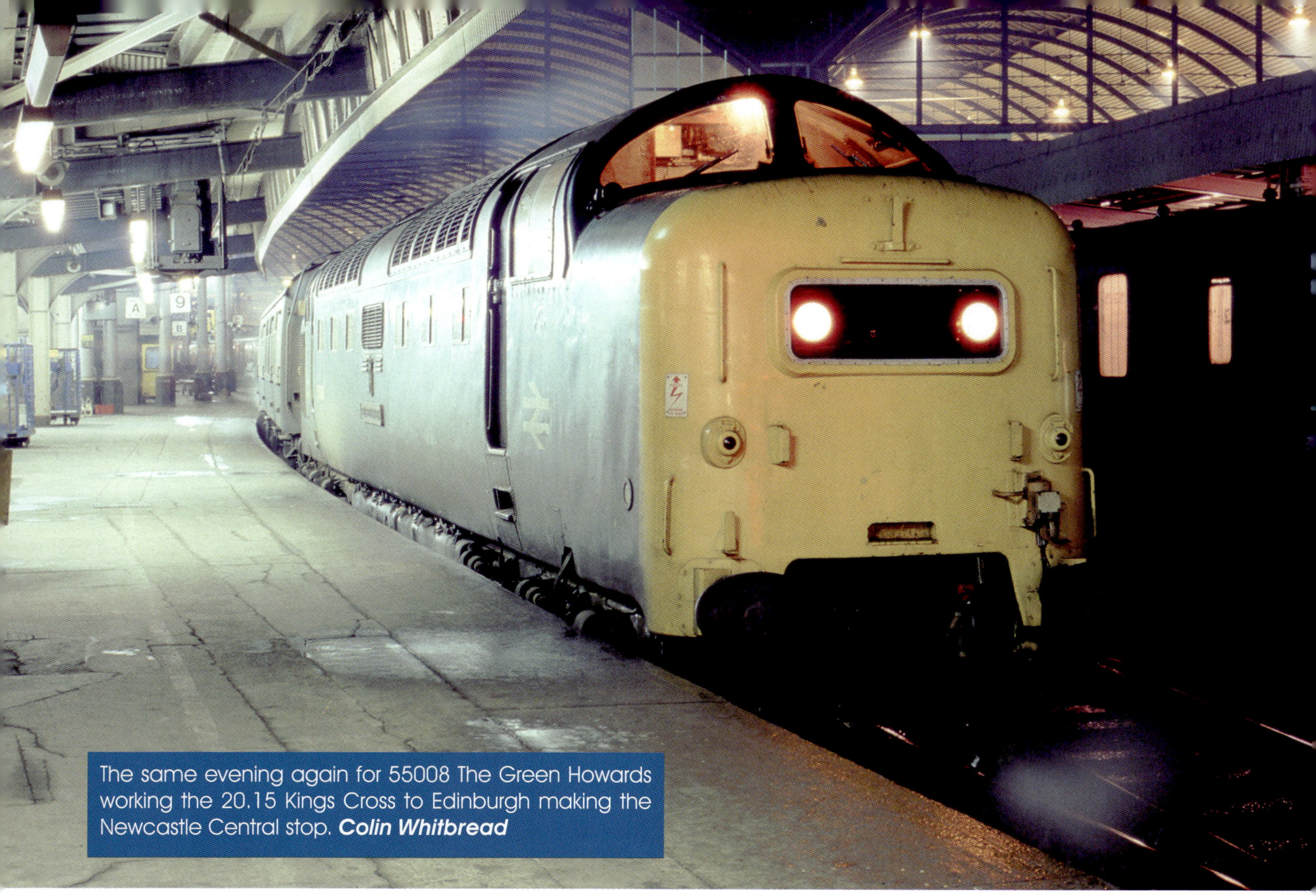

The same evening again for 55008 The Green Howards working the 20.15 Kings Cross to Edinburgh making the Newcastle Central stop. ***Colin Whitbread***

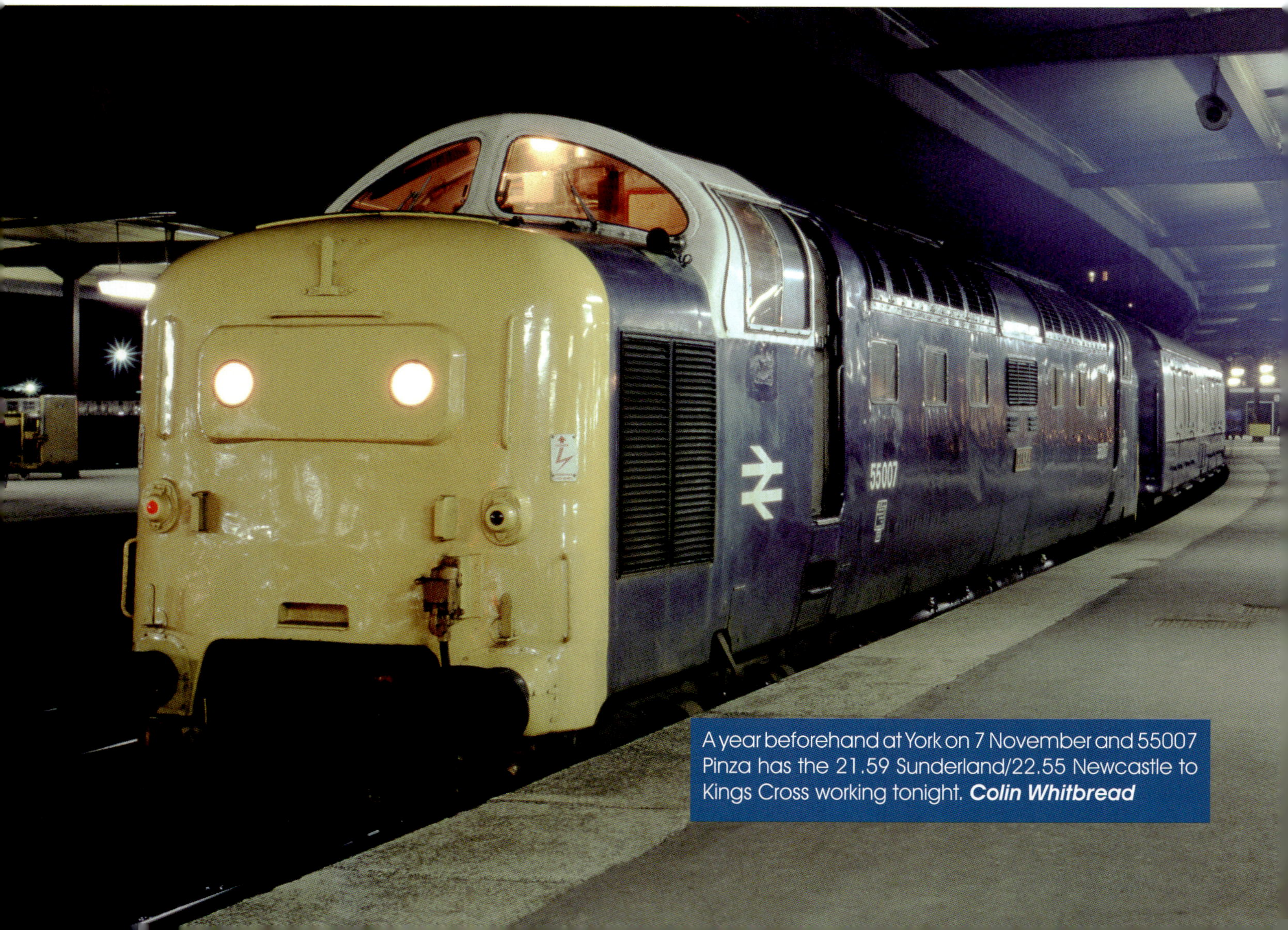

A year beforehand at York on 7 November and 55007 Pinza has the 21.59 Sunderland/22.55 Newcastle to Kings Cross working tonight. ***Colin Whitbread***

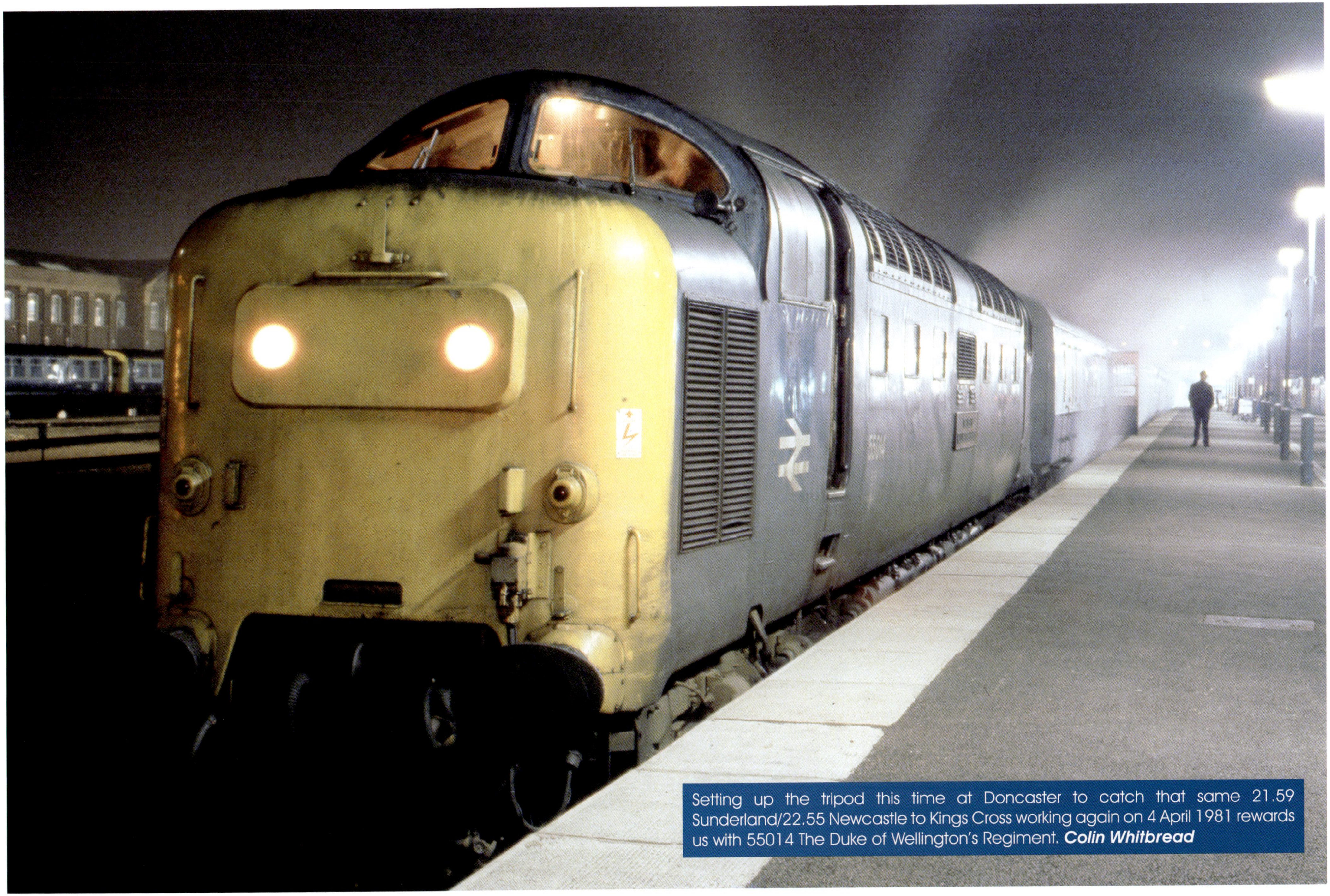

Setting up the tripod this time at Doncaster to catch that same 21.59 Sunderland/22.55 Newcastle to Kings Cross working again on 4 April 1981 rewards us with 55014 The Duke of Wellington's Regiment. ***Colin Whitbread***

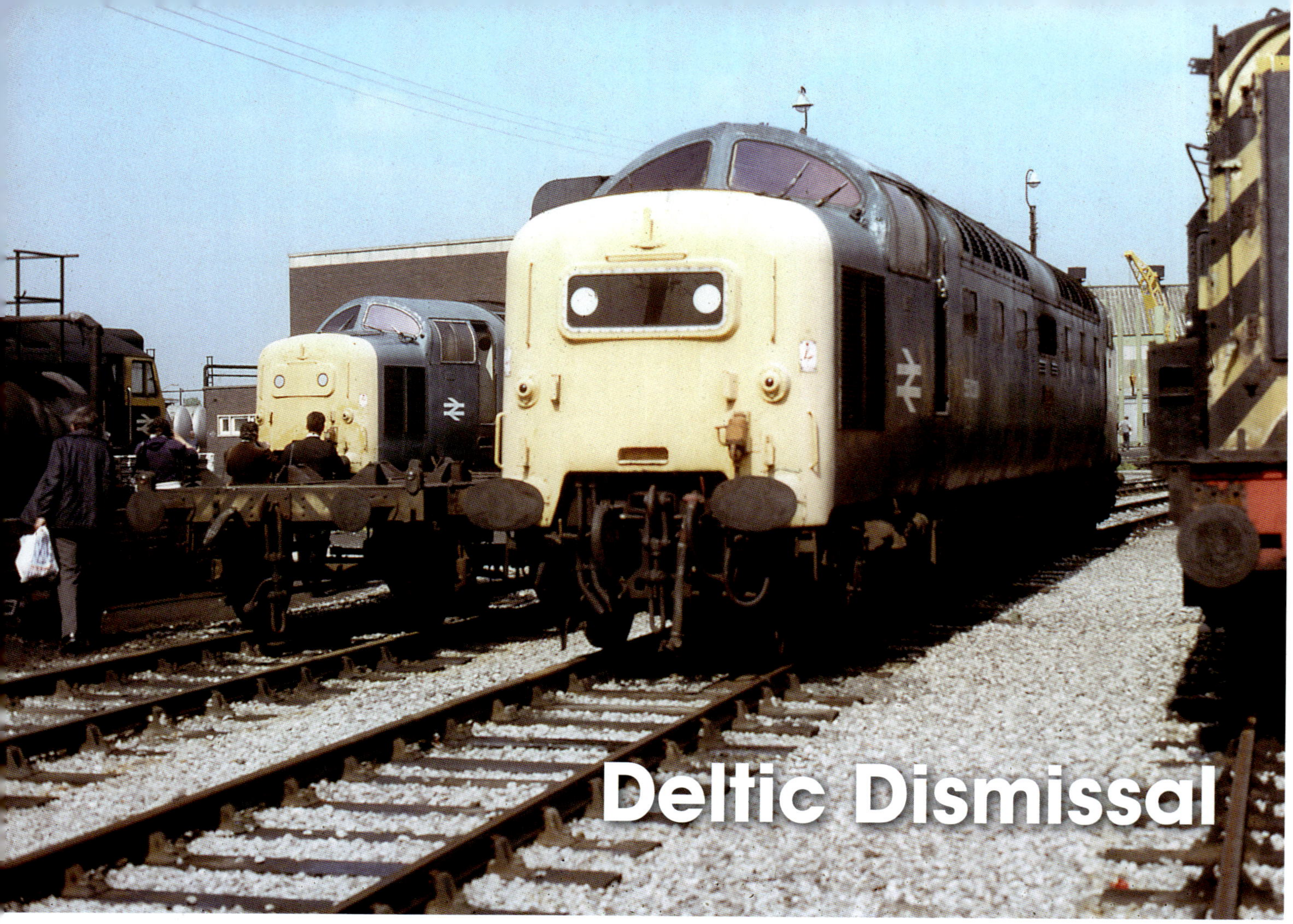

Deltic Dismissal

The first two Deltics to be put out to grass were 55020 Nimbus and 55001 St. Paddy, with the former arriving here at Doncaster for assessment on 26 April 1978 joining St.Paddy which had arrived a short while before in March. This was the scene in June 1979 as the pair awaited a possible sanctioning of repairs. This was not to come and enthusiasts learned that they were officially withdrawn as of 5 January 1980 and within a few weeks both had vanished at the hands of the works cutting staff. ***Bruce Smetham***

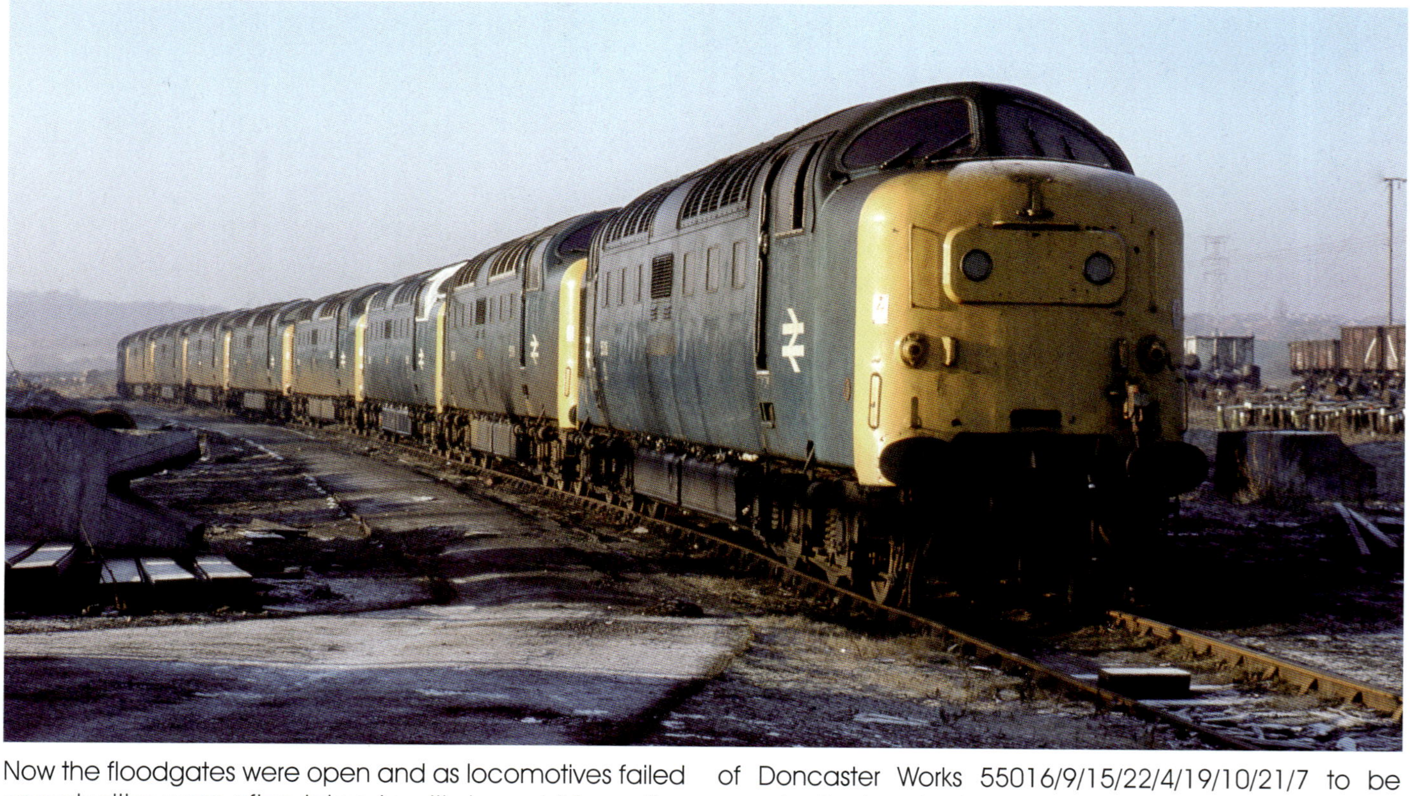

Now the floodgates were open and as locomotives failed opportunities were often taken to withdraw old favourites and by 10 January 1982 this was the line up at the back of Doncaster Works 55016/9/15/22/4/19/10/21/7 to be seen by the hundreds who bunked the fence to grab their shots. ***Jeffrey Lane***

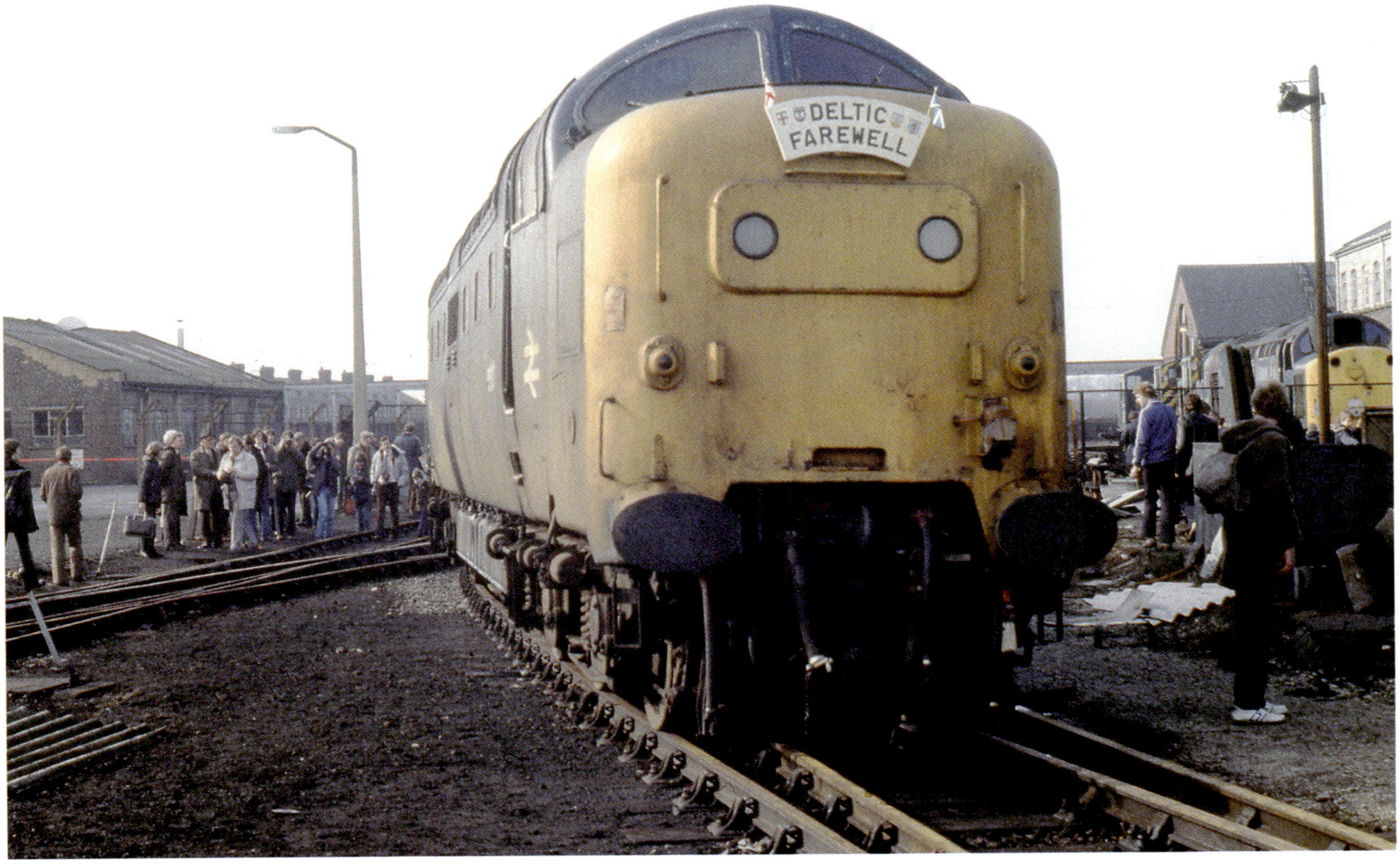

Such was the interest a Deltic Open Day was arranged for Saturday 27 February 1982 at Doncaster Works. Deltics were carefully positioned so as to cover up any open pits for safety and additional fencing and British Transport Police were provided to deter tresspassing elsewhere within the complex. With a Deltic Farewell headboard affixed 55007 Pinza took up its place in the parade ring. ***Matthew Hall***

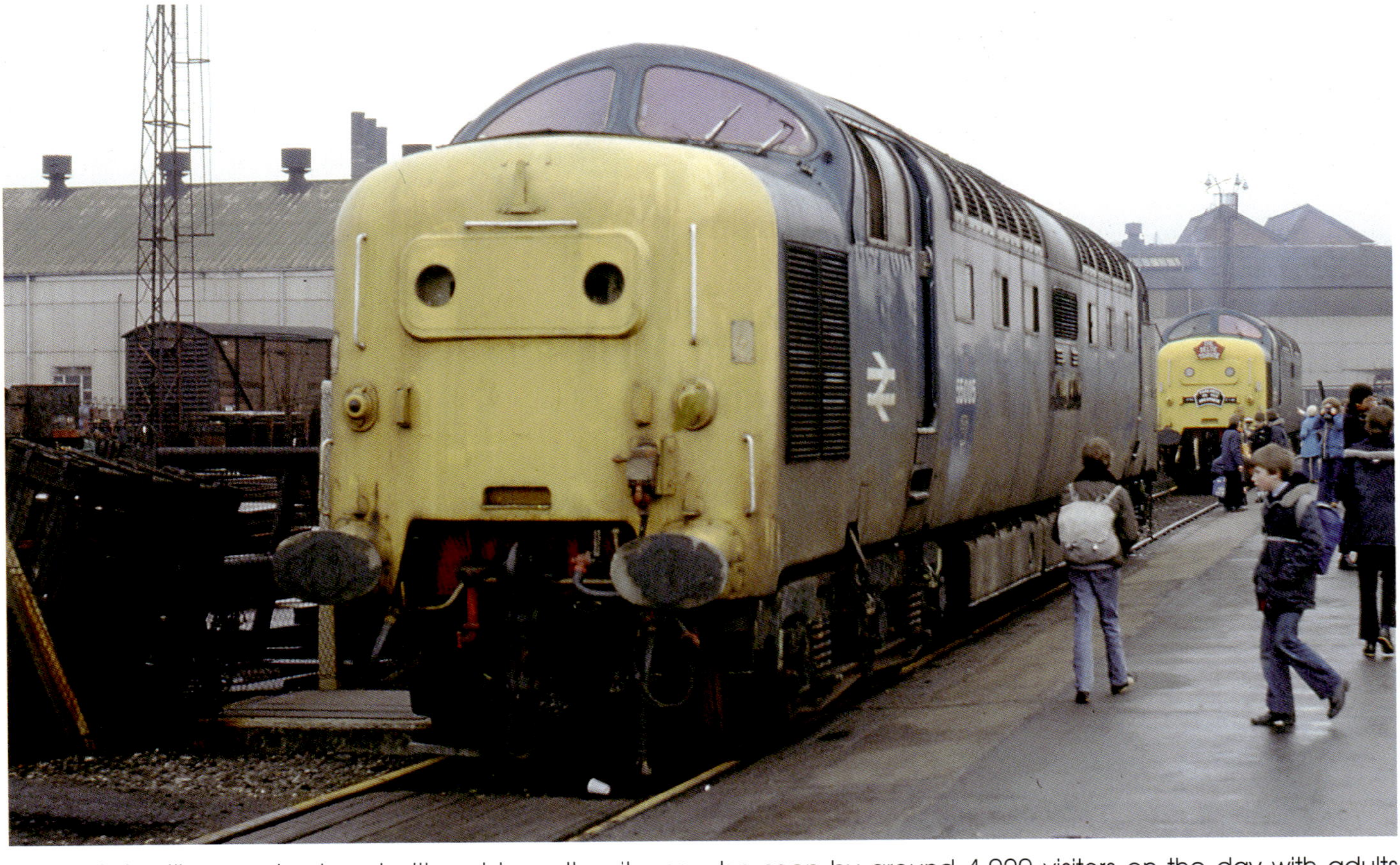

Although hastily organized and with cold weather it was expected that now shorn of any form of dignity 55005 The Prince of Wales's Own Regiment of Yorhsire may only be seen by around 4,000 visitors on the day with adults paying £1.00 and children to be charged 50p, with the proceeds going to charity. ***Matthew Hall***

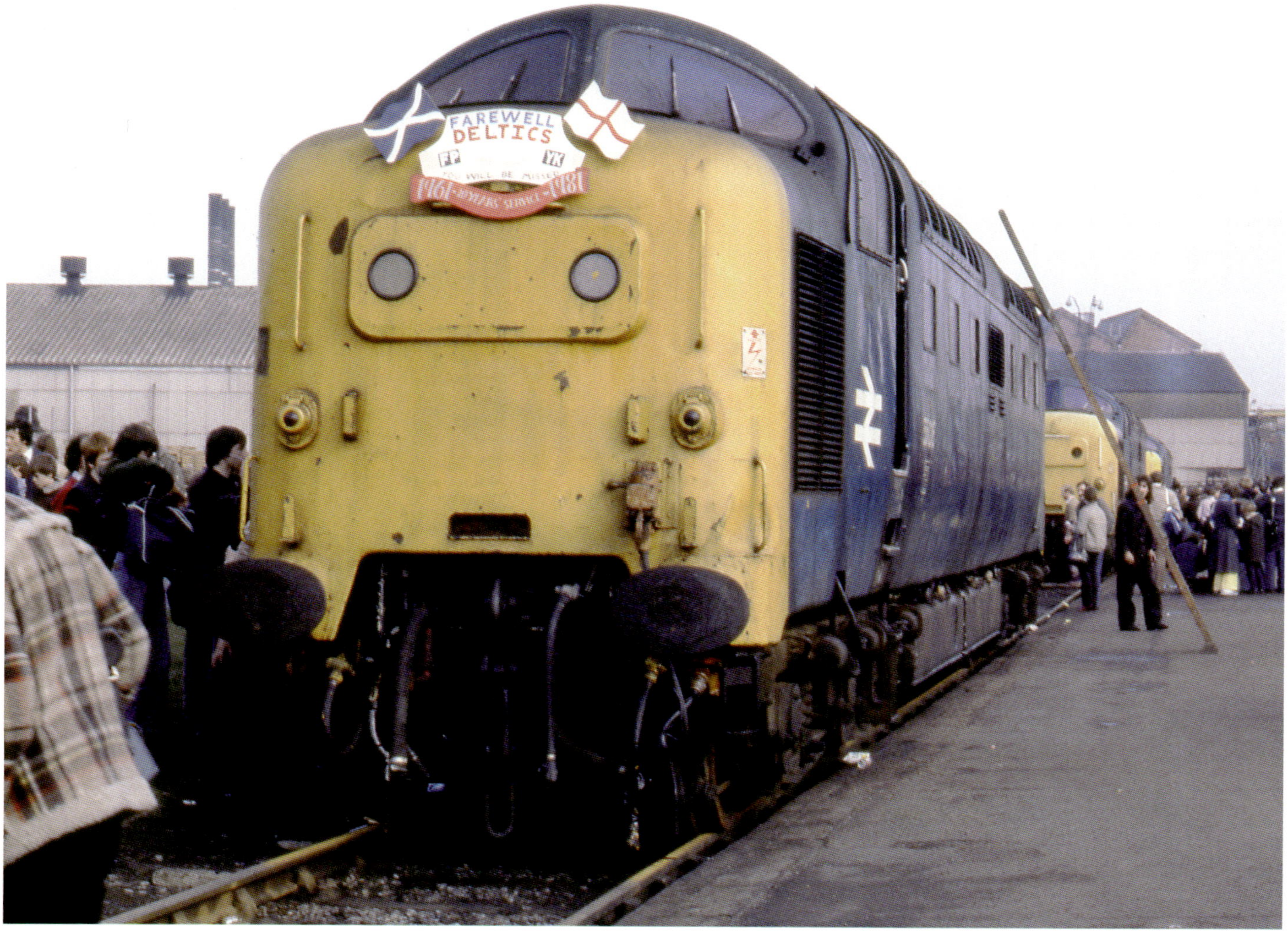

As planned the event would open at 10.00 and last admittance being at 14.00 due to the shorter winter daylight hours. Ready for inspection was 55016 Gordon Highlander, however it was apparent that by the lengthy que formed by 09.00 that the event was a hit, and the gates were opened early at 09.30. ***Stuart Broughton***

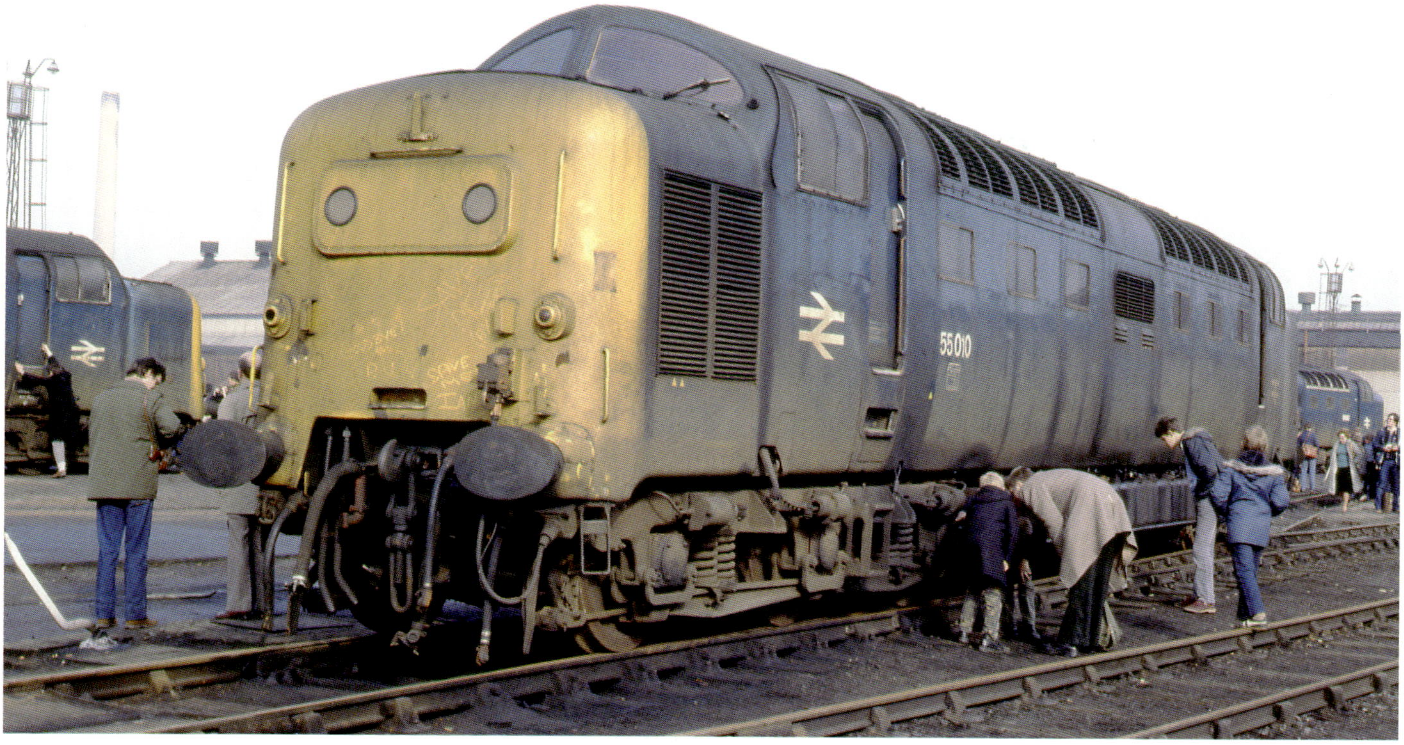

As the daylight hours drew to a close it was noted that over 9,000 people had taken advantage of this last chance to pay homage to 55010 The King's Own Scottish Borderer and the other sixteen Deltics on show that memorable day. ***Stuart Broughton***

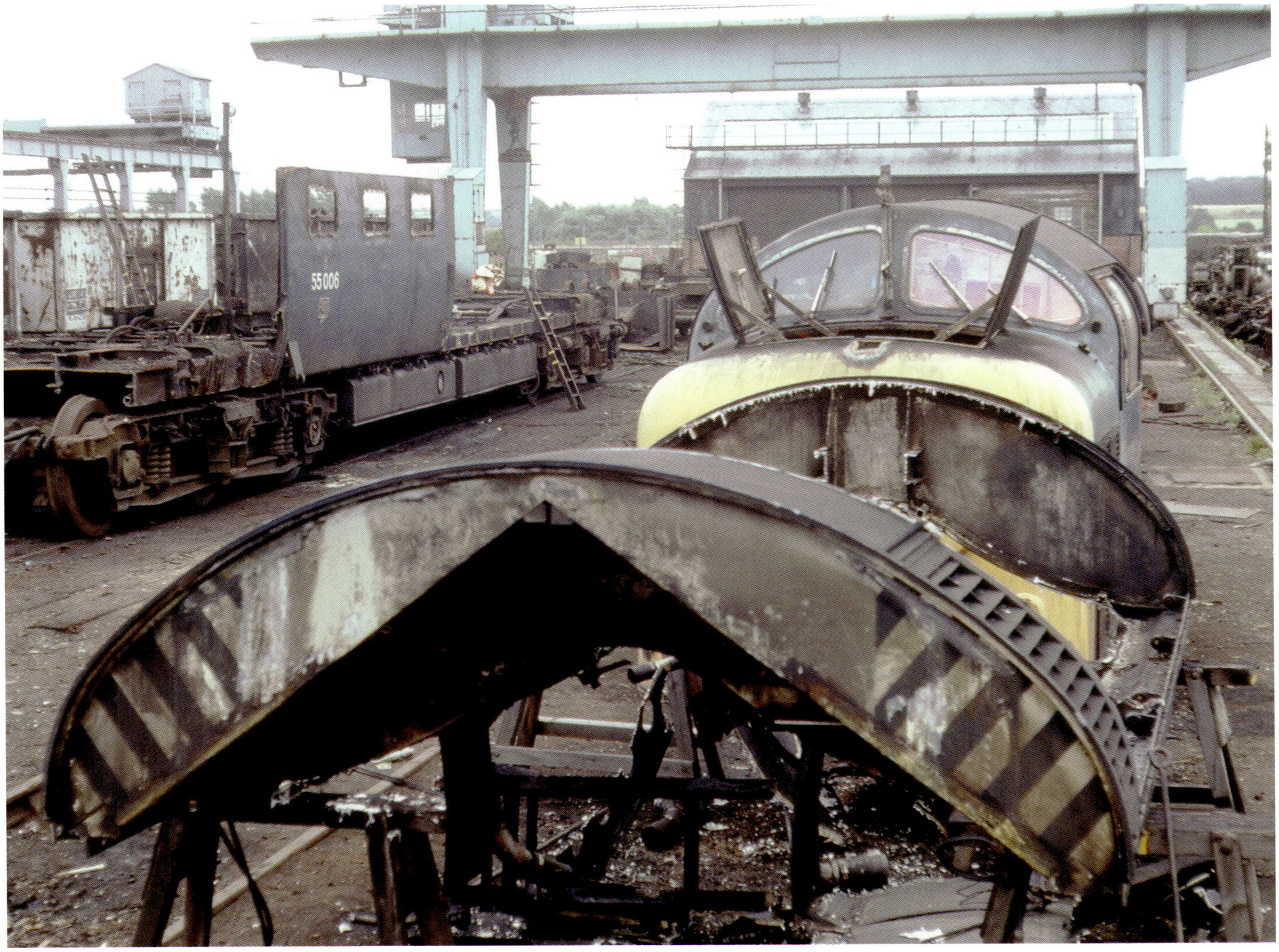

One of those not to survive long enough within Doncaster Works for the Deltic Open Day was 55006 The Fife & Forfar Yeomanry seen here on 19 July 1981 five months after being withdrawn. In the end sixteen Deltics and one Baby Deltic would perish at this site. ***Strathwood Library Collection***

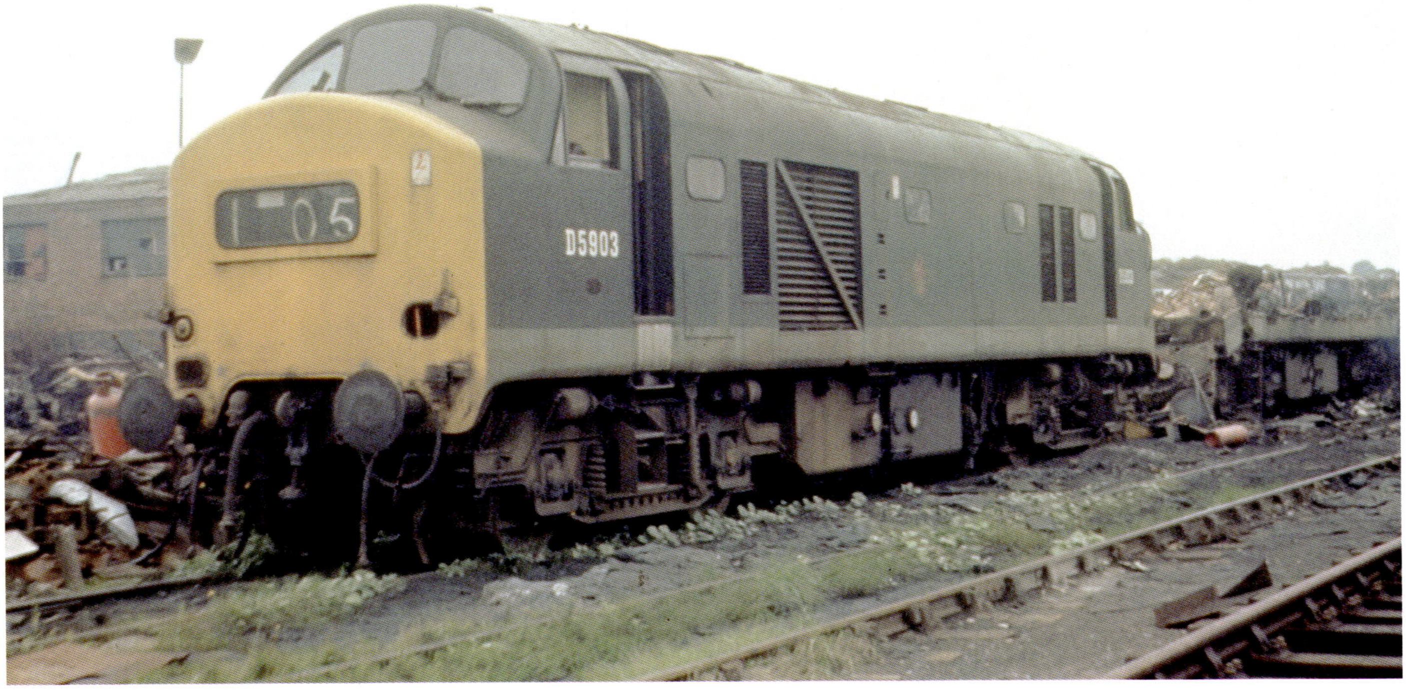

We have already reflected on the busy scrapyard of George Cohen at Cransley near Kettering as being the nemesis for Baby Deltics with D5903 awaiting its turn whilst D5900 had just been dealt with in August 1969. ***Grahame Wareham***

Deltic Specials Headboards

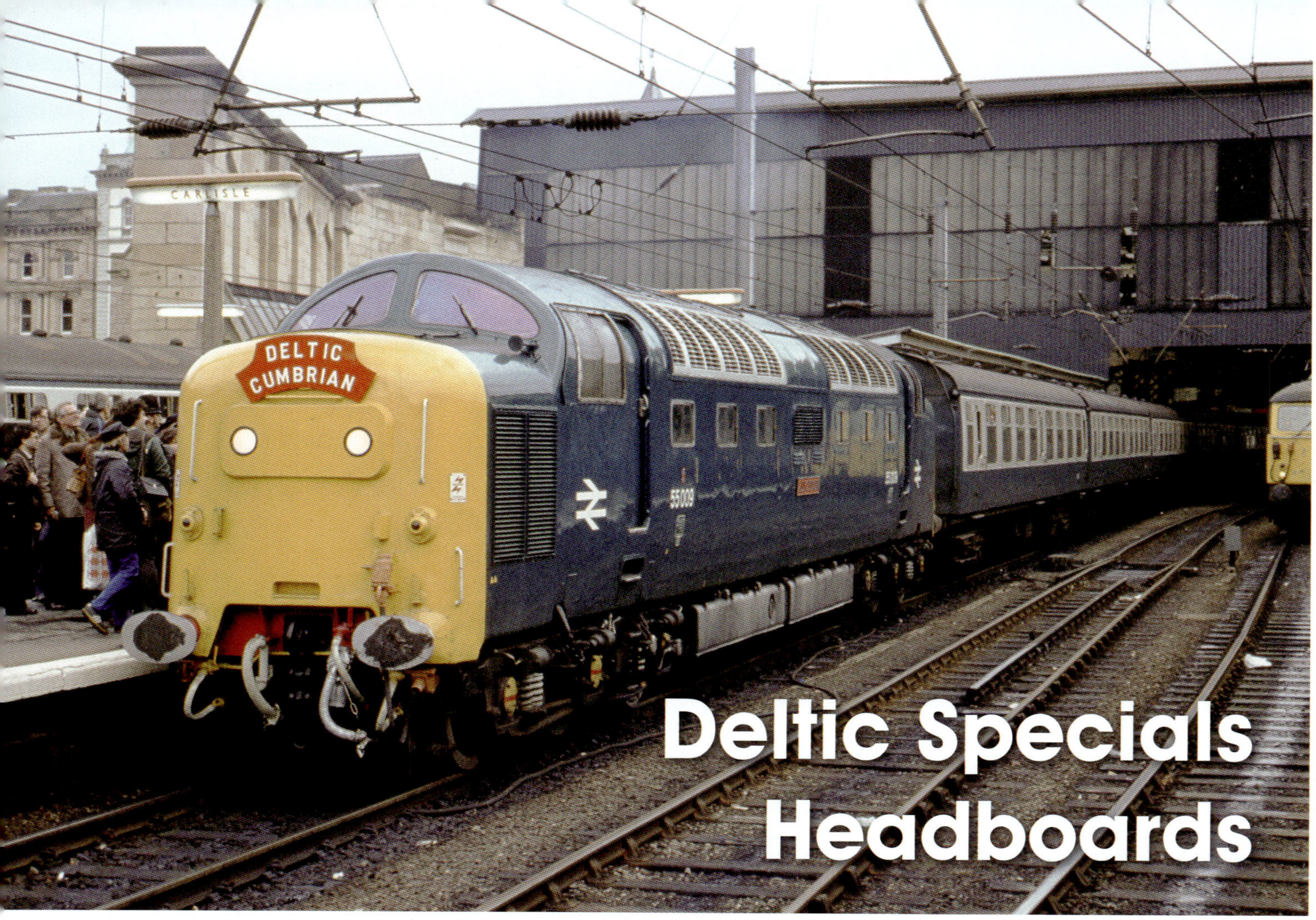

On 14 November 1981 55009 Alycidon was the motive power throughout for the Deltic Cumbrian from Kings Cross via Normanton and Skipton to arrive here at Carlisle, before a return via Newcastle Central and a gallop back along the ECML to Kings Cross. ***Arthur Wilson***

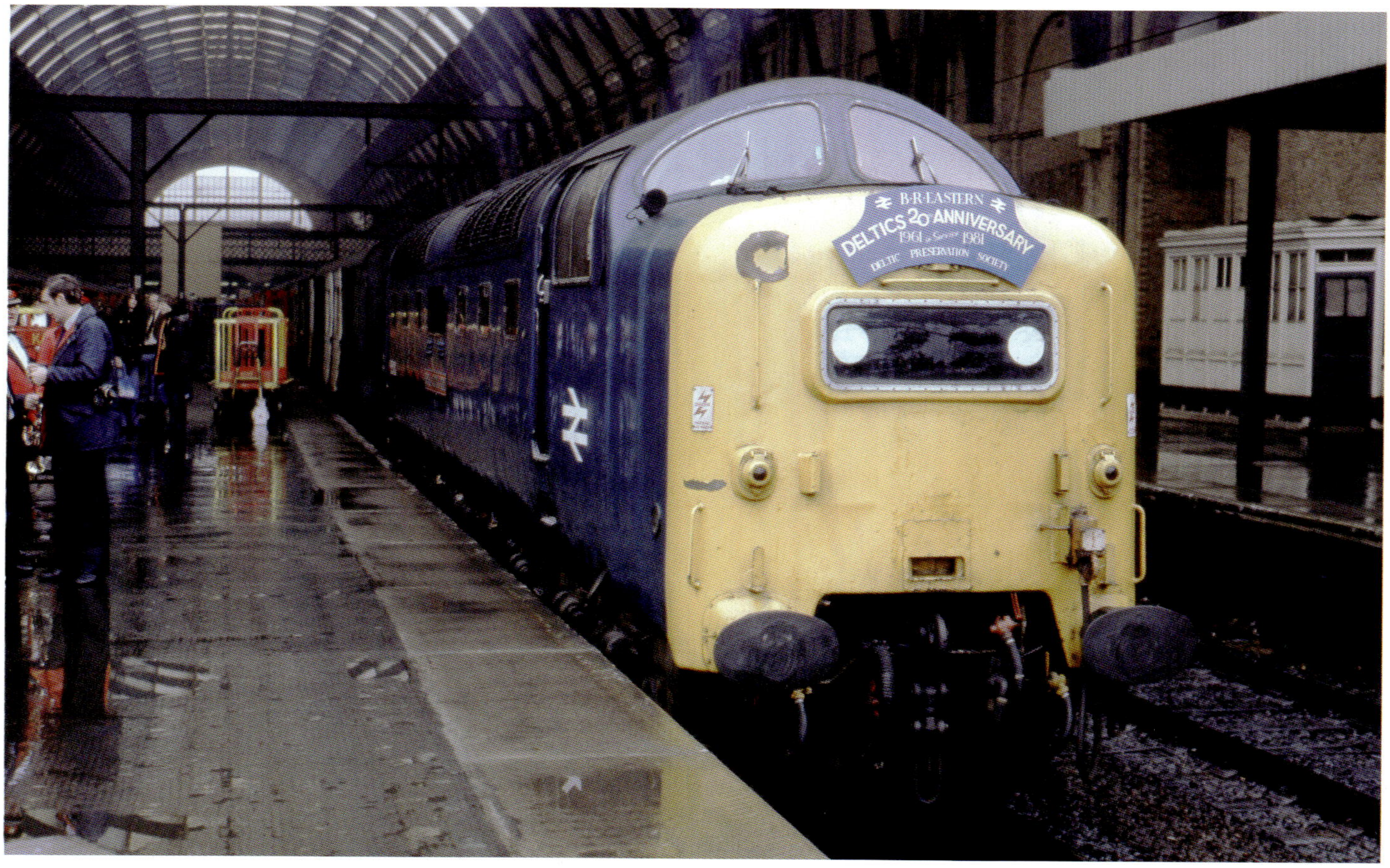

In recognition of the Deltics 20th Anniversary on the route on 28 February 1981, the 1L42 12:20 Kings Cross - York with 55022 Royal Scots Grey in charge at the London terminus carried this headboard provided by The Deltic Preservation Society. ***Strathwood Library Collection***

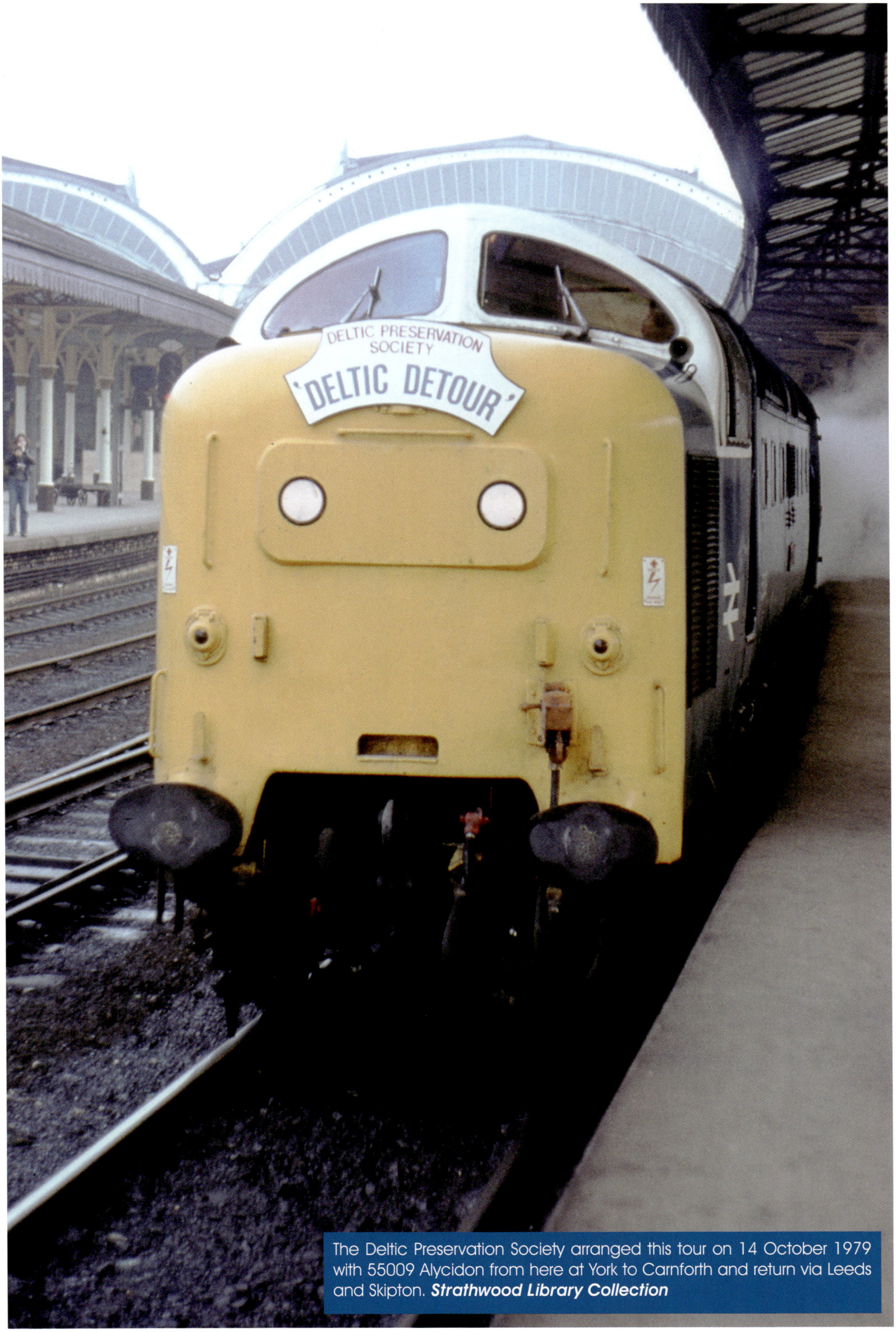

The Deltic Preservation Society arranged this tour on 14 October 1979 with 55009 Alycidon from here at York to Carnforth and return via Leeds and Skipton. ***Strathwood Library Collection***

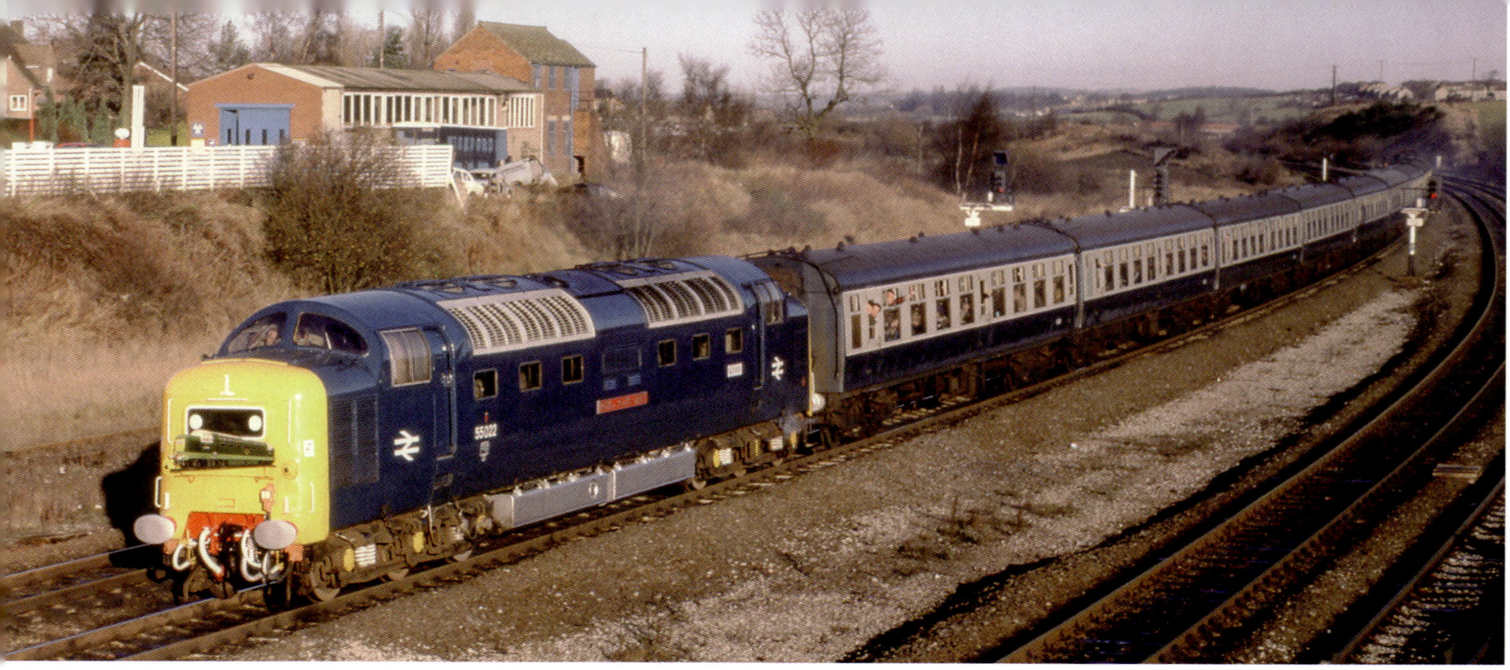

Perhaps the most photogenic was on-board 55022 Royal Scots Grey with the Deltic Venturer seen passing Clay Cross en route from York to Paddington and back on 28 November 1981. ***Ian Harrison***

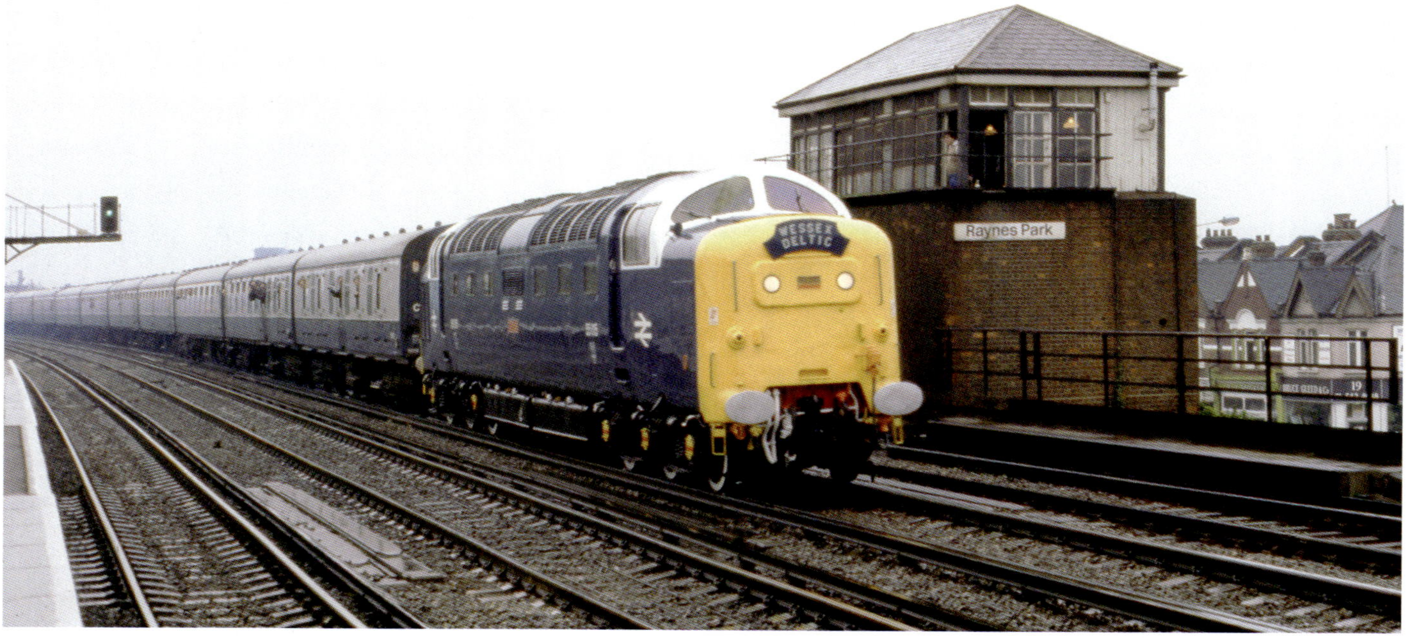

On a wet autumnal 17 October 1981 55015 Tulyar took the Wessex Deltic on tour of the Southern Region captured here running through Raynes Park in the London suburbs. ***Ian James***

Below: The Deltic Fenman of 4 May 1981 brought 55002 The King's Own Yorkshire Light Infantry around the curves at Stratford and out onto the Great Eastern mainline. ***John Harrup***

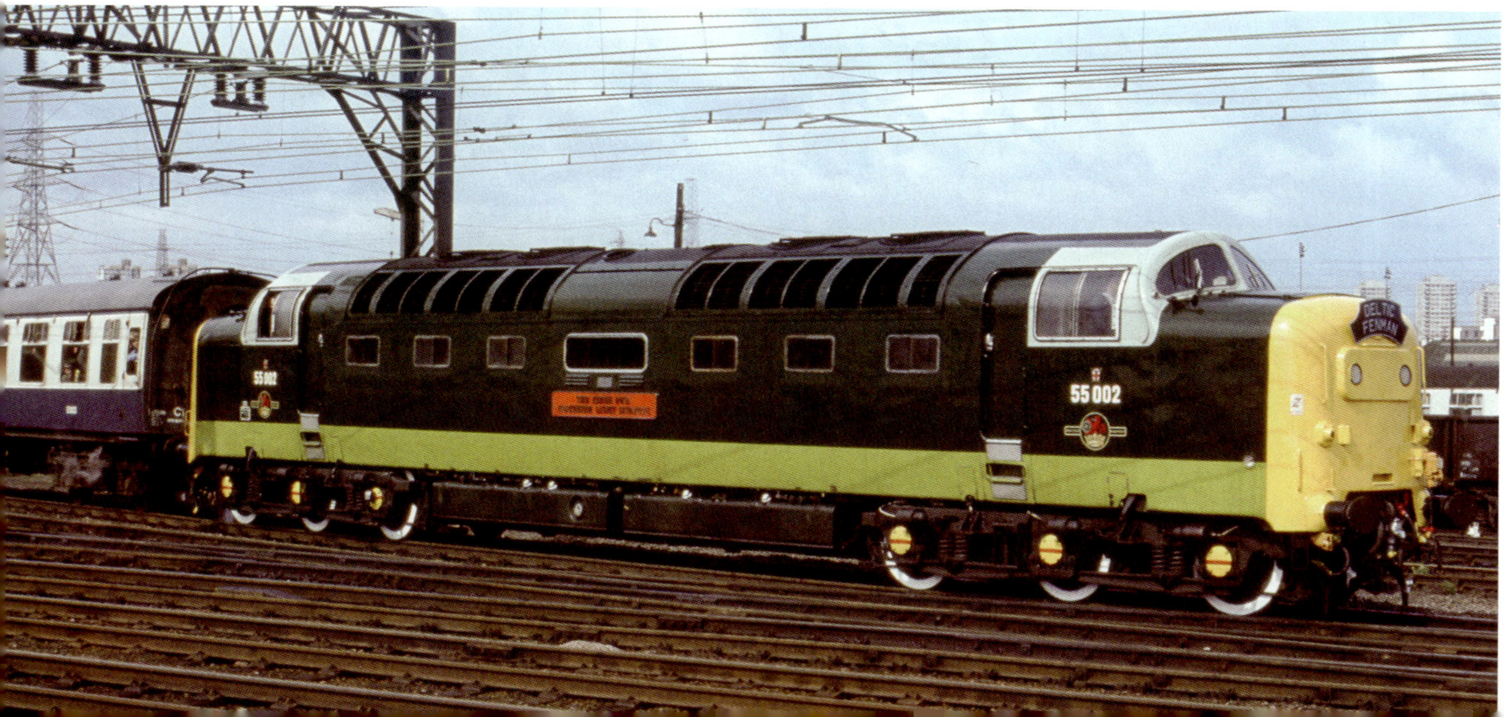

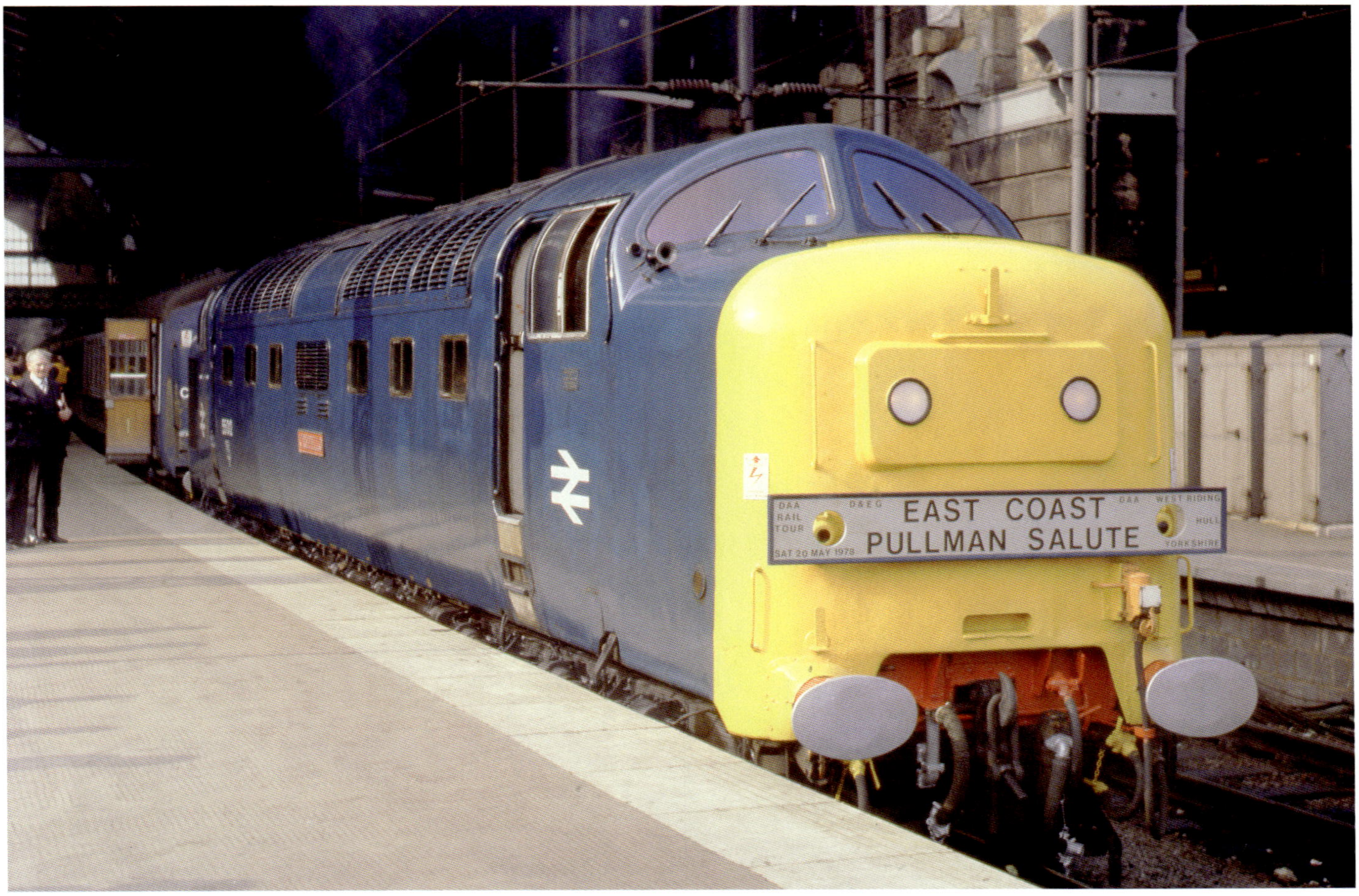

In charge for the outward leg from Kings Cross to Leeds on 20 May 1978 was 55012 Crepello which would reach 99.4mph racing through Tallington with the East Coast Pullman Salute. Two Class 37s would be put on at Leeds for the onward journey to York and Scarborough before this pairing would be run up to 90mph at Retford and Little Bytham on a likewise spirited run back to London. ***Ian James***

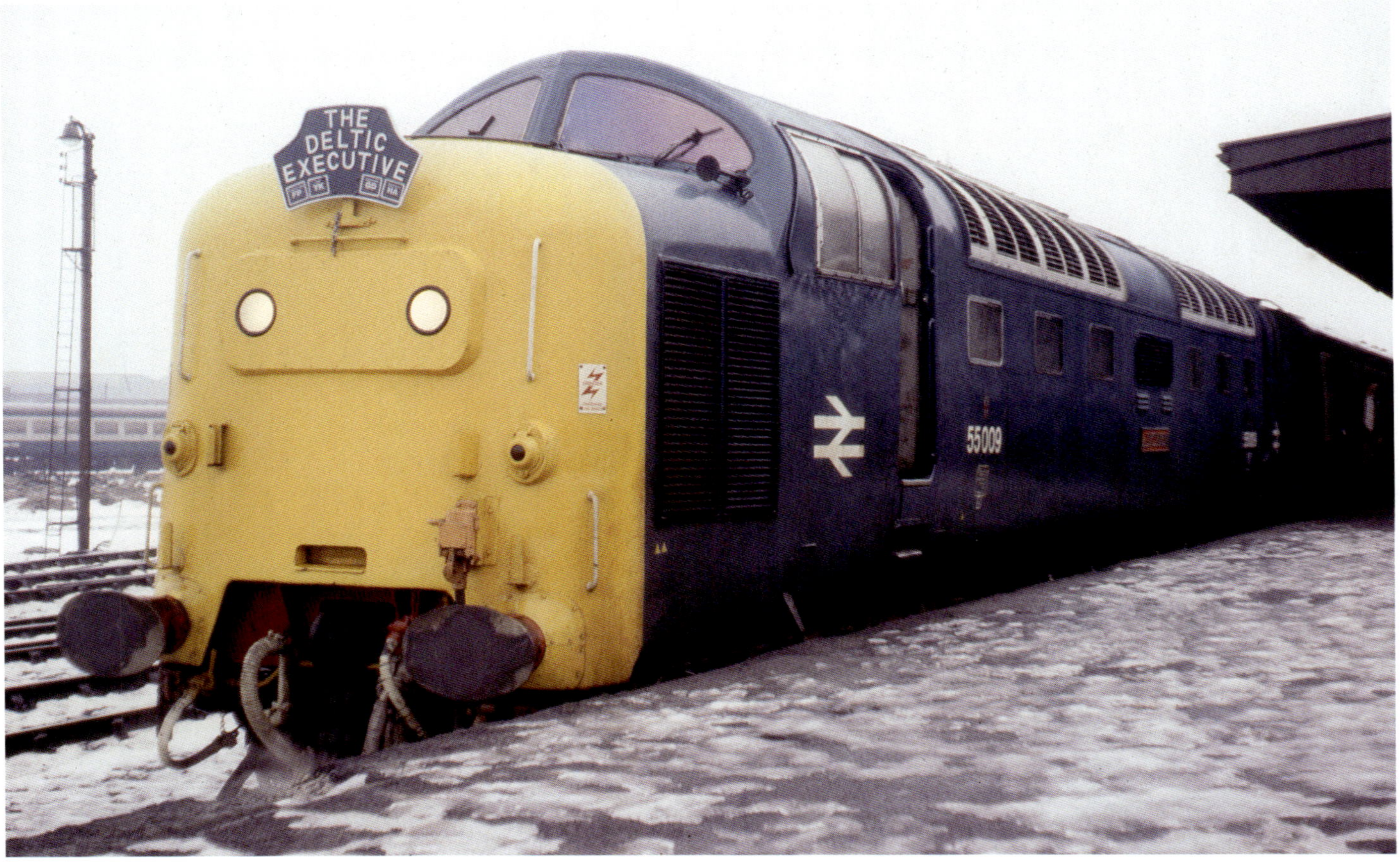

The motive power for The Deltic Executive on 29 December 1981 would be 55009 Alycidon bringing the train from Kings Cross to here at York before a run home again after taking in a trip to Hull after some resonable snowfalls in the north of England that week. ***Matthew Hall***

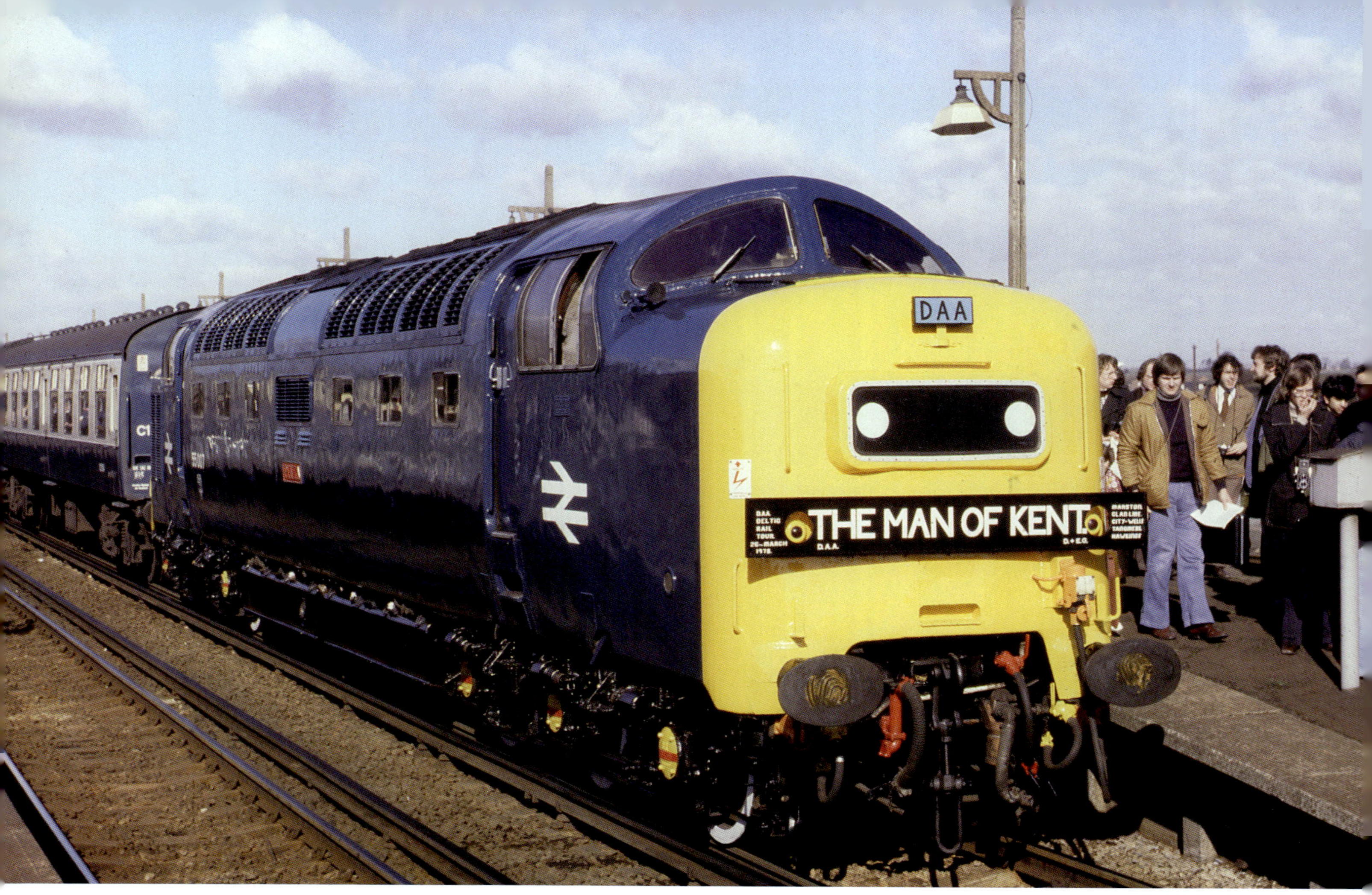

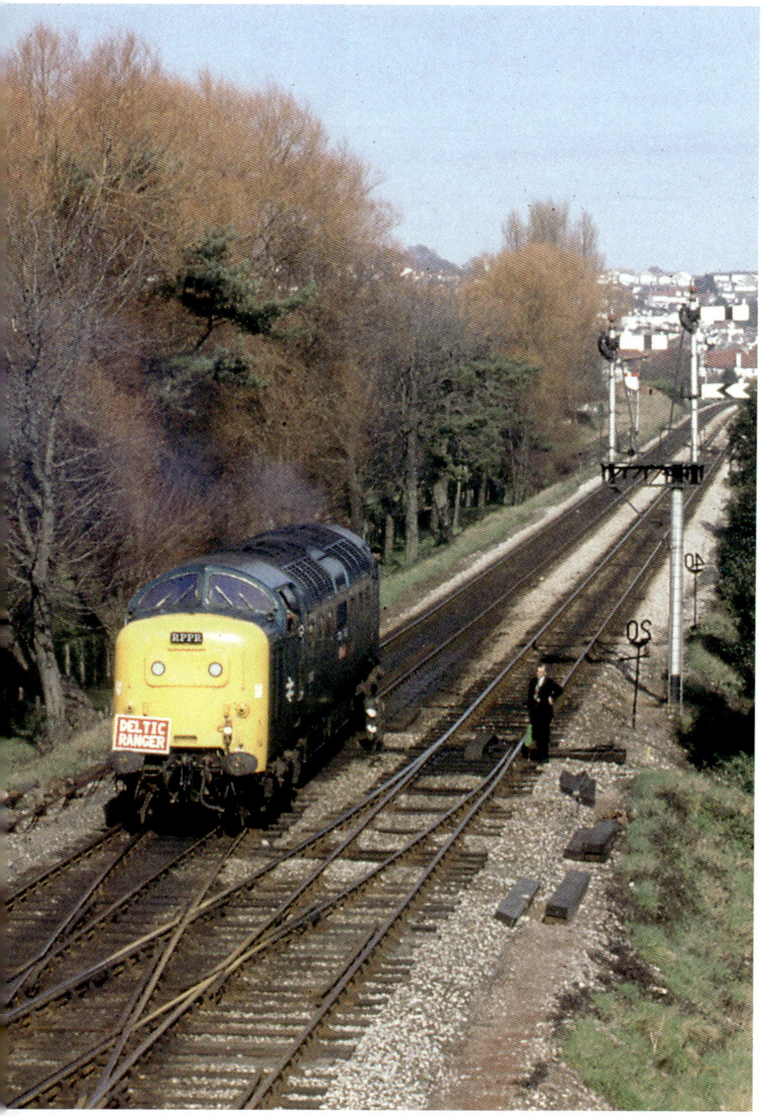

On a sunny 26 March 1978, 55007 Pinza embarked on a marathon eleven hour tour of the Southern Region with The Man of Kent making one of a number of stops that day, this one being at Sittingbourne for over two and half hours! ***Ian James***

Just a few weeks beforehand 55003 Meld was rostered for the Deltic Ranger Railtour Re-run on 3 March. This came about because the first tour a fortnight before behind 55018 Ballymoss was sent back due to heavy snowfalls in Devon as it was unable to make it here to Paignton, where Meld sets about running round. The planned Class 52 Western haulage had to be abandoned owing to a bridge being washed away on the Paignton & Dartmouth Steam Railway due to the thawing snow from a few weeks before, instead a run to Par and back behind 46003 was substituted. ***Bruce Smetham***

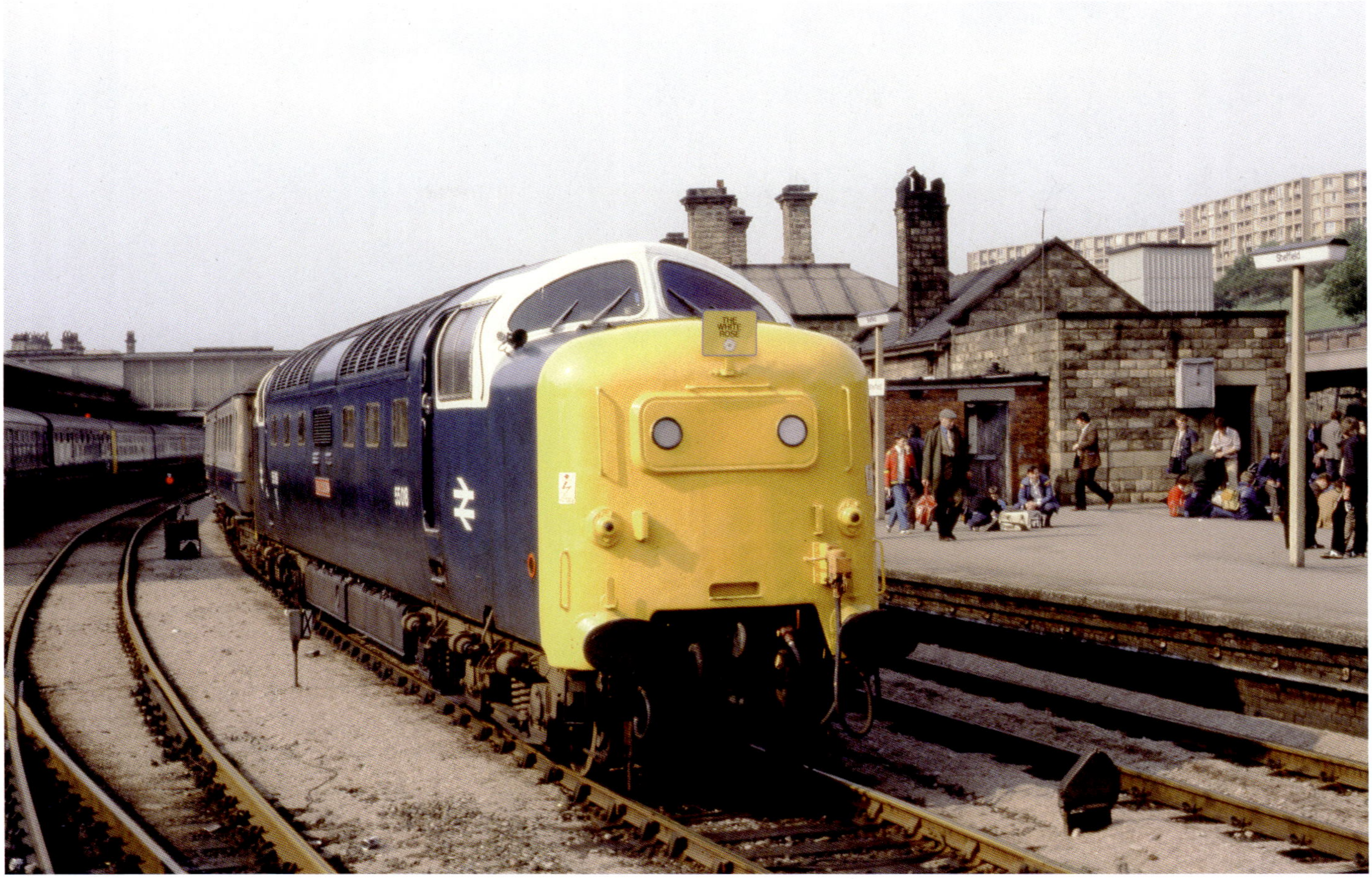

A very discrete yellow headboard for The White Rose on 15 June 1980 bringing 55018 Ballymoss to Sheffield Midland on a circular railtour of Yorkshire and the East Midlands that started and finished at Kings Cross. ***Denis Feltham***

An appropriate stand in locomotive for the failed 55002 The King's Own Yorkshire Light Infantry which had been booked for the the Deltic Devonian on 28 November 1981 was 55016 Gordon Highlander going well as the special ran alongside the Kennet & Avon Canal past Bedwyn that saturday morning. ***Colin Whitbread***

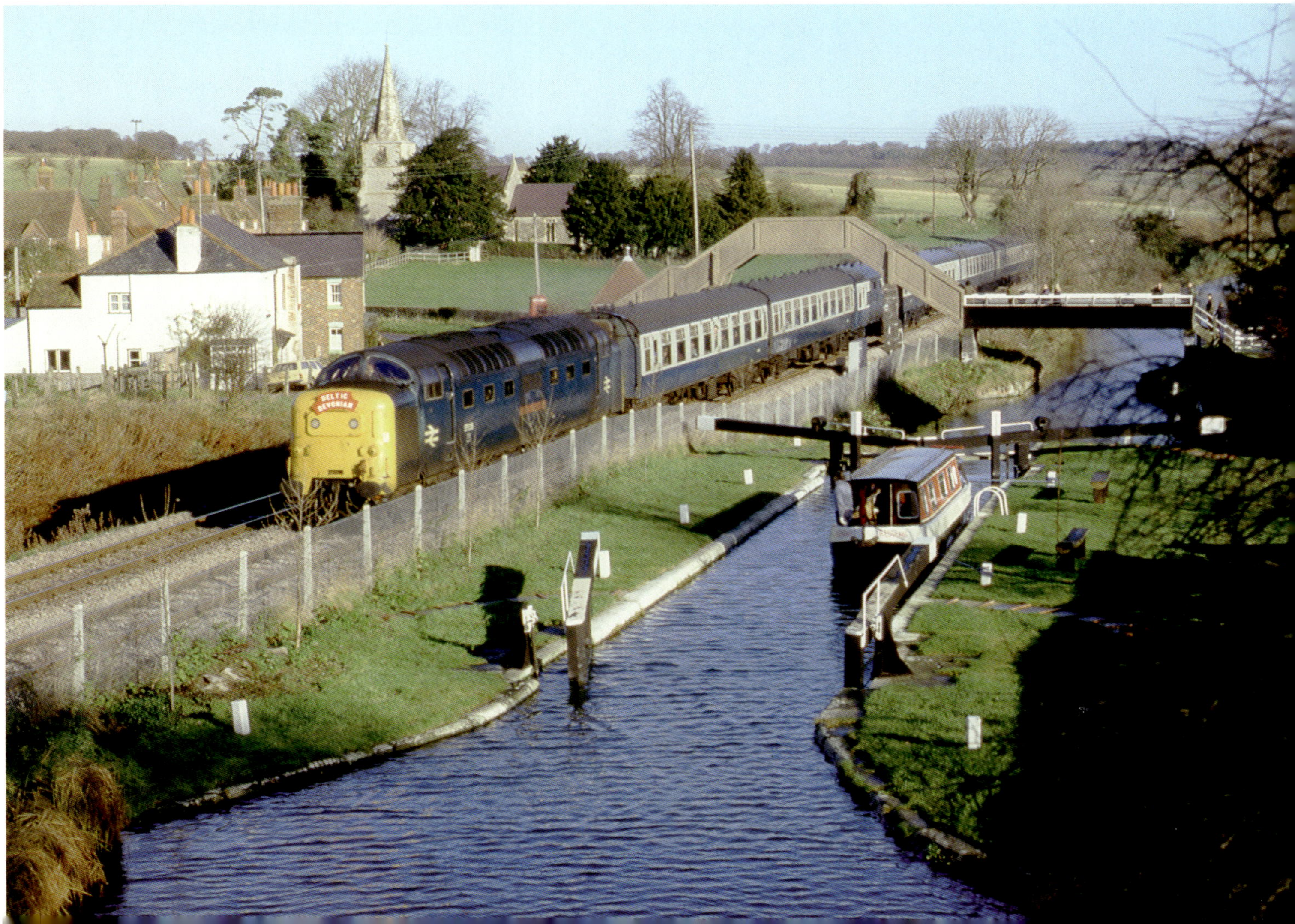

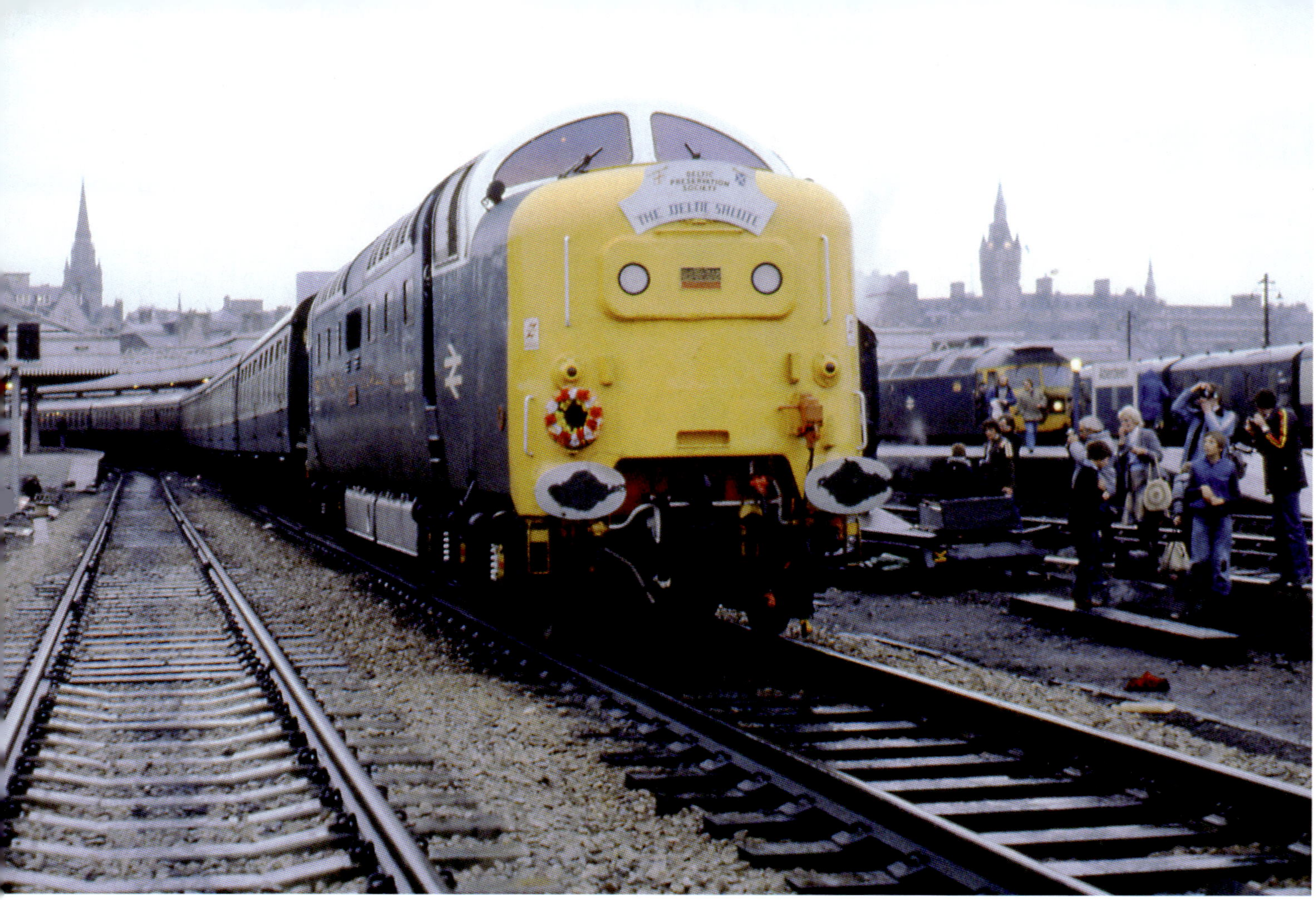

Its very wet across the Granite City at Aberdeen on 24 October 1981 as 55015 Tulyar stands in the drizzle for some time with what was to be the last railtour organiised by the Deltic Preservation Society to use a Deltic still in active British Rail service, The Deltic Salute, note the wreath. ***Strathwood Library Collection***

Heavy snow elsewhere would be the problem for 55002 The King's Own Yorkshire Light Infantry at the head of another Deltic Preservation Society tour in 1981, when on 25 April, The North Briton was forced to be re-routed away from the Settle and Carlisle line at Settle Junction due to snow and sent via Carnforth to Edinburgh and back here to York. ***Strathwood Library Collection***

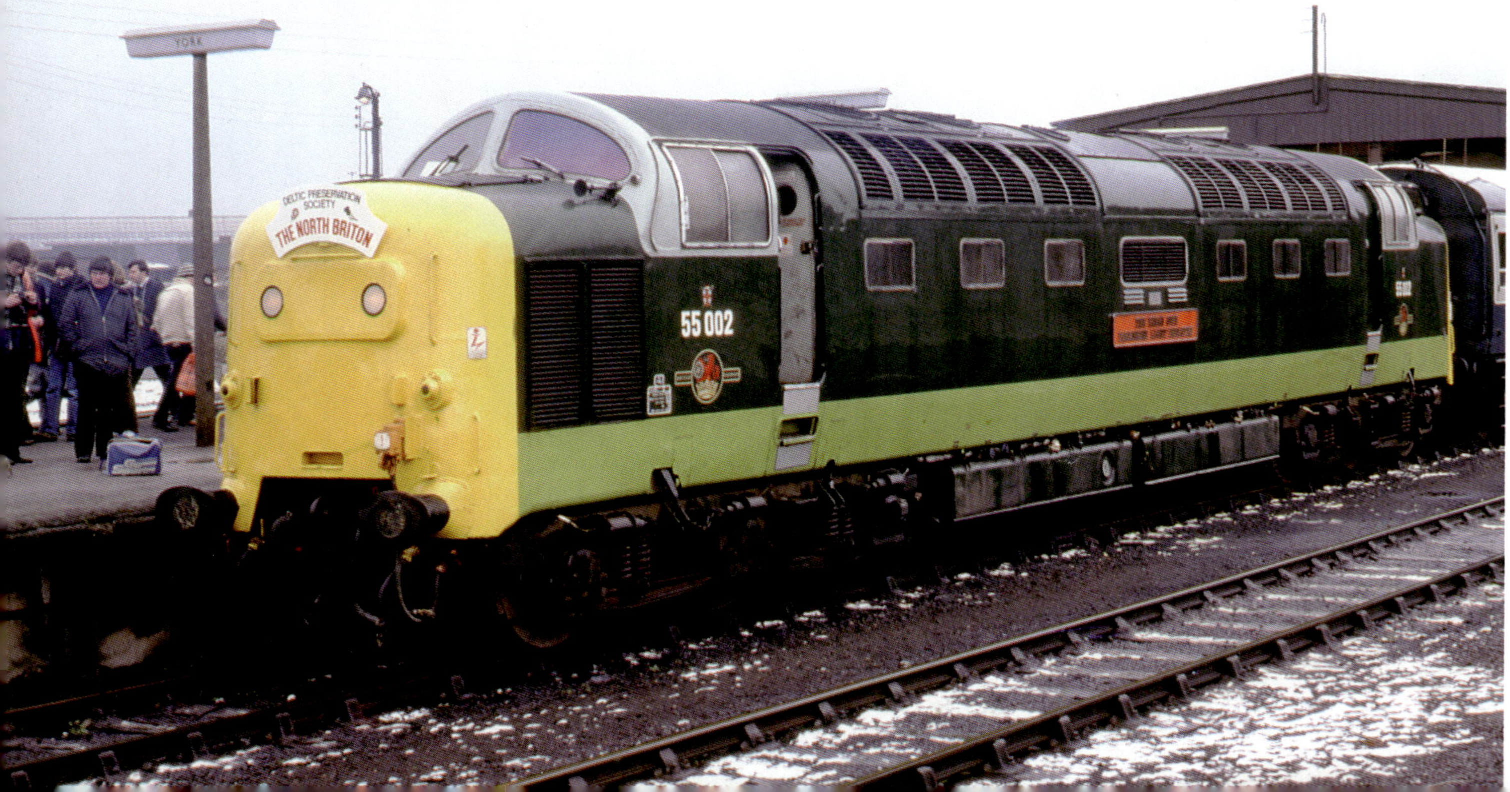

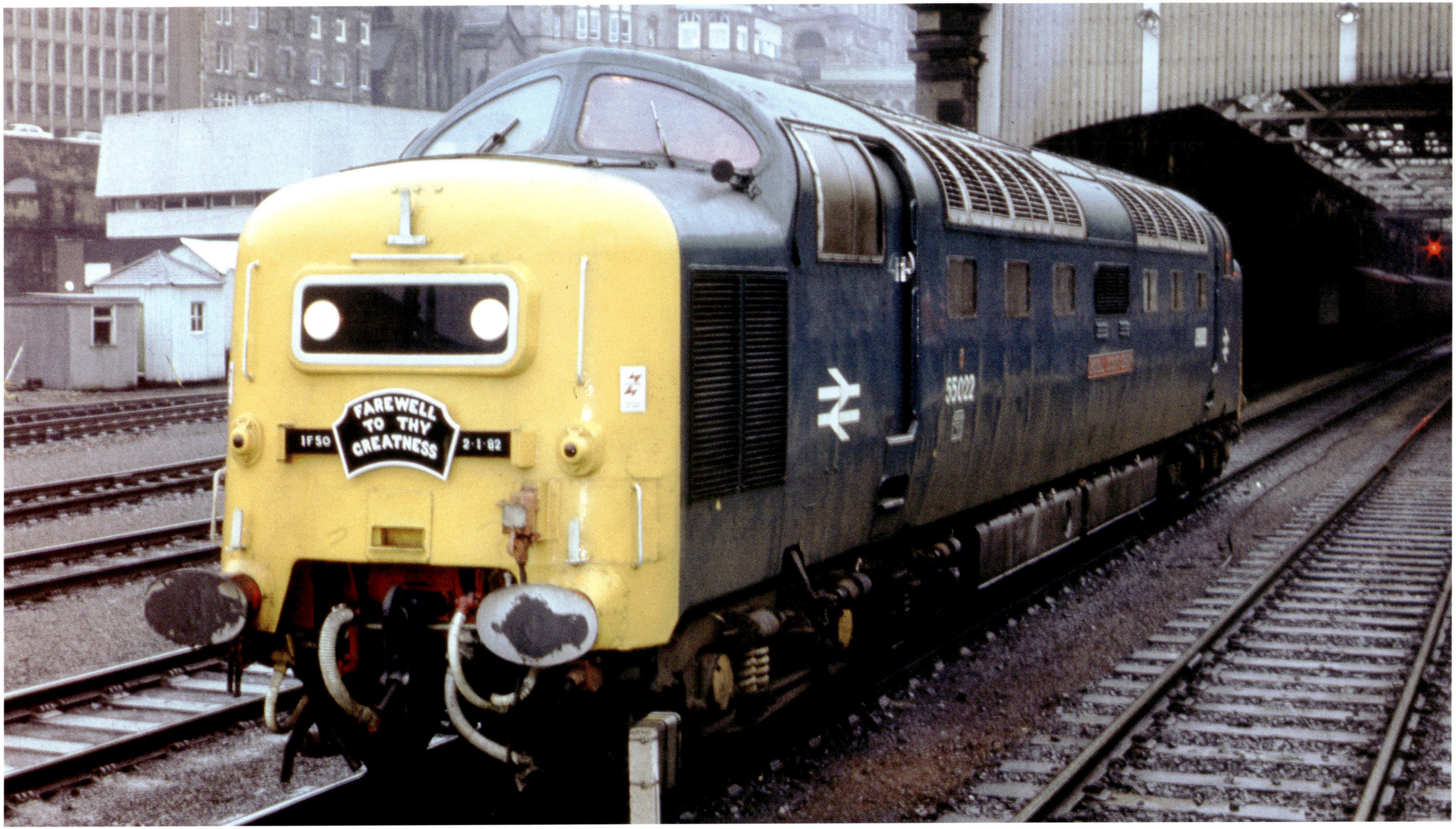

This final headboard says it all for the Deltics as affixed to 55022 Royal Scots Grey at Edinburgh Waverley on 2 January 1982 for the British Rail Eastern Region organised The Deltic Scotsman Farewell. The down train had arrived from Kings Cross behind 55015 Tulyar threeminutes late at 14.06 after being held for signals at Newark. A speedy change round in the Scottish capital saw 55022 Royal Scots Gey put on for the return to London departing two minutes late at 14.32 to arrive back at Kings Cross at 20.05 still three minutes down after passing thousands of well wishers along the route to enjoy what we thought would be the last mainline Deltic run along the East Coast Main Line. Just in case of failures 55009 Alycidon was the standby engine in the event of any problems with either of the tour locomotives but in the event was not called upon to work. Instead 55009 Alycidon worked light engine from Peterborough to Newcastle and back under the headcode 0F50 and carried The Deltic Tribute headboard. ***Len Ball***

Help To Preserve Our Railway Heritage

Strathwood not only publish books on our railway heritage but have also set up the Railway Photographic Preservation Association as a Charitable Trust to house an archive of images comprising over 200,000 photographic negatives and slides.

The archive was established to not only preserve the collections of over one hundred photographers both living and deceased, but to also make their work available to a younger audience for the future. To achieve this aim, we have begun an energetic programme to publish a considerable number of books. Allied to this we are making as many as possible of the photographs and slides we hold, available as copies to interested enthusiasts, individuals, societies and other publishers.

Many photographers have chosen Strathwood to care for their collections and to publish the best examples of their work for posterity.

If you have negatives or colour slides of transport subjects then we would like to hear from you. We purchase, accept on loan, or welcome donations of material to the archive. Photographers always receive recognition for their work when it is used by publishers (A N Other/Strathwood Library). To answer why so many images are just credited as Strathwood Library Collection in this volume, the reason is we do not know who the original photographer was. This is usually because their collection gets split up via auctions or collectors upon their death with no record of the late photographer for us to credit. Please do not let this happen to your collection. Make contact with us today to discuss what can be done to ensure you work is fully credited and recognised for both today and the future.

Please call us today if you would like to see your work in print, perhaps in a similar fashion to this publication. We also undertake publications to benefit charities and societies on behalf of our contributors. In addition we can store, and catalogue collections on behalf of clubs and societies by way of loan, thereby releasing such groups to concentrate on other aspects of their activities.

Strathwood Ltd,
Glenavon House,
Kinchurdy Road,
Boat of Garten,
Inverness-shire,
PH24 3BP.

Telephone 01479 831139

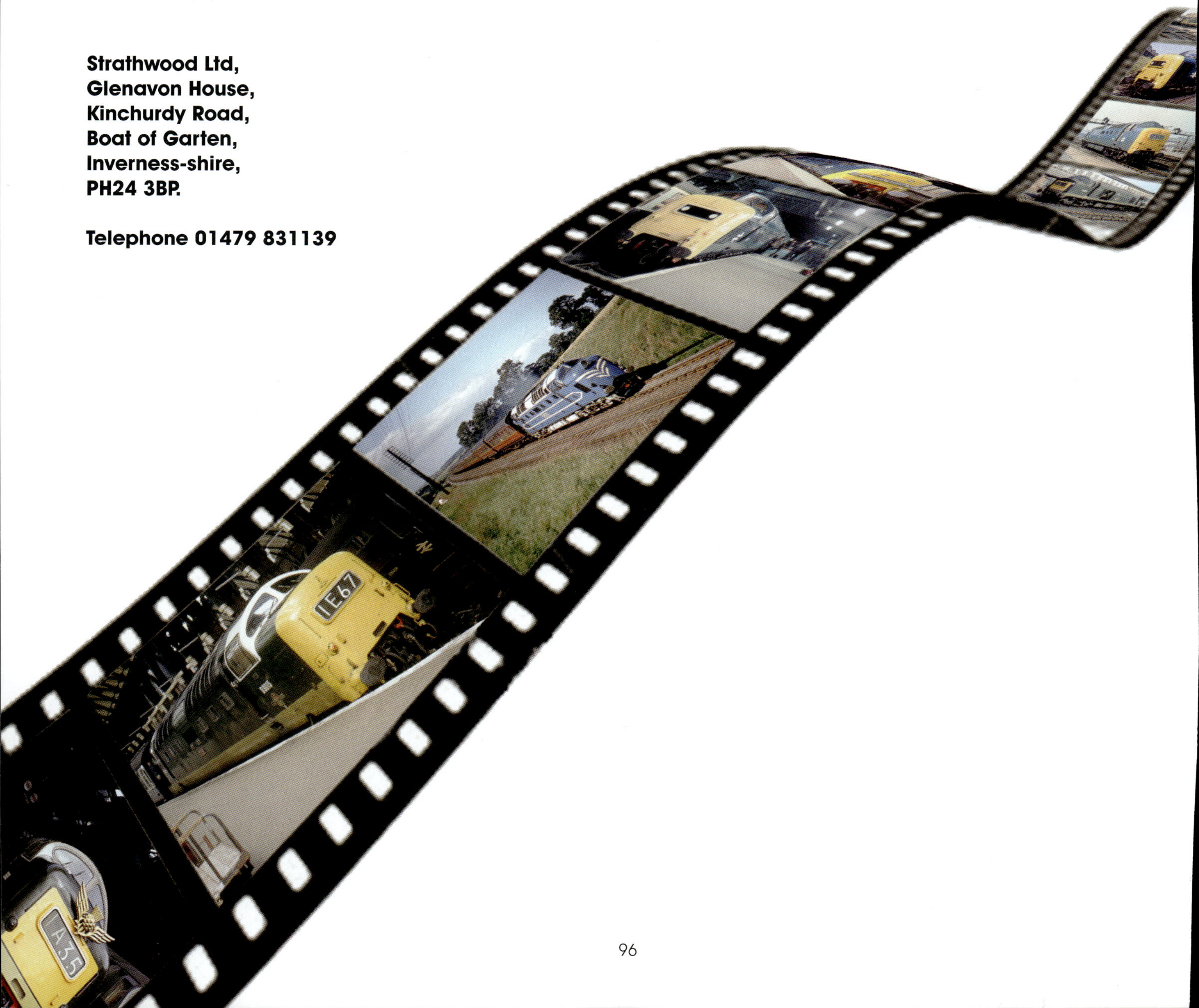